ƒP

Learning to Die in Miami

Confessions of a Refugee Boy

Carlos Eire

Free Press

New York London Toronto Sydney

ƒP
Free Press
A Division of Simon & Schuster, Inc.
1230 Avenue of the Americas
New York, NY 10020

First Free Press trade paperback edition June 2011

FREE PRESS and colophon are trademarks of Simon & Schuster, Inc.

For information about special discounts for bulk purchases, please contact Simon &
Schuster Special Sales at 1-866-506-1949 or business@simonandschuster.com.

The Simon & Schuster Speakers Bureau can bring authors to your live event. For
more information or to book an event contact the Simon & Schuster Speakers
Bureau at 1-866-248-3049 or visit our website at www.simonspeakers.com.

Book design by Ellen R. Sasahara

Manufactured in the United States of America

1   3   5   7   9   10   8   6   4   2

The Library of Congress has catalogued the hardcover edition as follows:
Eire, Carlos M. N.
Learning to die in Miami: confessions of a refugee boy / Carlos Eire.
p.   cm.
Continues: Waiting for snow in Havana / Carlos Eire.
New York: Free Press, © 2003
1. Eire, Carlos M. N.—Childhood and youth. 2. Cuban Americans—Biography.
3. Refugee children—Florida—Miami—Biography. 4. Miami (Fla.)—Biography.
I. Eire, Carlos M. N. Waiting for snow in Havana. II. Title.
E184.C97E36 2010
305.8968'72910759381—dc22
[B]   2009052286

ISBN 978-1-4391-8190-4
ISBN 978-1-4391-8191-1 (pbk)
ISBN 978-1-4391-8192-8 (ebook)

To the Infant Jesus of Prague,
fellow exile,
and to all who opened their arms
to the Lost Boys and Girls
from Castrolandia:
eternal thanks

Death is a dialogue between
The spirit and the dust.
"Dissolve," says Death. The Spirit, "Sir,
I have another trust."

Death doubts it, argues from the ground.
The Spirit turns away,
Just laying off, for evidence,
An overcoat of clay.

—Emily Dickinson

Preamble

Fearing that we'd be enslaved,
    our parents sent us away, so many of us,
        to a land across the turquoise sea.

Alone, all alone, we kids. No mom, no dad,
    no kin on the alien shore, beyond the horizon;
        willing, clueless fugitives.

Our exodus came to be known as the Pedro Pan airlift.
    Operation Peter Pan in English.
A ridiculous name for something
    so unlike a fairy tale.

Ferried to Anti-Neverland,
    we lost our childhood in a blinding flash,
        forever.

We dribbled out little by little, between 1960 and 1962,
    steadily, inexorably,
like drops of blood from a wound that wouldn't heal,
    unnoticed.

Fourteen thousand of us, boys and girls
    —a Children's Crusade—
exiled, orphaned, for what?

Freedom.

For us who flew away, our families, and our captive brethren
    freedom is no abstraction.
        It's as real as the marrow in our bones,
    or the words on this page, or whatever you ate today,
        and as crucial as breathing.

Everything in this narrative was preordained,
    including our inability to predict our fate.
    Most of us still marvel at our peculiar niche in history,
    as invisible footnotes.

Our would-be overlords marvel, too, as they choke on their bile.
    Poor devils.
    It irks them to know that we escaped,
    and they so envy our luminous scars
    and our ceaseless resurrection.

One

_____

Having just died, I shouldn't be starting my afterlife with a chicken sandwich, no matter what, especially one served up by nuns.

Is it a bad omen, this sandwich? Perhaps. But maybe it's a good one too.

How can I know?

I have no way of discerning good from bad omens, much less of intuiting that all auguries are really an extension of our own fears. I don't know yet, at this point in life, that misfortunes can prove to be gifts from on high, sometimes the greatest gifts of all, or that ironic twists of fate are sure signs of divine providence. A child of eleven has no way of knowing that, or of believing it. And that's how old I am.

It's late at night, and I've just arrived at the camp for airlifted Cuban children in deepest, darkest South Florida. Earlier today, I left behind my parents, my entire family, all of my possessions, and my native land, and at this moment I don't really know whether I'll see any of them ever again.

In other words, I've just died. I've passed through the burning silence that strips you bare of everything you've ever been. And so have the other two boys sharing the table with me: Luis Del Riego Martinez, age seven, and his little brother Roberto, age six.

The sandwich I've been served is very white. It's on that kind of bread that comes in square slices and is all spongy and tasteless, with a thin rubbery crust. American bread. *Pan Americano.* The chicken is almost as colorless as the bread, and so is the mayonnaise that oozes out, cautiously. It's been cut down the middle, diagonally, and the square has been turned into two triangles. It reminds me of the sandwiches served at my first communion reception, at the Havana Yacht Club, back when the world was still spinning in the right direction. Except those had ham salad inside, not sliced-up chicken, which gave you a hint of pink. I stare at it, this white thing, these symmetrical triangles, there, on the flimsy white paper plate, which is round, on a square table that's covered by a white tablecloth. It's so orderly, so controlled, so geometrical, so colorless, this plate of food. Two triangles that form a square, inside a circle, laid out on a larger square. It's the perfect disguise for the very messy and painful process that made this meal possible. Chickens aren't square or triangular. Chickens don't just lay themselves down on bread, in neat thin slices. Where are the feathers? Where are the feet, or the beak, or the blood and offal? Who dismembered this lumpy, clucking creature and turned it into a geometry lesson?

The plate has scalloped edges that curve upward slightly. The curving indentations on the rim are perfect, having been stamped by a machine, a contraption that is surely a masterpiece of modern engineering, made possible only by very precise computations and the manipulation of Euclidean geometry.

Bright fluorescent bulbs flood the room with a bluish yellow light that makes everyone look slightly jaundiced or just plain ugly. The bulbs are long and tubular: perfect circles stretched out, in which mercury vapor atoms go berserk. The fixture into which these tubes are inserted—as two parallel lines that could stretch to infinity—is rectangular. The other two boys look like zombies. The nuns look very kindly and very stern all at once, and very wrinkled, save for their habits and veils, which are the very definition of order, neatness, and control expressed in cloth.

"*Pan Americano,* Pan American: how hilarious, this double meaning," I say to myself, thinking of the bread on my plate and one of the two airlines that link Cuba and the United States. I've just flown on the other one, KLM, Royal Dutch Airlines.

This is only one of the many non sequiturs that are racing through my mind as I adjust to my death and rebirth, and prepare for torture.

Having just flown for the first time, I have airplanes on my mind. Aircraft are all about geometry and symmetry too, and about using exact calculations to transcend our limitations. Airplanes are all about leaving messes behind too, and forgetting they exist. I meditate briefly on the fact that if it were up to me to invent airplanes, there wouldn't ever be any, given my loathing of exact calculations and my inborn distrust of the laws of nature. No airplanes, no way, if it were all up to me. No triangular chicken sandwiches either.

"Ay, pero esto es pollo," I yell inside my head, very, very loudly. Oh, but this is chicken.

Talk about a rough landing.

This chicken meal offends me, greatly, and scares the hell out of me. My parents have always been extremely indulgent when it came to my food preferences. I've spent my entire childhood shielded from chicken flesh, which, as every well-educated person knows, is not much different from that of reptiles. Even the not-so-well educated know this, I suspect. After all, is there anyone on earth who hasn't noticed that bird feet are thoroughly reptilian? And how is the taste of reptile meat described by those who have sunk their teeth into frogs, snakes, alligators, and iguanas?

"Tastes just like chicken."

Big problem, this likeness between avian and reptile flesh: It's all part of the evolution that made us humans what we are—so different from birds and snakes, and yet so much like them. Even as a small child, the whole deal bothered me to no end: Eat or be eaten, and beware of serpents in paradise.

Somehow, I know of this affinity between fowl, reptiles, and our inner rottenness. I know it instinctively. It was the very first thing I saw when I opened my third eye, and it blew me away, at a very early age, in a stinking meat market where you chose which creature would be slaughtered for you, right there, as you looked on. *No me jodas,* I said to myself, as the butcher plucked the feathers from a freshly decapitated and still bleeding chicken. You've got to be kidding. *Whack, whack.* There go the feet too. *Ay.* What kind of cruel cosmic hoax is this?

Exactly the same reaction I had to the story of the serpent in the Garden of Eden, and the goddamned fruit, when I first heard it. *No me jodas.*

Being too young to attend school, where one is taught to discern between right and wrong, I had not yet learned that such words—used so freely by my fellow countrymen—could land you in hell for eternity. So I parroted my fellow Cubans with abandon, until I got to school a year or two later and the Christian Brothers set me straight.

Learning of the connection between words and damnation would open my third eye even wider, allowing me to reckon at an early age that most of the big things in life don't really make much sense and that seemingly stupid questions might turn out to be the most significant.

I often wonder, still, so many years later: Do chickens and snakes know that they are related to each other? Do they ever have a sense of déjà vu when they cross paths, or recognize a familiar glimmer in each other's eyes? Do chickens laugh at us, knowing that a cousin of theirs caused us to be exiled from paradise?

Big problem, then, my being fed a chicken sandwich by the nuns that evening. It's a harbinger of things to come, a foretaste of other unsavory dishes on my horizon. I haven't had a bite to eat since breakfast, however, and I know that there's no longer anyone to pamper me or shield me from reptile meat. I'm hungrier and more stunned than I've ever been in my whole life, and I'm eager to be as flexible as a newly dead and resurrected eleven-year-old boy can be.

No parents, no choice, I tell myself.

Damn it. This chicken sandwich is just as awful as I expected. Every cell in my brain is screaming in revolt, at full volume. But I gobble it up as the nuns stare at me, silently, with their eagle eyes, so exquisitely adapted to perceiving and preying upon the slightest hint of disobedience, a mile away. I know enough about nuns to suspect that if I spurn the damned thing, or leave a crumb or two behind, I might get whacked or be forced to write *I shall never again refuse a chicken sandwich* a thousand times on the blackboard. Maybe even in English, rather than Spanish.

I try not to gag, but I do, a couple of times. I can't help it. I struggle to disguise the gagging as hiccups. You never know what a nun might do to you if you gag on her sandwich.

I don't realize it, but these fake hiccups are my very first step toward becoming an American, my first successful attempt at being someone other than myself. And little do I suspect that six years later, in high school, when I go on my first date, I'll go into a hiccuping fit that will last longer than a week. Who knows what doctors Freud and Jung or any of their disciples would have to say about that, or about the fact that I ended up marrying and divorcing that girl?

I don't really want to know.

Outside, the night air is perfectly calm, but the din from the insects is deafening. Maybe the frogs are chiming in too, and the alligators, and freakish loudmouthed lizards and snakes that I've never run into before. I've never heard such a racket. The earth hums so loudly that I feel the vibrations on my skin. I imagine a squadron of flying saucers hovering nearby. That would be so great. But there aren't any spacecraft. I'm old enough to know that all accounts about flying saucers and interstellar travel are nothing but fairy tales. And I'm also old enough to know that there are no aliens here, save for ourselves.

We're perched on the edge of the Everglades, about an hour's drive south of Miami, in Florida City, the southernmost town on the U.S. mainland, right next to Homestead Air Force Base. The next town down Dixie Highway, the only road that leads out of town, is Key Largo in the Florida Keys. I don't know this, of course. I think I'm in Miami. There's a whole lot I don't know, including what awaits me right after I finish this gag-a-thon of a chicken meal.

The three of us who've arrived at that camp on the night of the sixth of April, 1962, have just been thrown onto a well-oiled conveyor belt that receives pampered Cuban children every few days, sorts them out, and ships them all over the United States, preferably as far from Florida as possible. Back in Cuba our parents had told us that we'd be sent to great boarding schools, on scholarships, or be taken in by wealthy American families.

Our parents have no clue either. Not one of us airlifted kids would end up at Phillips Exeter, Groton, or Choate Rosemary Hall.

I imagine my parents are calm, even happy. After all, they've been so desperate to catapult us off the island, for our own protection. It doesn't occur to me that they might be weeping and wailing, gnashing their teeth, and rending their garments. Many years later, after I've had children of my own, I'll look back on this moment and think about the gloom that must have descended on them whenever they walked past my empty bedroom, or what awful things they imagined whenever they gave any thought to tomorrow, or the next day, and the day after that. But that will be years later.

On this night, I'm still a kid, and I still believe what my parents have told me.

Everything will be all right. *No te preocupes.* Don't worry.

I try not to think about the fact that my brother Tony and I were separated at the airport, as soon as we cleared the immigration desk, and that he's been whisked away to a different camp. No one has yet explained why he was taken away in one van and I in another. In a little while I'll find out that he's gone to the camp for teenage boys, and that I've ended up at the one for girls and preteen boys. No one has to explain the logic behind this arrangement to me. I understand it instinctively. It's 1962, after all, and everyone knows that girls need to be shielded from pubescent boys and vice versa. I remember being told at some point that this is one of the ten commandments: Thou shalt not bring those with raging hormones unto temptation.

I'm still convinced at this point that the first commandment is "Thou shalt not utter filthy words," and that the second is "Thou shalt not have any dirty thoughts." I'd already had several years of Catholic schooling, after all, and learned all there was to learn about sin.

We finish our hellish sandwiches, and I feel extra virtuous. I've managed not to vomit, and I've even fooled these nuns into thinking that I enjoyed their meal. I think of my mom and dad and how proud and amazed they'd be if they knew that I'd just eaten an entire chicken sandwich and kept it down.

"*Muchísimas gracias,*" I say to the nuns as I leave their well-lit torture chamber. Politeness was always the most important virtue in my household, back in benighted Havana.

I'm taken to my sleeping quarters, and the other two boys to theirs. The camp is a cluster of tiny houses, dotted with a handful of larger buildings including a large one made of steel, which is the mess hall, as I'll find out soon enough. I'll also discover that this camp once served as housing for the families of married airmen from Homestead Air Force

Base. I'll also find out quickly that the prefabricated houses are ridiculously small, and that all of them are managed by Cuban couples who live there with their own children and with those of us who keep arriving and leaving in a steady stream, like water through a garden hose.

I'll find out that boys and girls are carefully segregated there, too, which means that brothers and sisters go to different homes.

When I get to my house, I can't believe my good fortune: My house parents are people I know, friends of my mom and dad. Familiar faces in a strange place: the Angones family. My brand-new foster father has known my father for many years. My dad called him Panchitín, a diminutive form of Pancho, the nickname for Francisco. But I can't call him that. Calling him Señor Angones sounds too formal, so I end up trying not to call him anything. Their son Frank had been to many of my birthday parties, back in Havana, before the world changed. I don't know any of them that well, but at least we're not perfect strangers. I know deep inside that they'll look out for me with extra care.

Frank's mom hugs me, and his dad reassures me that everything will be all right.

I can't believe how many kids are crammed into this house. We're packed tight in there, on bunk beds, and Frank has to share his space with all of us. He'd come on the airlift too, without his parents, and had been through all this before. And then his parents came, and they chose to stay at the camp and serve as foster parents for wave after wave of us. So Frank has to wait quite a while before he gets his own room.

We'd come and go through that house and all the others at that camp like heads of lettuce being picked, packed, and trucked away at some top-secret farm. And so did the teenage boys at the other camp, at Kendall, much closer to Miami, but still out in the bush. Kendall was so remote back then that the teenage boys cracked jokes about Tarzan being their closest neighbor. No one would notice us. We'd dribble in, invisibly, noiselessly, and be ferried out in the dark of night to camps in the jungle. Journalists would have no clue this was happening, or they simply didn't care. We were only Cubans, after all, aliens from an exotic location that most Americans couldn't even locate on a map. Who would want to read about us back then, in 1962? Nothing would change later, either: To this day, hardly anyone in the world knows that all of this happened.

Fourteen thousand and sixty-four boys and girls, some as young as three years old, were shipped off to the United States by desperate parents, warehoused out of sight, redistributed at lightning speed, scattered to the four winds. To me, this seemed normal. It's what nearly all of my childhood friends were going through too. It seemed so commonplace that it took me twenty years to come to grips with its monstrous abnormality, the questions I should have asked at the time, and the rage I had to bury deep inside.

But that night, as I drift to sleep in my bunk at the Angoneses' house in the Florida City camp, all I care about is the fact that I've escaped from Cuba, which is the same as escaping from hell, and that I'm in a new land with marvelous vending machines.

On the ride from the airport, as we zipped through Miami and out into the Everglades, I was in shock. Here I am. *Estoy aquí*. All of my life I'd longed to be *here* in the United States of America because the place had thrust itself upon me through movies, television shows, comic books, and a thousand and one products, from baseball cards to model trains and soft drinks. I'd been seeing images of this place, playing with its toys, and consuming its goods and entertainment since the day I was born. I'd fallen in love with its women on-screen, long before I ever fell in love with a real girl. It was the ideal world, and ours seemed but a pale reflection of it. Later, when I'd first learn of Plato's allegory of the cave, I'd understand the concept instantly, without any difficulty, because I'd already lived in such a cave and escaped from it. Once Fidel and his crew set out to pulverize everything that was a mirror image of the United States in Cuba—mostly out of sheer bilious envy—they'd make our cave much deeper, and darker. They'd succeeded in blocking the entrance to the cave and destroying our physical contact with the ideal world, but they couldn't take away what was stored in our memories, or at least in my memory.

In many ways this new place was home, and perhaps more of a home than my own native land. Or so I thought as I looked out of the van's window.

Yet, I recognized nothing. No images of Miami had ever entered my field of vision in Cuba, for America exported very little of Miami, if anything. Back then, Miami was a kitschy tourist trap that didn't figure much in American culture. The cityscape I saw buzzing past me on expressways and highways looked nothing like what I'd imagined. There were no skyscrapers, no mountains, no deserts. No cowboys, for sure, and no Marilyn Monroe. It looked shockingly familiar, a whole lot like the newest neighborhoods on the outskirts of Havana. But those Havana neighborhoods, which had suddenly stopped growing as soon as Fidel showed up, were already looking shabby and older than they really were. Without paint and constant repair, tropical homes deteriorate very fast. This place was different, all right. Nothing was old here, or shabby. So it seemed, anyway. All the buildings hugged the ground, as if afraid to rise too far from it. And the vegetation seemed very thick and jungle-like. But I really couldn't see much after a while. It was nighttime, and I could make out only whatever was lit by streetlights or the traffic on the road.

Except for the gas stations, which seemed like widely scattered galaxies that filled the empty space with their own light. There seemed to be a lot more of them here, and they seemed bigger, more brightly lit. It was the first noticeable difference that caught my eye, along with the strange brands of gasoline being sold: Phillips 66, Cities Service, Sunoco, Union 76. Their illuminated signs were practically all I could see once we got past a certain point and there were fewer and fewer buildings. And these oases of light were strung out at great distances from one another, like the bread crumbs in the Hansel and Gretel story, marking a path through the woods. But this was no fairy tale, and there were no witches in sight.

This was the real world, and I had finally crossed over into it.

I was alive, at last. Really alive. As I saw it then, Cuba had become some other dimension, far from earth: A parallel universe not unlike that of Bizarro World in the Superman comic books, where everything was the opposite of what one might expect on earth. And I couldn't wait to escape from it, no matter what. Losing everything, including my family, seemed like a small price to pay. Or so I thought.

Being in shock didn't help me gain a sense of perspective. What caught my eye most intensely were the soda-pop vending machines at the gasoline stations, all lit up in colors much more eye-catching than I had seen on any of their Cuban counterparts. Like everything else we'd missed for the past two years, these machines were way ahead into the future. These were space-age models. I wanted to jump out of the van, drop nickels in their sweet, sweet coin slots, fill my arms with their bottles, and sample those drinks I'd never, ever seen or tasted before, such as Bubble Up, and all those familiar ones that had once been available in Cuba, before Che Guevara made them disappear, such as Coke and Pepsi. Nothing seemed more desirable, more worthy of my attention. But I had no money at all, and the van was on a nonstop mission.

Where I'll end up and what might become of me doesn't trouble me much that night, at least not on the conscious level. I've just died—without knowing it—and am as stunned as Lazarus must have been when he emerged from the tomb, entangled in his burial shroud, his hair a total stinking mess.

Whatever Tony is thinking and feeling at that moment is hidden from me, and doesn't worry me at all. He's always been so headstrong, so daring, and so cocksure of his invulnerability that I can't imagine him hurting in any way, or being scared. I miss his company, yes, but I can't admit it to myself. God knows what might happen if I do. I tell myself that this is a great adventure, and that for once in my life I don't have to share anything with an older brother who, like all older brothers, is an expert tyrant.

Back home in Havana, my adopted brother Ernesto must have been celebrating his good fortune. Now, at last, he was the only child, the Dauphin, first in line to inherit everything. He must have surely relished his new place on the totem pole, and our absence, despite the fact that under communism one can't really own anything. He was clever enough to dodge all rules and get his way, and he knew it. As for our spinster aunt Lucía: Who could ever tell what she was thinking and feeling in her room at the rear of the house? She always rivaled the Sphinx when it came to opening up or displaying emotion. Our father, the man who not only believed in reincarnation, but claimed to remember all of his past lives, the onetime king of France, his majesty Louis XVI, the king of self-deception at all times, must have been hugging his pain, the way I've hugged mine so often, cursing and thanking God all at once. Our mother, the only sensible person in that house, and the most affectionate, probably contemplated what step to take next, the following morning, as she wiped away a flood of tears.

And the lizards, those goddamned ugly reptiles that ruled the island,

and that I desperately longed to wipe off the face of the earth, they were laughing their heads off, and partying in their own inimitable lizard way. Tony and Carlos—their largest and fiercest predators—were gone. No more torture, no more lizard holocausts. Let's dart our tongues in and out like yo-yos at a yo-yo tournament, they said to one another, wordlessly. Let's change colors with abandon, screw our brains out, and repopulate the neighborhood. Be fruitful and multiply, and gobble up as many insects as possible. Eat away, and mate away, as mindlessly as ever, oblivious to God above or the Evil One who hovers so menacingly all the time here below, like a roaring lion, oblivious to the little evil one with the stupid beard who thinks he can usurp our throne.

And if they'd known that I'd just eaten a chicken sandwich, the lizards would have laughed and partied with even greater abandon.

"Poetic justice," they surely would have said. "Carlos hasn't just kissed a lizard, he's eaten one, and now he's one of us."

And I, what would I have said to the chief lizard, if I'd been able to talk back to him?

"No me jodas."

Two

The sprinklers woke me up: *sh-swish, sh-swish, sh-swish*. A sound I'd never heard before. I jumped out of bed and ran to the nearest window.

What I saw floored me. It was a flat landscape, flatter than any I'd ever seen before. I had no idea the earth could be so featureless, so much of a pancake. Lush fields of green, kind of gray in the pale light of dawn, stretching all the way to the horizon, with a tree here and there, scattered about as if they were feuding or fearful of one another. Between me and the horizon, all I could see were scores of nozzles spraying water with a circular motion. Off to one side, our camp stretched for quite some distance, in a straight line, behind a tall chain-link fence. All I could hear was *sh-swish, sh-swish, sh-swish*. The graceful arcs of water shooting from the giant sprinklers were quite a sight, like nothing I'd ever seen before, in terms of size. I'd seen small sprinklers, of course, but none as huge as these.

Fountains, I thought. Americans are so advanced and so wealthy that they can dot the landscape with fountains, just for the hell of it, simply because they look so cool. Or maybe they were a secret weapon, spraying lethal acid to keep the Russians away. To me, it didn't matter what they were. They were simply there, like everything else in nature, a puzzle to solve, an easy target begging to be attacked. I hadn't read Don Quixote yet, but I'd seen the film on television once, back in the days before Fidel turned all entertainment into brainwashing. So I thought of windmills, and giants, and the need to wage war against them.

I had no Dulcinea to impress, no American blonde, yet, but I still felt the urge to tilt against the sprinklers, just for the hell of it. Even if they were keeping the Russians at bay, the sprinklers were asking for a fight, and deserved it. I could have had some fun with them, save for one fundamental obstacle: the sudden realization that I was now an orphan, at least for the time being.

That thought sent me reeling. And it didn't feel like something that had come out of my own head, but rather like a huge dark wave that had just crashed on me. All of a sudden I was swept away to some unfamiliar place even stranger than the landscape on the other side of the window—a realm so utterly void of anything or anyone as to make me feel smaller than an atom. Suddenly, I no longer saw or heard the sprinklers. Instead I felt totally alone in a dark void, crushed by a great force from all sides, annihilated by something totally impersonal and uncaring: the force of nothing, of nothingness itself. Worst of all, this oppressively vast emptiness felt eternal, and inescapable.

Existential vertigo, I suppose one could call it.

I prefer to call it Hell.

To be utterly alone, forever, and to be painfully aware of one's eternal loneliness, this is Hell, at least my Hell, the one I entered that morning for the first of many times. Nothing has ever scared me more, not even my kidney stones or the worst, most boring, most pretentious, and longest paper at a scholarly conference. Jean-Paul Sartre had it all wrong, lousy existentialist that he was. Hell is not other people. Hell is being utterly abandoned, forever and ever, *per omnia saecula saeculorum*. Hell is being by yourself forever, having no one to love and no one to love you back. Hell is eternal unrequited love, eternal absence, eternal unfulfillable longing.

Flash forward, nine years. I'm in a Chicago hospital, on the operating table, about to be knocked out by the anesthesiologist. I'm there to have an injury repaired.

Surprise, surprise. Next stop: Hell.

"Count back from ten," someone says.

"Ten, nine, eight . . ."

Bonk. I leave my body and float over it. I'm looking at myself, and at the doctors and nurses, and I hear everything they're saying. My body doesn't look too good without me in it. I look dead, or hungover, or both at the same time. I see and hear everything in great detail, including the jokes they're making about me. They laugh; I don't.

Bonk. I'm out of there, going down a spiral tunnel very, very fast, headfirst. It's a long way down, down, down. It seems to take hours, maybe days, or some timeless measure, and as I plummet it gets darker and darker, and I can't see anything, and my falling speeds up.

Bonk. I'm out of the tunnel, and there's nothing there. Nothing but me, without my body. Nothing but utter darkness and me, whatever I am: mind, soul, whatever, but certainly not a body. I left that behind on the operating table, looking poorly. No motion, no sound, no cold, no heat; nothing to see, nothing to touch, nothing to feel, nothing to taste. Not even wormwood, or my own salty tears. I have no eyes, anyway, no tongue. Nothing but pure thought and the awareness of my own existence and my own eternal loneliness.

Never, ever, have I felt such pain and terror, such pure panic. I pray for annihilation, but there is no one or nothing to pray to. All I can do is to wish for my extinction, and to know that I'll be eternally unable to annihilate my lonely rotten self.

Bonk. I'm out of Hell, and back on the operating table. I hear my own labored breathing, *gurgle, gurgle, gurgle.* It sounds as if I'm percolating very thick coffee in my throat. I'm shaking uncontrollably and feel as if I have ice running through my veins. Never, ever, have I felt so cold, so terrified. I open my eyes and see a masked face hovering over me.

"Does he always shake like this?" someone asks from the other end of the room.

"Only after surgery," I reply in a raspy voice that doesn't sound like my own.

Everyone in the operating room laughs, loudly. I fail to get the joke.

I'm tossed onto a gurney and wheeled into the recovery room, with only a flimsy sheet draped over me, all askew. The stupid open-back hospital gown I was wearing before I went into surgery—a garment that should be outlawed as cruel and unusual punishment—is nowhere to be found. I'm buck naked and shaking violently, out of control. But what I feel inside is far worse: sheer terror, and a kind of spiritual pain that I'd never imagined was possible. I shake for hours after I'm brought out of the recovery room, until, finally, I'm given a pill and the shaking stops. My roommate, a full-blooded Sioux recovering from a severe beating, has asked the nurses to do something. My shaking was getting on his nerves. But a different sort of shaking continues to plague me inside for some time afterward. I go home with a small wound on the outside and a gaping, quaking hole in my soul. And it takes months to banish this memory to my Vault of Denial, which is the large vestibule to my Vault of Oblivion. This trip to hell is one item that can't fit into that deepest, darkest of vaults. No way.

Years later, I would come across accounts of near-death experiences that were eerily similar to what I went through that day, but they wouldn't cheer me up at all. Just the opposite: They'd unnerve the hell out of me, literally. Most of them spoke of floating over one's body and entering a long spiral tunnel, yes, but they also tended to describe a bright light and a paradise at the other end of the chute, a light I never even saw a glimmer of, and an incomparable feeling of well-being and companionship with God and all of one's dear departed.

I guess I took the wrong tunnel. Oops. I hope so, anyway, fervently.

Bad trip, as we used to say back then, in 1971. *Coño.* Bummer, man.

Back to the window in Florida City: What I felt that morning, there, looking at the sprinklers was but a foretaste of later visits to hell, including that most dramatic one during surgery. Much of the rest of my childhood would be shaped by these recurring attacks, which became as much a part of me as any of my physical features. From that morning forward, throughout my life, even up until now, the slightest, subtlest of cues will suddenly open the door from which this hell comes roaring out. Its unpredictability gives it a fearsome power over me that I can't tame, no matter how much cold hard reasoning I apply to it.

Reason alone can take you only so far, especially when you're dealing with hell, or matters of the heart.

Everyone in that flimsy house woke up immediately. When you're packed in so tightly, all it takes is for one person to stir, and that's it. Good morning. *Buenos días.*

I have no memories of what followed, since I was still stuck in hell, inside my mind and heart. Nothing I saw or heard registered, save my own inner turmoil. I do remember what broke the evil spell, however: It was a surprise call from my parents in Havana, who somehow managed to get through to the Angones house. I still have no clue how that call was arranged. Phone connections between Cuba and the United States were very difficult at that time, since the Cuban government wanted to keep them to a minimum. But miracles happen. My parents called, and I spoke with them, and merely hearing their voices pulled me out of hell and back to earth again. It was a three-minute call, the only kind you could have back then, but those three minutes seemed much longer. They were a lifetime, in fact, my entire life up until then, for those three minutes reminded me of the fact that I had not really died and gone to some afterlife, but was still actually on this planet with all those I had left behind.

Later experiences would cast doubt on this feeling of connectedness to Cuba, and on the illusion that I was still in the same dimension as my loved ones back home.

Bits and pieces of that first day linger in my memory, totally fragmented and mixed with memories from the following two weeks. I've blocked out a lot, and I'm sure I've consigned most of the emotional memories to my Vault of Oblivion. But I do remember a few of my first experiences at that camp, which speak loudly about the process of death and rebirth.

Cereal boxes. I'd never seen anything like these boxes. In our mess hall, we could choose from dozens of different cereals, all packaged in single-serving boxes that could be used as bowls. Cardboard boxes with a perforated seam that could be simply ripped open. A foil package within, which could also be easily ripped with your fingers, full of cereal. You could open the box, lengthwise, tear the foil, add milk, and, presto, eat directly from the package with a plastic spoon. It was the most beautiful thing I'd ever seen, I thought. Such simplicity, such pragmatism, all made available through a mysterious economic process I couldn't comprehend at the time. All I knew was that the Cuba I'd just left behind had no cereals at all—even though it once had them—and that it couldn't produce anything like these little boxes full of foil-wrapped cereal, let alone plastic spoons with which to eat the contents.

This is a truly superior country, I thought.

Then I met some of the children on the other side of the chain-link fence, and I had to adjust my thinking. Kids from the Homestead Air Force Base called us spics, gave us the finger, and told us to go back where we belonged. Even worse, they spoke in a tongue I couldn't fully understand. I'd been studying English since first grade, so I had some of the basic vocabulary and grammar under my belt. But reading Dick and Jane books doesn't exactly prepare you for dealing with children your own age who hurl insults at you in English. Some of the other kids at the camp whose English was much better than mine translated the insults for the rest of us. We all left that fence feeling pretty low. Maybe as low as one can get.

It was 1962, after all, and we were in South Florida. Racial segregation was still legal. And we Cubans tended to be viewed by the locals as non-white intruders, even if we had blond hair and blue eyes. The lower you went on the social scale, the stronger the biases against us tended to be, but prejudices against Hispanics permeated the entire culture, from top to bottom, in a much more open way than nowadays.

All of my textbooks at school would confirm that fact during the next few years, once I got the chance to go to school with the kids on the other side of the chain-link fence.

Coins. I loved them, these American coins. I'd seen them all before, in Cuba, when we used them along with our own currency. Before Fidel and Che came along, the Cuban peso was equal to the dollar, and American coins were as common in our hands as Cuban coins. It was so great, once again, to handle these very familiar manifestations of the only universal religion on earth, which always has its local variants. What I had missed the most was the American nickel, with Thomas Jefferson on one side and his home, Monticello, on the other. Once, when I was about five years old, I made a wish on one of them.

"I hope someday I get to see this building, on this coin."

Ha. I'm still laughing. Be careful with your wishing. As divine providence would have it, I'd end up spending fifteen years in Charlottesville, Virginia, former home to Thomas Jefferson, and every time someone came to visit from out of town, the only thing to do was to take them to Monticello. Eventually, I got to see Monticello more times than I could count, and one of my children would break one of Mr. Jefferson's windows.

I loved them all, these coins, but they puzzled me then and puzzle me still. Human beings have irrationally concocted some way of placing value on pieces of metal or on strips of paper, and these objects can get you things. It's a complex belief system, but its complexity can't hide the fact that it's based on belief in symbols and their ability to represent something unseen. It's the only religion all humans share in common.

Save for communists, of course. I was driven out of my native land by people who hated money and the belief system it represents. Coins are all about the distribution of wealth, and about belief and symbols. If you don't have them, you're out of luck. But if you have them, the world can be yours for the asking. We had coins in Cuba, of course. But Che had changed all the currency and seized everyone's bank accounts, and the new Cuban coins were worth next to nothing in the world market and also at home. Money is kind of useless when everything is rationed and there's no private enterprise or private property. Che's plan was to do away with money altogether, and he came damn close to succeeding by making everyone equally poor, save for those who, like him, ran the country. It felt great to once again handle these little symbols of everything hated by Che and Fidel.

The grocery store. I couldn't believe my eyes. My house father, Panchitín Angones, took a bunch of us to a small grocery store in downtown Florida City that was jam-packed with produce and merchandise. Where does all of this come from? Why is this store so well stocked, and why is every store in Cuba so empty? What the hell is going on?

The store left me bewildered. Dizzy, even. For the past two years I'd seen everything vanish from the stores in Cuba, very quickly. I'd also seen lots of stores vanish, for there was nothing to sell. I'd had to stand in line for the simplest things, ration card in hand, and wait hours and hours for nothing at all. If you got in line too late, there'd be nothing left for you, no matter what your ration card entitled you to. The economy in Cuba was entirely in the hands of the government: All production, all supply was tightly controlled from above, and all stores too, along with prices. The result was an immediate collapse of the supply-and-demand system, and endemic shortages.

The difference between the place I'd just left and the place where I now found myself couldn't have been starker. Something worked here, something I couldn't understand. Every kind of fruit and vegetable, piled high. Shelves groaning under the weight of packaged goods. This was no supermarket, mind you. No. This was a rinky-dink store in downtown Florida City, at the very edge of the map. Yet what I saw amazed me, and once more convinced me that I'd died and gone to some other dimension. Surely, such disparities couldn't be found on planet earth: Aren't we all rational beings? Can't we all figure out how to make this happen?

Surely, yes, I thought. Or maybe not, I also thought.

And Panchitín Angones had to throw in an extra lesson in the virtues of American culture, as if the store shelves didn't speak for themselves. As we all piled out of the car, he said: "Look, kids, here in the United States, you don't even need to lock your car, and you can leave the keys in the ignition."

I couldn't believe my eyes, but this is precisely what Panchitín did. He left his keys in the car with the doors unlocked and walked into that store with all of us, feeling as carefree as a medieval lord surrounded by all of his knights.

"Damn it. Damn it. It's not fair. Not fair, at all," I thought. Why couldn't this be my place of birth?

So I decided, right there and then, at that rinky-dink store, that I'd become an American and forget about being Cuban, at least for the time being.

A fateful decision, but the only one I could have made, given the circumstances.

Flash back, just a couple of years. My father, the onetime king of France, Louis XVI, has just hauled out his Ouija board from its hiding place. For him this isn't a Parker Brothers game, but a sacred object. He really believes that he can receive messages from the dead through this very simple contraption: a cardboard chart of all twenty-six letters in the Latin alphabet and all the numbers zero through nine, with a plastic heart-shaped doodad known as a planchette that has three stubby legs and a tiny window of sorts in the middle.

My father really and truly believes that when he places his hand on the planchette and asks a question, the spirits of the dead will guide his hand over the board and pause the planchette's tiny window letter by letter, and that he will receive an answer that can be spelled out and depended on. The Ouija board also has a *yes* on one corner and a *no* on another, for simple questions. Of course, most of the questions my dad asks are about the future, and what lies in store for us.

How it is that he and his entire family have come to take this game so seriously is too long a story to tell. All I need to say at this point is that my father's family succumbed to that late–nineteenth century religious fad known as Spiritualism, especially that brand of it peddled by the Theosophical Society in America, which had its most successful overseas mission in Cuba, right after the Spanish-American War in 1898.

My father's family was truly ecumenical when it came to alternative religions. I suppose that they might be dubbed New Age nowadays. They believed in everything, and never, ever believed that anything actually contradicted the Roman Catholicism that they also observed at the same time. Reincarnation? Sure. Voodoo curses? Watch out, they're real. Séances? Yes, please, the more the merrier. Transubstantiation? Sure. Papal infallibility? Why not? But wait, let's add Madame Helena Blavatsky to the list of authorities, right along with the Pope. Protestants? They sure can sing, and they certainly have a legitimate right to complain about Catholicism and the Pope.

The sacred Ouija board has been opened on my father's rococo desk, in his study. It's just me and him, and my adopted brother Ernesto. I don't know where Tony is at that moment. Probably torturing lizards, or riding his bicycle to Pinar del Rio, forty miles away. He had a habit of disappearing, and of worrying our mother to death.

My father asks the board some preliminary questions. The planchette moves under his hand, or so he says. I question this proposition.

"Hey, you're just making this up."

"No, I'm not moving it; it's guiding me to the right letters. The planchette has a force of its own and you can't resist it. If you do, the power builds up and you get in trouble. Once, I tried to hold it down and it shot out of my hand like a rocket and crashed into one of my display cases on the other side of the room, breaking one of my Meissen figurines."

"*No me chives*," I say to him. You've got to be joking. I can't say what I really want to say out loud—*no me jodas*—because the verb *joder* is one of those words that can send you to hell. Its equivalent in English is the all-purpose f-word.

After a few simple questions are "answered," I venture to test the spirits of the dead.

"Ask what lies in store for me."

So he does, and the planchette under his hand moves ponderously from letter to letter, spelling out a very clear message.

"Your two sons have a future in another land."

"Ask them who I'm going to marry," I say, thinking that this is too tough a question for any spirit to answer.

"Your two sons will marry women from another land."

Damn. They had an answer. And a vague one at that.

"Ask how many children I will have," I say, testing the spirits further.

"Can't say," respond the spirits.

"Bastards," I say to myself, in Spanish, risking an eternity in hell. *Cabrónes.*

I found it odd that the spirits would predict a future in another land for me and Tony, the two sons of Louis XVI, the Ouija medium, and none for Ernesto, the adopted one. But I chose not to dwell on that, especially given my loathing for Ernesto, who seemed happy enough with these predictions.

So, you see, the spirits were right—whoever they were, wherever it was they came from, whether from the netherworld or my father's inexhaustible imagination. I had no choice. My destiny was to end up in a foreign land and to find my soul mate there, across the turquoise sea. Or maybe the spirits planted the seed in my mind about my future being in some other land. Since the spirits spoke when the so-called Revolution was well under way and Cuba was quickly sliding into its long nightmare, I'm not too surprised by their prophetic prowess, or by my father's deftness with the planchette.

Seeing all the merchandise at that rinky-dink store in Florida City, and watching Panchitín Angones leave his keys in the ignition as we went into that store just sealed these prophecies for me.

I had no choice, you see.

Sure. Just as I had no choice in writing this, or you in reading it.

Three

Hard edges, right angles. No curves to speak of, no outrageous colors. Nothing superfluous. No curlicues, no filigree, no gilding. Nothing old. No stifling past. No ghosts. No black magic. Blinding sunshine, but hazier than what you're used to, less sure of itself.

The clouds? Just about the same, sure, but more imposing, thanks to the flatness of the landscape and the lack of tall trees.

I couldn't help but notice these things. The place felt free from the crushing burdens of the past, free from fear of the unseen, from everything that was unnecessary. All you had here, in this new and very flat land, was the present and the future and billowing cumulus clouds towering overhead. Everything was as simple as the straight lines that defined every building, fence, and street. And just as slightly hazy as the atmosphere.

I'd never been in a place so new, so free of ghosts, so wide open, so much a proof that less is more and much less is much more.

Of course, the fact that my father was not there immediately cut down on ghost sightings and tragic stories from the past. This made a big difference. I'm sure he'd have found ghosts there, at that camp, and even remembered a prior life in these glades, probably as a vanquished Indian chieftain or a lost Spanish explorer. He'd always been important, in each of his lives, and all of his deaths had been tragic.

Exile is not so bad, after all.

I never expected to find this kind of freedom. For the first time in my life I no longer had shadows to fear at every turn, or someone else's baggage to mind or haul. Being free of the soul-crushing oppression of Castrolandia was all that I'd expected, and that was great enough. Being free of the past and the spirit world was a wonderful bonus.

Of course, being at the very edge of the map, in a hastily erected and refurbished military camp, helped a lot. I don't think I'd have felt the same way if I'd gone directly from Havana to Savannah, New Orleans, or witch-obsessed Salem.

Many years later I would drive into Savannah with my wife and kids, get the willies, and drive right out, at top speed. "Let's get outta here," said Jane, my lovely wife. The old city seemed as plagued by dark spirits as my deeply haunted Havana. The similarity between the names of the two cities had nothing to do with it. It was the vibes, pure and simple, the fallout from the past. Slavery. Human beings bought and sold. African gods driven into hiding. Too much dissembling. Too much cruelty mixed with gentility, too many slighted poets, too many duels and grievous endings. A lost war, and a lost cause. Endemic languor. More ghosts than living residents.

Florida City had no such baggage, and none of the frills that went with it. And I loved it for that, even though I knew I'd be there for only a short while.

It was a fast-spinning turnstile, a shuffling machine, the sole purpose of which was to move children as quickly as possible to other places. It was as efficient as all of its buildings, and as brutally simple. All of us there were waiting for an assigned destination that we could neither question nor refuse. They told us where we were going, and we went. Our parents back in Cuba had no say either, and most often no knowledge of the arrangements.

It was well-organized chaos.

Some of us went to orphanages, which were then in steep decline and had plenty of room available. Some went to Catholic boarding schools, which at that time were begging for boarders and thus had plenty of empty beds. Some ended up in institutions for troubled youths—"juvenile delinquents," as such kids were known then. The luckier ones ended up in foster homes, usually with American families who already had children of their own but were willing to take us in, thinking it would be only a few months until our parents arrived. I suppose many of these families viewed it as a foreign student exchange program. The luckiest ones of all ended up with relatives. But there were damn few of those.

Colorado, Montana, New York, Texas, Nebraska, Kansas, New Mexico, California, New Jersey, Idaho, Louisiana, Illinois. This place, that place. Here and there, anywhere. We ended up all over the map, like darts thrown by a gang of drunken sailors at an Irish pub ten minutes before closing time. Anyone willing to receive us got us, and the federal government of the United States paid for our upkeep. It was a great deal for many of those who took us in. A fabulous deal. But the turnstile had to spin fast, week in, week out, to keep pace with the arrivals, who only kept increasing in numbers.

None of us caught in this whirlwind of an airlift had any idea how large it was, or how complex the logistics were. We came and went so quickly, we couldn't catch a glimpse of the big picture. Years later, when I'd first learn that there had been over fourteen thousand of us, more or less, I found it hard to take in the numbers. I'd always thought that, at most, maybe three thousand of us had been airlifted. Then I learned that there were at least eighty thousand more children waiting to leave who never got the chance, and my head nearly exploded from a volatile mix of rage, grief, and astonishment. Good God. Jesus H. Refugee Christ, rushing down to Egypt, what can one make of such numbers?

A whole lot.

Abraham, we're told, was willing to sacrifice his son Isaac, simply because God asked him to. And God amply rewarded him by making him the father of the Chosen People, the most persecuted, most widely and continuously dispersed race of exiles in human history.

And then, we're told, God took his turn by actually sacrificing his own Son, so that the invaluable Chosen status could be extended to the whole human race, adding vast numbers to Abraham's progeny. And the deal included turning this Son into a refugee for a while, and also a homeless vagrant, and, finally, an enemy of the state. Then, to top it off, those who chose to believe in this Son became enemies of the state too, and sacrificial victims for three long centuries, and on and off after that, down to our own day.

We who've been sacrificed have a divine pedigree, you see. None of the particulars have to make much sense, and the sacrificial offering doesn't even have to undergo death; it's the offering that counts, the sheer willingness of the parent to give up what is most precious, especially if the circumstances are impossibly painful and illogical.

And the sacrificial victims somehow help to redeem the world. Somehow. Always in a very weird way that seems unacceptable to most people, including the victims themselves.

My ticket out was just about the best I could have hoped for. I was one of the lucky ones. Really lucky. And so was Tony. We won the second prize in the placement lottery: American foster homes. It was all so incredibly simple and improbable at the same time.

A good childhood friend of our mom's, Marta Monjardín, had married a lawyer named Juan Becquer, back before the world changed. Young attorney Becquer had dealt with the construction of the Havana Hilton Hotel, and in the process had come to know Sidney Rubin, one of the American interior decorators. When the Becquers fled Cuba, the young attorney, like all other Cuban lawyers, found himself unable to practice his profession in the United States. He'd been trained in Napoleonic law, not common law. So, like every other Cuban lawyer in exile, Juan Becquer went searching for any kind of job he could get in Miami, and he contacted every American he had known in Havana, including Sidney Rubin, and Sidney offered him a job as a janitor in his warehouse. It was the only job available, and attorney Becquer took it.

I'd visited their house in Havana many times before they left. It was so beautiful, so heartbreakingly beautiful. And on the eve of their departure, we helped them sort through the stuff they were leaving behind, much as one does when someone dies. What I remember best is a box filled with swizzle sticks from Havana's nightclubs. I wanted to take it home, but my mom, ever sensible, nixed the idea. "What would you do with those things? Besides, you'll be leaving soon too."

Ay.

So, while the Becquers are living in a shotgun shack in some Miami slum, along with their two small children and Marta's parents, and Juan is stacking boxes and sweeping the floors at Sidney Rubin's warehouse, my mom stays in touch with them and warns them of the imminent departure of her sons. Fully aware of the cheekiness needed for any such request, Juan Becquer asks his boss Sid whether he knows of anyone who might be willing to take in two Cuban boys for a few months, while they wait for their mother to arrive. Sidney Rubin, a Jew whose family was chased out of Eastern Europe by pogroms, one of the Chosen, one of the perpetual refugees, offers to take in one of us. And he convinces his close friends, Louis and Norma Chait, to take in the other. They too are of the Chosen People, eternal exiles.

I've already had my share of adventures at the camp by the time I'm informed of this great deal, so I'm more than ready to move on: In less than two weeks, I've found metal fragments in my lunch, gotten a ring-shaped piece of glass stuck on one of my fingers, smeared bubble gum on my hair when a giant bubble popped on me, ripped one of my only two pairs of pants, seen a cloud shaped like the island of Cuba, and learned how to kick soda pop bottles loose from one of the camp's vending machines. I've also learned to bury my feelings much more deeply than I ever had before. And I've had a very intense religious experience, thanks to one of the nuns, who—despite the fact that she was not a man—preached the best damned sermon I'd ever heard. Of course, I won't admit that some of the seeds she has sown have landed on fertile soil. I'm dumb enough to believe they've gone straight into the Vault of Oblivion.

Fool yourself long enough and you'll be proven a fool for sure. Just when I thought I had all my problems licked, I got sideswiped by all of my buried emotions. Walloped. Sucker punched. Flattened. I'm taken to meet my prospective foster parents and I melt down as I've never, ever done before. Suddenly, I'm wailing like a banshee and feeling as if all the cells in my body are dissolving their bonds with one another. There, in their living room, right under a framed reproduction of Picasso's *Three Musicians,* a piece of art that my father would not only have ridiculed, but thrown into the flames, something goes haywire inside my mind and I start sobbing uncontrollably, saying again and again—in Spanish—"No, no, I'm not worthy of living here, this is far too good for me."

Chew on that one, doctors Freud and Jung, and please have an argument over it. I'd love to hear your opinions. Is it a piece of cake, or a jawbreaker, this eruption of mine? I'll help you out by adding this:

What I felt most intensely was absence. Faced with the undeniable fact that I was about to get new parents, suddenly, as if from nowhere, this gaping void, this vortex of nothingness—of pure Absence—filled the room and tore me apart. Louis XVI and Marie Antoinette, my very flawed and very dear parents, were not there at all, and I longed for their presence, their bodies. I ached for them, physically, and for their flaws as someone might ache for all four limbs if they were suddenly to be severed, or for a soul mate who can never, ever be embraced again. To stay in that house, to get new parents, was to admit that my real parents were really, really gone. Out of the picture. It was also to admit that perhaps I might be better off without them, that I'd happily betray them forever.

Son of a bitch, that Void. *Sónomambíche*, in Caribbean Spanglish.

Fortunately, Juan Becquer saved the day. He took me out to the backyard and gave me a sound verbal thrashing that straightened me out and helped that gaping Void to vanish as quickly as it had appeared. "You can't throw this away," he said. "Don't be such an idiot." *No sé tan comemierda.* So I went back in, all calm, and everyone acted as if nothing had happened, and the pleasantries flowed once again, and the next thing I knew I was leaving the camp and moving in with Louis and Norma Chait, their two recently adopted children, Philip and Eric, both younger than two years, and their German shepherd, Victor. And Tony was moving in with Sid and Carol Rubin and their two teenage children, Alan and Sherry. Tony and I wouldn't be reunited under one roof, as we'd hoped, but at least we'd be only about three miles apart, living with folks who were good friends and got together regularly.

I've said it before, and I'll say it again and again, until the day I die: such good people, such brave people, such transparent proofs for the existence of God. Little did they know what was in store for them, entangling their lives with ours. And little did Tony and I know what lay in store for us during the next few months, day in, day out. It was a giant leap of faith for everyone involved, even Victor the dog, a leap from great heights without parachutes or bungee cords or hang gliders or anything else that could break your fall or turn it into a joy ride. Not exactly a leap into the Void, but a fearsome leap all the same.

But that Void I felt there, in the Chaits' very small living room, in that tiny house in the Westchester area of Miami, which was then at the out-ermost edge of the city, that Absence, that Void, which deserves its capi-tal V, would keep resurfacing again and again, walloping me every time, flattening me again and again. Age hasn't made it any easier to take. I rec-ognize it now for what it is, but knowing what it is makes it no easier to stand up against its knockout punch, which seems to be getting stronger and stronger. I put up a fight every time, even though I know I can't win; I dodge and bob and weave and throw punches that always miss, but I swing away all the same. And the Void always cheats, pounding me with a lightning-fast punch when I least expect it.

"You, again. Okay, here we go. Dukes up." *Pow.* Lights out. *Coño, que mierda.*

But every now and then I land a winning punch.

Flash forward, forty-three years.

I'm holding my mother's hand in a Chicago hospital, waiting for her to die. It's a stormy Midwestern spring night, lightning bolts fork-ing everywhere between the tall buildings and above them, there, near the edge of Lake Michigan, a fickle body of water that sometimes looks awkwardly turquoise, almost like the sea that caresses Havana, but also has a habit of turning steel gray and freezing over. The sparks given off by the elevated trains, less than half a block away, respond in some kind of code to the lightning bolts, as if joining in a subtle, sublime harmony that only God and the angels can hear.

Earlier that day, the room had been full of Cubans, my mother's friends. Tony was there too, briefly. He couldn't get away from his nurs-ing home for very long, and couldn't take the stress either. We weren't all supposed to be there, but we had snuck in one by one, fooling the secu-rity guard downstairs, with the help of a very kindly nun. The room was jam-packed, and the walls reverberated with our voices as we prayed the rosary, loudly, in Spanish, at breakneck speed, stringing together all the words as if there were no spaces between them, going from *Ave Maria* to *Amen* in a split second. It wasn't how I like to pray, *rat-tat-tat*, but this is what they'd all done together for years with my mom, once a week, and it was beautiful, the best possible "bon voyage" gift at that moment.

At one point, a nurse had opened the door and jumped back, as if she'd stumbled upon a kennel full of barking, spike-collared Doberman pinschers. She didn't dare return after that. And I laughed at that, out loud, as everyone kept the *Ave Marias* going at full speed, *rat-tat-tat*.

But as I hold my mom's hand, I'm the only one in the room. It's nearly midnight, and everyone else has gone home. I've been told she has only about six hours left to live, maybe ten at most, so I'm ready for a long vigil. She's unconscious, and her breathing doesn't sound anything like breathing. It's a loud gurgling of the sort one expects to hear from sewer pipes, or from one of the machines at her factory, where she worked for many years. The Void hovers close by, circling ever tighter. It's tensing up, getting ready to pounce, but it hesitates. I'm praying wordlessly, asking for nothing. Nothing at all, save for God to do the praying for me.

I've never been more awake, more ready to take on the Void.

Dukes up.

Zap! Whoosh! Snap!

Sweet Jesus, my God. Hail Mary, full of grace. A powerful electric current surges from my mother's hand into mine—*zap, whoosh, snap*—and it courses through my whole body in a flash, and lingers, and fills me with a sense of wholeness and well-being the likes of which I have never, ever felt. I'm there and not there all at once. I'm home. Home. I've always been here and always will be, and there is no Void. None at all. The Void is exposed for what it is: Nothing. And against this Fullness and Light there can be no Void of any kind, no Absence, no Darkness, no Unrequited Love. And time is stripped of its hypnotic power, and in this eternal Now there is no longing, no pain, no guilt of any kind, only pure Love that seems like annihilation, but is just its opposite. And all my little loves and infatuations are exposed for what they've always been: tiny shards of the real thing, grossly misshapen by my own selfishness.

Then the current that has been flowing through me forever suddenly stops, and I know my mother has just given me the best embrace ever.

Of course.

I look over and she's no longer breathing. The gurgling has ceased. Her body looks a lot like mine did when I hovered above it during surgery, at another Chicago hospital, thirty-four years earlier.

I go out to the nurse's station and ask them to confirm the obvious. I make all the necessary arrangements, all of which are exceedingly mundane and not as painful as I'd feared, and I walk out of the hospital.

It's about a quarter past two in the morning, Central Time. I've already spoken on the phone with Jane, back east in Connecticut. I can't call Tony at the nursing home until sunup. So, it's just me and Chicago. There are very few people on the wet streets, and few cars too. The el train rumbles past, its sparks flashing wildly on nearby buildings and on the trees, which are swaying as wildly as the sparks, and casting fleeting inkblot shadows here and there, above and below, left and right. The sky is pink, the way it always is when it's cloudy in Chicago at night, thanks to its legions of street lamps. The thunderstorms have quit, but the wind is trying to keep the party going. The air is moist, thick, and sweet-smelling. The trees are all doing their early spring thing, spewing all kinds of scents as they unfurl their new leaves. I pause to fill my lungs with the sweet night air and look at the skyline, once so familiar, now so surprisingly alien.

This became home, long ago, and is home forever and nevermore.

Sweet, sweet exile. Blessed exile. Sacred entryway to Now, my Ishtar Gate. Eternal blues bar. Sweet home, Chicago, my promised land, my Babylon, gained and lost, by the rivers of which I laughed and wept, and sang no songs of Zion. Sweet and holy privilege, exile. Blessed are the Chosen, for they shall always yearn for home, everywhere and nowhere in particular, and always find it in the most unlikely places. And blessed are the sacrificial victims, for they shall have no choice but to accept their role, and smile, knowingly.

In the dark of night, silhouetted against the pink sky, all I see are straight lines and right angles. No curves to speak of, no outrageous colors. Nothing superfluous. No curlicues, no filigree, no gilding, even though I well know that the city is full of such things. Sheffield Avenue, the street I'm on, seems to stretch to infinity. That's how most of the streets look in Chicago, which is as flat as South Florida. It's designed as a perfect grid, with lines so straight and true that you can use them to guide your stargazing on clear nights. But it's all an illusion. Forget infinity down here. A few blocks to the north, between the point at which I'm standing and infinity, Sheffield runs past Wrigley Field, home of the Cubs, the ultimate losers, the baseball team that turned me into a sports atheist. Nothing is more finite than Wrigley Field, or more charmingly heartbreaking.

The city feels eternal, not old, and as free of its stifling past as it is of ghosts, including those of Abe Lincoln, Al Capone, and my mother. I'm so, so happy, and so, so grief stricken all at once. So much at home, so displaced, so eager, and so unwilling to go where my mother has gone.

The Void will knock me out again, for sure. I know it. It'll roar back when I least expect it, and its inevitable sucker punch will land true and hurt like hell, as always. But the next time—maybe tomorrow, or an hour from now, or next Christmas—I might be able to last a round or two against my familiar adversary, and taunt it a little.

Sónomambiche. Cabrón. Dukes up. *Ay.*

Lights out.

Four

I'd never seen a garbage disposal before. It was one of those contraptions that never made it to Havana, thanks to the Revolution. One of many technological advances that had been deflected by Castrolandia's new communist force field, which was directed from Moscow. The free world moved ahead at breakneck speed, inventing and selling all sorts of neat stuff, while Castrolandia headed backward toward a Neolithic standard of living.

The garbage disposal inside the kitchen sink drain was one of many, many wonders in the humble Chait household, my new home. It made a lovely sound I won't try to imitate, for chances are that you've probably heard it, a harmonious blend of whirring and grinding and chopping, which spoke of sheer annihilation. How I wanted to toss stuff down that drain and flip the switch. Hoooo Weeee! Any item would have done. But I knew myself well enough by then: If I were to throw in just one item, I'd have to follow it up with another and another. And soon enough the kitchen would be emptied of contents or the grinding machine would be smoking and crying for help, or both.

And then I'd be in the doghouse.

One of the first things my new mom Norma showed me was the doghouse plaque in the kitchen. It had six little wooden dogs hanging on hooks to the right of a doghouse with a hook in it. The six dogs had our names on them. Everyone in the house had a dog avatar, even Victor the German shepherd. If anyone misbehaved in any way or caused trouble, their dog figure would be moved into the doghouse and hung on its hook.

I didn't know what shamed me the most: my dog hanging in the doghouse, or the empty hook left behind among the other dog figures. It was a painful thing to look at, any way you sliced it. I'd have that debate with myself until the day I left that wonderful house, and my dog was retired, all scuffed and worn-out at the edges.

The Puritans who once ran the New England town in which I live would humiliate all reprobates by shackling them to pillories on the village green, where everyone could scold them and pelt them with rotten food and other unpleasant stuff. The Chaits had no pillory, but they did have the doghouse plaque in the kitchen. Over the next few months, my dog would be in there way too frequently. The only other member of the household who came close to rivaling my record was Victor. He was a good dog, but a lot like me. Too curious, too clueless, and too bent on following his instincts.

The sliding glass doors that led to the screen-enclosed patio in the back had paper appliqués on them: human handprints and figures of birds, all in tropical colors. Victor liked to chase whatever moved in the yard, even beyond the screened-in patio, and he'd crashed into the glass doors too often. The silhouettes pasted on the glass were there to remind Victor that there was a wall of glass between him and the great outdoors. I think he'd crashed through one of them and injured himself, but I'm not sure about that because when Norma and Lou told me that story, I still didn't understand everything they said.

By the way, the name on my dog plaque was *Charles*, not *Carlos*. I didn't speak much English, but I knew what the English version of my name should be. And when my new foster parents asked me what I'd like to be called, I said *Charles*.

I wanted to fit in, not stand out in any way. I was hell-bent on becoming an American.

Too bad I was branded on my face as well as on my tongue. A four-eyes since second grade, I was permanently saddled with eyeglasses, and mine couldn't have looked more foreign or bizarre. I had the same frames that Fidel Castro wore, which were exclusively Cuban: an oversize, bulked-up version of Ray-Ban Wayfarers made of genuine tortoise-shell. No American kid had anything like it.

My eyeglasses were utterly ridiculous on this side of the Florida Straits: the ugliest possible proof of my alien status that I could have asked for. Hanging a dead rotting dog from my neck would have been preferable, and less humiliating. All I had to do was show my face and everyone knew I was not from *here*. I wouldn't even have to open my mouth, which would also give me away instantly.

My blond hair fooled most Americans, though, confusing the hell out of them. "Huh? What's wrong with this picture?" Cubans weren't supposed to be fair-skinned and blond. We weren't supposed to be smart either.

Ignorance and prejudice are joined at the spleen.

And my ignorance of English was a serious problem. I knew how to form basic sentences, but I couldn't really communicate with anyone who didn't speak Spanish. I could say simple things, such as "He is my brother." I'd actually used that line at the Miami airport, right after we landed and were going through immigration. Tony had always failed at English because he couldn't have cared less about it, so, at the airport, I had to serve as his bumbling interpreter. Tony wasn't fazed in the least. He'd never cared about such things. He'd make up words when our aunt Lucía would help him review his English vocabulary for tests at school.

"*Cómo se dice* ventana *en Inglés?*" How do you say *window* in English?

"*Ventan.*"

"*Cómo se dice* caballo?" Horse.

"*Quey-bal.*"

His English version of numbers one through ten sounded something like this: *un, du, tri, qwat, sink, sez, siet, og, nuvi, diz.*

And so on. Much of it came out sounding like a deranged version of French, but it was pure coincidence. He stunk at French too.

Being able to speak and understand simple sentences from Dick and Jane books is one thing. Actually living with people who speak only English is quite another. My first attempts to communicate with Norma and Lou were pained, but agreeable enough. We all knew what the basic problem was and worked around it, with a combination of pantomine and constant pausing at unfamiliar words, coupled with a lot of pointing at objects and the routine invocation of the proper names for everything that was pointed to. Their sons, Philip and Eric, were no problem, because neither one of them was old enough to speak yet. I had no trouble communicating with Victor either, my kindred spirit and doghouse cell mate, who quickly became a good friend.

My first evening at that house seemed otherworldly, more of an entrance to the afterlife than anything I'd experienced in the past three weeks. I don't remember arriving at the house, or having dinner. But I do remember being shown to my room, which must have been only about ten by twelve feet, yet seemed palatial to me. It was my own room, something I'd never had. I also remember watching television in the bright, open living room that night. The Chaits had a mechanical remote control for changing the channels on the TV, another marvel that had been deflected by Castrolandia's Soviet energy field and Fidel's determination to return Cuba to the Stone Age. I clicked and clicked. It made a very loud and reassuring sound, that remote, which was linked to the television by a cable. Back then there were only three or four channels to choose from, but I tried them all, again and again.

Clack, clack, clack. If it hadn't been my first day, I'd probably have ended up in the doghouse.

Norma and Lou were also nice enough to buy me a transistor radio, a compact battery-operated Japanese model that fit in the palm of my hand and had a dial for station-searching. It was brown and ivory, with gold trim, and you could listen to it through an earphone. I'd never seen those either. You know why by now. Blame all of this astonishment of mine on Castrolandia and its fascination with Soviet backwardness.

I loved that radio. It made my heart sing, and it made me love Norma and Lou. Every night, at bedtime, I'd turn it on for about twenty minutes before going to sleep and dial away, searching for good music. Much to my dismay in the beginning, there were no Spanish-language radio shows of the kind Tony and I had listened to at bedtime back in Havana, before Fidel squelched all genuine entertainment.

Before Fidel or, in shorthand, B.F.: Something that needs explaining, I suppose (A.F. in Spanish: *Antes de Fidel*). Ask any Cuban. It's a reckoning of time that is as essential to understanding us as A.D. and B.C. used to be for understanding Western civilization.

We had all sorts of radio shows in the era B.F.: action, comedy, Westerns, soaps. Tony and I listened mostly to the action and comedy shows, especially to *La Tremenda Corte* (*The Tremendous Court*), a hilarious show that brought the same characters to a courtroom every single night. The accused was always the same man, José Candelario Tres Patines; the judge and prosecutor were always the same too, and so was the plaintiff, Luz María Nananina. The concept was absolutely insane, for Tres Patines would always end up saddled with crushing fines and jail sentences, only to return the very next day, accused of some new crime, but the insanity worked beautifully, somehow. We also listened to an adventure show about a white man who was king of the jungle in Africa, a total Tarzan rip-off. Once, the star of the show came to our house and all of our friends came to see him. He was an ordinary-looking guy, and kind of small and wiry, and that surprised us. We expected a musclebound Cuban equivalent of Johnny Weissmuller, the real Tarzan. We asked him to prove that he was indeed the king of the jungle. "Do your yell! Do your jungle yell," we pleaded. "Prove that it's really you."

So he went into my father's study, closed the door, and—after a moment of the deepest silence that house had ever witnessed—yelled his lungs out, basso profundo.

Haa-oooo-a-ooo-arrrooo-ah!

My hair stood on end, and so did everyone else's. It *was* him! He *was* the real thing! We stared at one another in disbelief. How could that little guy belt out such a roar? It was magic, pure and simple, we had to admit. The same wimpy guy that had walked into the study walked out, looking no worse for wear, with every hair still in place. He wasn't any taller, or beefier. But for an instant, there, behind that closed door, he had transformed into someone else we could only imagine.

How wise of him, not to rob us of our imagination. I still thank him, every now and then, for not breaking the spell.

There was nothing like that on Miami radio in 1962. So I gravitated to the rock-and-roll stations. And in a matter of days, I got over my dismay concerning Spanish-language radio. All this great new music, and years of lost music to catch up on. Charles needs to catch up, if he's going to be Charles instead of Carlos.

That first night I also met one of the neighbors. Norma called him over from down the street. He was the only other Cuban boy on the block, and his name was Freddy. Like me, he'd already changed his name from Federico. He'd also come to the United States without his parents, and he was living with his uncle and aunt in a house that was nearly identical to that of the Chaits, a few doors down, across the street. He was also almost exactly the same age as me. From the very start, however, we didn't hit it off very well. I don't really know why. And I'll never figure it out either. Most of the time, I think, we had the same feeling, as if we were positively charged magnets that repelled each other. We'd end up having some good times together, but we'd also end up fighting a lot. But on that first night with the Chaits, it felt so good to know that there was another Cuban boy on the street, someone to whom I could speak in my own tongue, and from whom I might pick up a few survival tips. He'd already been in Miami for more than a year, so he knew a lot.

I'd learn a lot from Freddy.

It was Freddy who would reveal to me, about two months later, that Desi Arnaz spoke English with a very thick Cuban accent. Until he broke the news to me, I thought Desi spoke perfect, unaccented English. "I can't wait till I can talk like Desi," I used to say to myself. "That guy has really nailed the language deal, and picked up a redhead too, as a result."

I was stunned beyond belief. I had such a long steep climb ahead of me.

It was Freddy who would show me where everything was in the neighborhood, including all the best shortcuts and how to ride bikes up and down the side walls of the concrete drainage ditches behind the Westchester shopping center. He'd also straighten my head out more than once, about my identity.

Once, he had to slap me on the side of the head, really hard, and yell at me, full throttle, to remind me that I was still a Cuban, despite the fact that I lived with an American family.

Thank you, Freddy. *Mil gracias.*

Living as he did with his aunt and uncle, Freddy could never fully forget that he was Cuban. They still called him Federico at home, and they all spoke Spanish constantly. But living with an American family made it easy for Charles to forget about Carlos. Freddy and I spoke Spanish all the time, and that was the sole reality check I had, other than talking to Tony on the phone twice a week. Lou and Norma made me call my brother twice a week. They'd sit there and watch me, and wait until I connected with the Rubin household, for they soon realized that I needed prodding when it came to some tasks.

I find it very odd now, but back then, I thought it was perfectly normal and more than all right for me *not* to call Tony regularly. He was in his world, and I was in mine. And he never called me. It was always up to me to stay in contact with him, never the other way around. "Well, let him call me," I'd think. "Have you called Tony yet?" Norma would ask. If it weren't for her, I'd have probably never called.

I knew I was going to see Tony at church on Sundays, anyway. We always got together on Sundays, as part of a most unusual ritual arrangement. So unusual that it ended up shaping my character, and my take on religious differences.

Since both the Chaits and the Rubins were Jewish, I thought I had it made. I knew that Jews didn't go to church. I'd had Jewish friends back in Cuba, and so had my parents, and I knew that Jews went to synagogue instead, on Saturdays. So, I thought for sure my new parents would do me the great favor of acting neutral, like the Swiss, and not send me to either church or synagogue.

I hated church so much. Nothing was more distasteful, more awful, more creepy, or more boring than church. Jesus scared me most of all. That cross, those nails, that crown of thorns. All that blood. Jesus was the ultimate creepy monster, worse than anything Hollywood had ever come up with. Frankenstein and Dracula had never haunted my dreams, but Jesus certainly had.

The church's ritual didn't scare me. It was the symbols: the churches themselves, and their thousands of spooky images, many of which were life-size and decked out with real human hair and glass eyes. Madame Tussauds wax museum couldn't compete with any church in Havana when it came to macabre realism. Jesus being whipped. Jesus on the cross. Jesus dead in the tomb. Mary with seven swords piercing her body. Mary holding the dead Jesus, who has already started to turn green. Saints with their eyes on a platter, or their heads under one of their arms, or their tongues chopped off. Mutilation, torture, mayhem. Saints being flayed alive, or torn apart, or boiled, or disemboweled, or beheaded, or filled with arrows like a pincushion. Some saints' images were so grotesque that—if they hadn't been so scary—they would have made me laugh, like the one of the saint with an ax sticking out of the back of his head.

Eventually, I'd end up writing my doctoral dissertation on how and why Protestants attacked and destroyed Catholic images in the sixteenth century. Then, after that, I'd dedicate my professional life to studying this subject.

I don't need to ask doctors Freud and Jung about that choice of mine.

Catholic ritual was not scary at all, but it sure was annoying. The mass was just mind-numbing drudgery. The same damned thing every time, again and again, and always in Latin. *Dominus vobiscum.* Yeah, sure. Go *vobis* yourself. Whatever. Go ahead and mumble some more in your ridiculous outfit, you girly man, up there with your back turned to us, wearing your stupid frilly albs, copes, and chasubles, or whatever you call them. I call them dresses. *Vestidos,* that's what you wear. Dresses, not vestments. Yeah, and why don't you get some real shoes? What's with those sandals? Those are for *maricones,* not for real men. Wash that gold cup, girly man, glide your handkerchief over it compulsively, again and again, and make sure you do the same to those gold plates. But don't take too long, please. We've already been here far too long, and it's hot. It's always ten times hotter in church than anywhere else.

It's like hell in here.

Confession and communion were a major nuisance. Confession kept you from doing all sorts of great things that you wanted to do, but would be too embarrassed to tell a priest later. It also made you take yourself too seriously, forcing you to blame yourself for all kinds of sins that were really out of your control, or not really your fault at all, but God's, for making the world the way it is and you the way you are. And communion not only made it necessary for you to go to confession, but also to fast for three whole hours. No water, even. Not one drop of water, no matter what. Too bad if you were dying of thirst. Plus, you had to be careful when you brushed your teeth before going to church, because if you allowed a single droplet of water or toothpaste to go down your gullet, you were toast.

Sinner. Unworthy. You've got to miss communion. You'd better pray that you don't get hit by a bus or die from an *embolia* at the beach before your next confession.

Even worse, if you did make it up to that communion rail, you had to act all pious and solemn, and after all was said and done, the host was no prize to be coveted, like the neat stuff you found in cereal boxes. It was like thin cardboard that melted on your tongue. All that waiting for it, all that fasting, and poof, the ever-disappointing wafer was gone in a few seconds.

Body of Christ? *Corpus Christi?* Yeah? All right, if you say so, but it sure tastes like cardboard, and if I were crazy enough to chew on a cereal box, I'm sure I'd feel exactly the same way after swallowing that.

That's how I saw it all, back then, blasphemer that I was. One could say that the devil had me by the short nether hairs, but I was too young to have any of those at that time. And this was the main problem. Before one starts sprouting hairs in the nether regions, down yonder, or other such things that come along at puberty, it's immensely difficult to understand or appreciate religion or astrophysics or other complex matters. So, by the time you get your nether hairs, it's very hard to recognize the darkness inside yourself and the devil who's had you by the throat all along.

I'd already envisioned not going to church as one more of those freedoms that were guaranteed in the United States. Another bonus. Especially while living in a Jewish household.

So, what's one of the very first things that the Chaits and Rubins do to us? They make us go to church, because that is just what our parents would like us to do. *Ay!* Both Tony and I thought we were in the clear. Jews aren't supposed to send you to church. And they certainly aren't supposed to give you money to put into the collection basket either. But this is what they do.

Damn.

And they do this to us on the one day out of the whole year that has the longest, most mind-numbing, and creepiest of all liturgies: Good Friday.

We'd moved into their homes on Holy Thursday, the Catholic equivalent of Passover. Rescued from Egypt on our Passover, set free from our bondage at the camps, only to be subjected to a very familiar sort of bondage, that of the pew, on Good Friday. Both families actually arranged for some Catholic friend of theirs to pick us both up and drive us to St. Brendan's Church in a large station wagon, along with his wife and kids.

We're doomed, I think. Not only do we have to sit through three hours of *Oremus* this and *Miserere* that, kneeling and standing, and genuflecting, and crossing ourselves and kneeling some more, and being suffocated with incense, we also actually have to do so with perfect strangers who don't speak our language and will try to be very nice to us. Perfect recipe for a massive display of awkwardness on the part of all involved.

Just what we need today, of all days.

As soon as I get into that station wagon, however, I notice something very, very strange. The car radio is on, and it's playing some kind of jazz. Wait a minute. What is going on? Are these people really Catholic? Maybe they're Protestants, I think. Why else would they be playing jazz in their car on the way to church on Good Friday, of all days. You're not supposed to play any music on Good Friday, save for doleful sacred hymns. You're not supposed to do anything pleasurable at all on Good Friday. No. You're supposed to mope all day long, and fast, and pray, and meditate on the suffering and death of Jesus. No television, save for shows on the passion of Christ, or long sermons on his final words on the cross. No movies, unless they're about Christ. No radio, unless, somehow, Christ's death is the main feature. No games or amusement of any kind. No way, no how. And God help you if you try to use any sharp tool or instrument on Good Friday, such as a knife or a saw, or if you try to pound a nail into anything. God will exact retribution. Anything that would have made Jesus Christ bleed is cursed on Good Friday.

I'd seen this divine curse at work once, back in Havana. My nemesis and adopted brother, Ernesto, had set his mind on building something on Good Friday. My father tried to warn him about the curse, but Ernesto wouldn't listen. He went out to the back patio and began to saw and hammer away. I can't remember what he was making, and it doesn't matter. What I do remember very clearly is the inevitable gash in his hand, and the blood spurting, and my father trying to stanch the flow.

"See, I told you so," said Louis XVI to the Dauphin, as he wrapped the wound.

Louis XVI also reminded us every single Good Friday that the sun would always disappear at three in the afternoon, the time of Jesus's death. This didn't have to involve a solar eclipse, of course, but merely some cloud cover. From a very early age, I'd always waited with great anticipation for three in the afternoon on Good Friday, to see if Louis XVI was right. And every Good Friday some clouds would show up, all right, and darken the sky. As soon as I got to the United States, however, the clouds and the sun refused to engage in such hocus-pocus.

On that first *Viernes Santo* I spent in the United States, the sun blazed at three in the afternoon, unobstructed, in a joyously clear sky, and its light filled the nave of St. Brendan's Church.

As the sun played by different rules here on Good Friday, so did everyone else. This was a great revelation to me, an epiphany unlike any I'd had up until then about the Catholic faith in which I'd been reared: Catholicism was not exactly the same everywhere. It took a long time for that to sink in, but once it did, I began to reconsider my loathing for religion.

The Spanish *Viernes Santo* that Tony and I had grown up with was all doom and gloom, a lethal combination of self-denial, ritual excess, and superstition. It was all about death and suffering, never about the Resurrection on Easter Sunday. Hell, I never knew Easter existed until I came to the United States. I don't mean the Peter Cottontail Easter, although that, too, was a total surprise. Eggs? Bunnies? *Qué coño es esto?* I mean the celebration of Christ's triumph over death, the assertion that he didn't stay dead, and we won't stay dead either. As far as I knew, Jesus Christ died every Good Friday and stayed dead all year long, until the next Good Friday came along, and so on. His sole function as redeemer was to die and stay dead, and die again and again, and hang on the cross, bruised and bloodied, until the end of the world, when he'd come back to judge the entire human race and send sinners to hell. It didn't make sense, but then again, neither did anything else related to religion.

The jazz in that large American car was the first hint I had of Easter, ever. Our driver kept mentioning "Good Friday" too; it was just about the only thing he said that I could understand. He was confusing me. I could have no more called *Viernes Santo* "good" than I could have called Satan "God." Polar opposites. My Cuban Good Friday was

"Holy Friday," and there was nothing good about it. But that jazz, whatever tune it was, began to change my viewpoint. It was a crucial first step toward enlightenment, reinforced by all the other American kids in the car, who seemed to be having a perfectly good time on the most depressing day of the year. Even the kids knew that Easter begins on Good Friday.

The second step toward enlightenment followed as soon as we got out of the car and into St. Brendan's Church. Good God, what was this? St. Brendan's was light and airy, and totally free of frightening images and bad vibes. We had modern churches in Havana too, mostly in my neighborhood, but they didn't have this feel to them.

The Good Friday liturgy was just as awful and as long as I expected, but the space in which we were trapped was not at all oppressive. I have no way of explaining it, but the people in that church also gave off very different vibes. No one looked morose, no one beat his or her breast, visibly. I think it might have a lot to do with the simple fact that they were there to celebrate "Good" Friday. Funny thing, the world of difference words can make.

Tony and I survived the liturgy and the ride home with the nice family, and the awkwardness quotient was kept to a minimum. All of us kept our lips sealed, and that seemed to be fine with everyone. We had jazz to listen to, of course. The jazz never stopped on the way back to our Jewish homes.

I wouldn't admit it to myself, but I was very, very confused. What I'd just seen and heard and felt was all very familiar, but also very strange and new, all at once. Even though I was a total dolt at the time, I began to understand the marvel of that moment on the way home: the sweet, sweet irony that I should have been forced to go to a Good Friday service at St. Brendan's by a Jewish family.

The irony only increased in sweetness from that day forward, Sunday after Sunday, as Tony and I would ride our bikes from our separate foster homes and meet up at St. Brendan's for mass. We were both sorely tempted to pocket the money our foster parents had given us to put into the collection basket, but I don't think we ever did. Well, at least I prefer to remember it that way. We were also sorely tempted to skip mass. But Sunday mass became our lode star, the sole fixed point that linked our present and our past. We'd see each other at other times too, whenever the Chaits and Rubins got together, but not all that often. Mass became our strongest bond, even though we never said much to each other.

And we'd sit and kneel and stand and genuflect and cross ourselves and watch the girly man do his thing in Latin, and never give a second thought to the miracle on the altar or the miracle of our being there, together.

We did stop going to confession and communion, though. And our sins piled up furiously in our hardened souls.

We each had our own life to lead, and we lived in different houses. That's just the way it was, and that was that. Our parents were back in Havana, doing God knows what, thinking and feeling God knows what. We had no way of knowing. From the instant we left them behind at the Havana airport, we'd had no real, meaningful contact with them. We had the occasional three-minute phone call, but what can anyone say in three minutes, once every two months, with someone listening and laughing at the other end? We had letters, yes, but letters are a very poor substitute for parents when you're eleven and fourteen. Adults can get by on letters, or even have better relationships with each other through letters than by living together, but children need to press the flesh and to have Mom and Dad there, day in, day out. Without that sort of contact, Mom and Dad become ciphers, mere concepts. And once they become that, you can kiss Mom and Dad good-bye for good. You don't really need them. And you immediately learn that you don't need any other blood relations either, especially if they, too, are out of the picture. All you need is whomever is housing and feeding you and looking after your needs, day in, day out, or maybe not even them. Not at all.

That's just the way it was. And that's the way it is, period. Sorry. Absence doesn't necessarily make the heart grow fonder for children who have every reason to think that they've been abandoned. At least not consciously. Below the conscious level, all sorts of stuff remains alive, restive, volatile. And you deal with it any way you can, especially by making light of it all, trying to get others to laugh along with you.

Sigmund and Carl, please step back. Don't even touch this one. On this issue, I'm the expert.

Flash forward, forty-four years. I'm the keynote speaker at the annual meeting of the Florida Psychoanalytic Society, in Miami. The focus of that year's conference is childhood trauma and, more specifically, the fourteen thousand airlifted Cuban children. I deliver a tailor-made speech, but it contains bits and pieces from other talks, especially jokes that have brought the house down every time on other occasions. These are sure-fire jokes, tried and true, guaranteed to evoke spontaneous, uncontrolled laughter. I step up to the microphone as confident as ever, knowing I have a quiver full of golden material. Then, one by one, my killer jokes fall flat. No one laughs. No one responds in any way, whatsoever, to anything I say. Dead silence. I keep the jokes coming, as I always do, ramming them in at the most seemingly inappropriate and unexpected moments, to relieve tension. Not one laugh. Not a one.

I realize I'm addressing a group of professionals who specialize in showing no response whatsoever to anything anyone says to them. That's how they earn their living, by hiding whatever emotional response they might have to anything a patient says. They can't let their guard down, especially at their annual meeting, with all of their colleagues around them.

I close by saying that it's been a delight to speak to two hundred and fifty Freudian analysts knowing that I won't be billed for two hundred and fifty hours of therapy.

Silence. I get the feeling that there's no one out there in that cavernous banquet hall. Somehow, I've managed to warp back in time to some point before the Big Bang, when nothing existed.

The very next day I give a talk at a bookstore in Coral Gables, using many of the same tried-and-true jokes. The audience laughs this time, along with me. Prolonged outright laughter, from start to finish. All of us there have a marvelous time laughing at misfortune.

Go figure.

Or go throw something down the garbage disposal and listen to the sweet, sweet sound of annihilation, which, as I learned at St. Brendan's on that Good Friday, can always hold the promise of a resurrection.

Hooo Weee.

Five

Oh no. Good God in Heaven. No. Please no.

I can't believe my eyes.

My foster parents have arranged for a festive meal with the Rubins, to celebrate the arrival of Tony and Charles into their households. It's a Norman Rockwell painting, save for the palms and the mango tree in the yard. The table is beautifully set. It's a bit crowded, but cozy and cool. In Florida you seldom want it to be cozy and warm. Cool is better, much better.

And the main course is trotted out, as per Norman Rockwell's instructions.

It's the biggest goddamned chicken I've ever seen. I didn't know it was possible for chickens to get so huge. It's the whole deal: the animal itself, in its entirety, save for the head and feet. It's golden brown, and glistening.

Norman Rockwell would have been thrilled if he'd been invited. Every detail seems to have been copied perfectly from that painting of his, which I will see three years later, reproduced in a *Saturday Evening Post* retrospective on his work for that magazine.

Because of that painting, I refuse to go to the Norman Rockwell museum in Stockbridge, Massachusetts, even though I drive past it very often, on the way to my daughter's college. I don't ever want to see that abomination up close.

You know what I'm talking about. Everyone has seen that image of the all-American Thanksgiving dinner with the matriarch bringing out the big bird, the patriarch at her side, perhaps joined to her at the hip, and a table full of grinning, happy faces.

A picture of hell to me.

"I don't eeat cheeken," I announce, loudly, as everyone is busy beaming.

Norma looks crushed and puzzled at the same time. Everyone turns and looks at me with expressions that are just the opposite of those of the diners in Rockwell's painting.

"It's not a chicken. It's a turkey," says Norma.

"Is a cheeken . . . a beeg one," I protest.

"No, it's a turkey. You know, a turkey?"

"Turkey, turkey, turkey," others chime in.

"No . . . eh . . . arr . . . I don' eeat birds," I try to explain.

And everything goes downhill, swiftly. The details are now lost, trapped in my lovely, blessed Vault of Oblivion.

Hell of a way to start a relationship with two generous, loving families who've never run into a gnostic heretic before, or a firm conscientious objector to the consumption of avian flesh. It's the first real test of everyone's mettle: of their resolve to help us, and of our resolve to be helped only as we see fit.

I'm not alone in this, after all. There are two spoiled brats at the table.

Tony has the same problem with birds that I do. In fact, he's been my mentor in this area. Right after the incident at the meat market, which opened my third eye, Tony has been my guru, revealing the deepest darkest secrets about the stygian sources from which spring each and every piece of meat served up to us. He, too, had his third eye opened at that same meat market, three years before me. And in the time between his awakening and my mine, he had learned many other valuable secrets.

His lessons on inner organs will prove unforgettable, especially those on brains, kidneys, and livers.

"Do you know what you're eating?" he asks me, as I sit in my high chair, back in our museum of a house, in Havana.

"Mom calls them *frituritas*."

"No, no, not fritters; do you know what they *really* are?"

"*Muy buenas*," I say. Very good. "*Deliciosas.*" Yummy.

"No, idiot. They're *frituritas de seso.* You're eating a calf's brain, all cut up and deep-fried. A calf is a baby cow, and you're eating the squishy organ that's inside its skull. Do you know what a brain is?"

"No."

"The brain is what we think with and feel with. It's where all memories are stored too."

"Oh."

"Before it gets cooked, it's all pink and slimy, and wrinkled. It looks like a huge ball of worms. Or little snakes."

"Oh . . . ughh . . . oh . . . *vrrroughshhhh.*"

How well I remember that sudden rush of nausea, and the vomit that spewed out. Tony remembers it too.

Tony is the chief gnostic, the high priest of discernment when it comes to *carne* of any kind, the master of all flesh-related knowledge, the *fleischmeister.* But right now, at this table in Norma and Lou's house, Tony's main problem is that he can't speak a word of English, and that he has to leave all of the confessing and protesting to his lone disciple, who lacks the requisite eloquence.

And there's no equivalent of the Holy Spirit in our strange food cult, no Paraclete who can help us speak in tongues, or make us understood in languages other than our own.

The dinner disintegrates into a sad occasion, marred by our refusal to eat the main course and our inability to explain our revulsion.

Eating a bird sandwich is one thing; seeing the bird carved up and served to you is a whole other step, much steeper, which I can't take. And watching others gnaw on drumsticks is more than Tony and I can take. We try to shield our eyes as we eat the potatoes and the other stuff that's harmless.

Welcome to the adjustment period. *Ay.*

Being such good people, the Chaits and Rubins are not about to give up on us. So they make accommodations, and try again to have a nice group dinner, very soon after this fiasco. By that time, somehow, I've managed to draw up a list for Norma with the help of a dictionary. It's a list of the foods I can't eat, which include all birds, all water-dwelling creatures, and every inner organ I can think of. It's a good and thorough list, I think. And even though I'm a snot-faced brat, I have enough sense to be grateful for Norma's openness to my very peculiar food phobias. I know I must seem like a Martian to her.

So, a second gathering is arranged. This time, I say to myself, I have nothing to fear. My list is so clear, so complete, there can be no repeat of the last fiasco.

Same setting. Same inner beauty to the gathering, and to the people around the table. Everything feels so right, and looks so swell. So Norman Rockwell perfect.

Out comes the strangest and ugliest piece of meat I've ever seen. It's huge and purple and kind of tubular, and it has a very lumpy and fatty appendage at one end.

"*Qué coño es esto?*" Tony and I both ask ourselves, silently. The *coño* is a mortal sin, but it slips out, much like an *ouch*. What the hell is this?

"Eh . . . wat eez deez?" I ask, nervously.

"Tongue," says Norma. "Boiled tongue."

Qué coño es tong? I ask myself, risking hell again. I'm sure Tony is asking himself the same question.

For the life of me, I can't figure out what this piece of meat could be. It looks like a gargantuan slug, with a yellowish tumor on its rear end.

"Eh . . . wat eez tong?" I dare to ask.

Norma sticks out her tongue and points to it.

"*Lengua! Dios mio! Lengua. Quién come eso?*" I didn't know it was possible to eat tongue, or that the thought of doing so would cross anyone's mind.

Whirrrrr! Lou fires up the electric carving knife and begins to attack that huge cow tongue as if it were a nice piece of rump roast. *Slice, slice, slice.*

"Here, try it."

I can't really refuse it, since it's not on *the* list, my equivalent of the Geneva Conventions. A deal is a deal, and these people are so nice, I can't dig in my heels on this one, even though I've been blindsided by my own ignorance of the depths to which humans will sink when it comes to turning animals into food.

So I try it. And Tony tries it too.

I've never tasted anything so foul, so vomit-inducing, in all of my brief time on earth. It's not just the taste, but the texture. It's like rubber, coated with toxic slime. There's no way of chewing it up quickly and just swallowing it. The flavor is strong, aggressive, impossible to ignore. Every bite makes it gush out, and there are so many bites to take.

Mary, Mother of God, help me.

I chew and chew and so does Tony. We're watching each other, carefully. "If he can take it," I tell myself, "so can I." Tony's thinking exactly the same thing.

Then I look at the carved-up tongue on its platter, and I begin to lose my resolve. The sight of it is worse than the chamber of horrors inside my mouth.

I try to pretend I'm hiccuping, as I did with the nuns on my first night at the camp, but the gagging that takes over me is much too powerful to disguise.

I spit the rubbery chewed-up tongue into my napkin, as I pretend to wipe my mouth, and I slip this disgusting mess to my good friend Victor, under the table. I pray that no one sees this maneuver, as Victor chews up what I've just given him.

Fade to black. Total blackout. Past this point, I can access nothing that happened, save for feelings of shame and revulsion, and regret. This one is at the very bottom of my Vault of Oblivion.

Flash forward, forty-seven years. I'm speaking with Tony on the phone, as I do every night. "Oh, man," he says in his perfect Chicago accent, "do you remember that tongue dinner?" Tony uses the f-word a lot, so please insert that very special expletive in that sentence and all others spoken by him at the appropriate places. Use your imagination on this assignment, or refrain, however you prefer. "That's the worst thing I ever had to eat. Jeeezus, I couldn't believe it, that fat tongue, there on the table. What a sight, what a disgusting sight. Oh man, I can't think of anything worse than that tongue, ever."

And he goes on about the tongue for about five minutes, finding very creative ways of expressing his disgust, and his dismay at what it meant for him and for me at that moment, in those foster homes. It was as much a turning point for him as it was for me: proof positive that we'd entered the Twilight Zone, some sort of alternate dimension where you could never get your bearings because everything was so weird, so mind-blowingly and unpredictably strange.

Whenever I need a good laugh, I bring up the tongue dinner.

"Hey, Tony, how about that tongue?"

We speak in English now, all the time. The only time Spanish comes up is when we're talking about something someone said, long ago, in that other world we both lost so suddenly.

Funny thing: Both Tony and I became addicted to the television show *The Twilight Zone* at that time, right after the tongue dinner, even though we still didn't have full command of English. We've talked about it many times. The show made us feel more at home than almost anything else, back then.

Leaving the cave and entering the "real" world requires major adjustments in thinking. Plato had foreseen that, of course. He knew that those who escaped from the world of illusion would have trouble adjusting to the light and dealing with the real world. But he failed to go into the gritty details, as many philosophers do. He said nothing about having to eat tongue.

And he also said nothing about those in the real world who would have to contend with the refugees from the world of illusion. What crazy bastards, those cave dwellers. If Plato had been more thorough, he might have addressed this problem: the nonsense that people in the real world would have to put up with whenever those annoying refugees would emerge from their cave.

"Eh . . . wat eez deez?"

"Go back to that stinking burrow that you came from, you troglodyte. Ingrate. Ignoramus. *Kvetch*, chronic, whining complainer."

Allow me to explain that sudden slip into Yiddish.

Tony and I learned Yiddish along with English. That was a delight, and a surprise, later, after we'd left those foster homes. Tony and I thought that all of the Yiddish words we'd learned were English. Well, to put it that way is misleading. We simply thought every word uttered in our households was English. Why wouldn't we?

Surprise, surprise, surprise! *Oy!*

Every now and then, someone is shocked by my Yiddish. Just as shocked as I was to learn that all those wonderful words were incomprehensible in central Illinois.

"So-and-so is such a *schnorr*."

"Say what? Is that Spanish?"

After the tongue dinner, *the* list became complete. All possible surprises were eliminated by one simple category: no inner organs of any kind, even from all permissible quadrupeds. Tony and I would end up eating a lot of egg dishes. And we'd learn to fend for ourselves in the kitchen, for the first time in our lives.

We learned how to make scrambled eggs. Norma taught me how to do it, and I couldn't believe that she'd trust me with a frying pan. Back home, my parents wouldn't have ever allowed me near a stove. I could detonate huge firecrackers, climb tall trees, walk along narrow high ledges, and engage in rock fights all the time, but handling fire on the stove was too dangerous. I never asked why. Anyway, after a few days, my scrambled eggs began to evolve from so-so to very good. Soon enough, my eggs were the best I'd ever tasted. The same thing happened to Tony.

I learned how to make my own sandwiches too, with cold cuts. And I found a new mysterious foodstuff called peanut butter, which tasted great.

The best thing of all was learning to be independent, and to be given some responsibilities.

Norma taught me how to take out the trash and put me in charge of that. It was a big threshold for me to cross, another one of those Twilight Zone moments. Back where I came from, only servants would handle the trash. The fact that I was being asked to sink to the level of a servant was shocking at first, even though I knew that the Chaits had no maids, nannies, or gardeners. But as soon as she asked me I realized that something was different here. The Chaits didn't have any servants of any kind. They were a middle-class American family, and in this respect they were very different from their Cuban counterparts. In Cuba, even lower-middle-class families often had servants of one sort or another, at least until Fidel came along. I caught on to that right away, and chalked it all up as yet one more indication that this was a more advanced country. Everyone must do their own work, and no one seems to mind. It seemed ennobling to me.

Or so I thought.

Flash forward, forty-one years. I'm talking to Norma and Lou in their kitchen, in Cooper City, near Fort Lauderdale, reminiscing about the time I lived with them. Norma tells me that I recoiled with horror at the prospect of taking out the trash and that I put up some strong resistance to it. The way she remembers it, I never got over my revulsion. I'm shocked. How can her memory be so different from mine? I've remembered this as one of the most important steps I took in life, and as something that I came to treasure and love, and for which I thank God above.

Funny thing, memory. Go figure.

Slowly, gradually, we became more accustomed to one another's weirdnesses.

And immediately, Tony and I were sent to school. Both of us had missed an entire year of schooling in Cuba, and now it was late April and the school year in Florida was almost over. But that didn't matter. We were both plunked down in English-speaking public schools: Tony went to Rockway Junior High and I to Everglades Elementary. Both of us set ourselves back a whole year, knowing we had a lot of catching up to do.

I was supposed to be in sixth grade, but asked to be placed in fifth; Tony was supposed to be in ninth, but asked for eighth. We did it knowingly and willingly. We'd missed too much schooling and didn't know enough English. It hurt me to take a step back, but I knew it was the right thing to do. It was the very first important choice I made on my own, and a good one, as it turned out.

In high school, a few years later, I'd be the first one in my class to get a driver's license, which instantly improved my social life.

Everglades Elementary School was aptly named. Back then, the Everglades were not all that far from it. Soon after my arrival there, a forest fire broke out in that nearby jungle and the wildlife began to scatter. Warnings were issued at school: Watch out for panthers at recess time. If you see one, go immediately back to your classroom. Alligator sightings in the canal that ran right past the school were also common, even though I never saw one.

I went straight into one of the portable classrooms outside the main school building. It was a cabin on stilts, filled with Cuban children. The main objective in that classroom was to teach us English and prepare us for the classrooms in the main building. Our English teacher was a very young and very gentle guy named Aaron: a Russian Jew who'd spent time in Argentina and spoke Spanish fluently. We Cubans jokingly called him *El Ruso*, the Russian, and he understood the ironic undercurrent in that name. We were all there fleeing the Russians who had taken over our nation, and here we were learning English in the United States from a Russian. It made us all laugh.

Aaron seemed larger-than-life to me. He knew many languages and had multiple identities. He was patient. He was compassionate. He was very, very funny too. And, best of all, he sure knew how to teach. I'd had some good teachers in Cuba, but this guy was undoubtedly the best I'd ever had the good luck to run into. Even though I arrived at the end of the term, he made me feel at home right away, and he helped me catch up. We had a Cuban teacher in the classroom too, but I can't remember her having much of a role. Aaron was in charge of teaching English, and we spent most of our time doing that.

One of the very first things the other kids told me was that Aaron had jumped into the canal to rescue a drowning boy, and that he hadn't given a second thought to the alligators that prowled the waters. So, on top of it all, the guy was a hero.

And I can't for the life of me recall his surname. That's how friendly and informal he was with us, a very rare thing for a teacher back then.

English all the time, from bell to bell. Some math, science, and social studies, yes, with some music and art thrown in. But English was our main focus. Let's get these kids ready for life in the United States, let's mainstream them as soon as possible. Drill after drill after drill. Constant exposure to grammar and vocabulary. Let's make sure these kids don't stay marginalized; let's give them a real fighting chance at becoming Americans.

No bilingual coddling crap. Learn English, it's what you need in order to climb out of the bottom. Spanish is wonderful, yes, and you shouldn't forget that, but you're here now, and Spanish won't get you anywhere. None of us in that portable classroom disagreed with that. All of us were on fire to learn English and to get out of that cabin on stilts.

Don't ask me what I think about my fellow Hispanics who insist on bilingual everything, or about how I feel every time I see a public sign in Spanish or am asked to choose between English and Spanish on the telephone. Don't ask, please. I get too angry. There's no better way of keeping Hispanics down in the United States than to tell them that they don't have to learn English. No better way of creating an underclass. No better way of making everyone else think that Hispanics are too dumb to learn another language, or maybe even the dumbest people on earth.

I had an advantage over most of the kids in that class. When I went home, no one spoke Spanish. So I learned English very, very quickly. By the time June rolled around and school was over, I was already fluent. Yes, I made mistakes all the time and I still had an accent, but I could communicate easily in English, read in English, and understand television and movies without the aid of subtitles.

Aaron helped me overcome my fear of seeming foolish, which is always the greatest obstacle in learning how to use a new language. He didn't work all that hard on our pronunciation, knowing that it would straighten itself out soon enough. Speak it. Say it. Never mind your mistakes. Everyone makes them at first.

And I made a whopper of a mistake that made Aaron laugh out loud one day. He'd asked us to write an essay in English describing and analyzing the content of some work of art. We had several famous paintings to choose from. I chose *Dempsey and Firpo* by George Wesley Bellows, a rendition of the 1923 heavyweight boxing match between the American Jack Dempsey and the Argentine Luis Ángel Firpo. I'd been hearing about this fight all my life because my grandfather had been a great fan of Firpo's and had even named one of his dogs after him. As if this were not enough, this was a very cool painting. What could be cooler than violence of any sort, depicted on canvas? Or cooler than a boxer getting knocked out of the ring?

I began to search my dictionary for the translation to *pelea*, which is what we called a boxing match in Cuba. It was a key word. Without it, I had nowhere to go. And there, under *pelea*, I'm given some choices, and I make what I think is a good one. I go on to write one hell of an essay in English, in which I exhaust whatever anyone might be able to say about this masterpiece, which surely ranks up there with da Vinci's *Mona Lisa*, Gainsborough's *Blue Boy*, or Whistler's *Mother*—the only three other paintings I could name at the time, other than the ones hanging on the walls of my house back in Havana. It's a fabulous essay, unlike any ever written on the subject, especially by a kid struggling with the English language.

As soon as I'm done I hand the essay to Aaron, and he begins to read it immediately. And the first thing he does is laugh out loud. Not just one laugh, but one of those long laughing fits that seem eternal.

"What's so funny?"

Aaron reads back the first line: "This painting is about two boxers who are quarreling."

"Quarrel, yes," I protest. "It's the English for *pelea*. I looked it up in the dictionary."

Aaron laughs some more, and then he explains the difference between *quarrel* and *fight* in such a light-hearted way that I start laughing too.

And I'm laughing still, as I write this. "Some quarrel," I say every time I stumble onto cage fighting on television.

My Spanish-English/English-Spanish dictionary becomes part of me. I don't wear it around my neck, but I might as well do so. I never let go of it, whenever I'm not playing outdoors or sleeping. Pretty soon it begins to disintegrate, but it doesn't matter: As I wear out the pages I also store away every word I look up, and every phrase in the appendix of slang and colloquial expressions.

I'm broke becomes one of my favorite expressions, along with *to kick the bucket*. Some words are sublime, like *skinflint* and *tightwad*. But every word, no matter how homely, seems a treasure to me. I'm smitten, enraptured by this tongue that bristles with Germanic barbarisms and makes no rational attempt to coordinate spelling and pronunciation. I fall in love with words that match sounds perfectly: *thud, bump, crash, bang, splat, click, clap, clang, ring, bark,* and so on. Their equivalents in Spanish had always sounded awkward to me, unconnected, stolen, phony. Some words are awfully difficult to pronounce, however, and can even get you into trouble. *Sheet* is the most treacherous word of all. *Fork* comes in a close second. Words beginning with two consonants are always a challenge: *stupid,* for instance, always comes out of my mouth as "es-toopit." Final Ds and Ts are a problem too, for my tongue can't distinguish between them. I just can't get the right sound to come out. Final Gs, which are so common in English, are also tricky. *Steal-*

ing always emerges as "es-teelin" and *explaining* as "es-playnin." Some words are designed to trip you up: *squirrel, stress, eschew*. The hardest word of all is *Worchestershire sauce*. I never ask for it by name. It's just "de braun soss."

Learning to bend your tongue and to rewire your brain is a struggle, but it's also very exhilarating because there's no way to lose this wrestling match. Even when you slip up, you always learn something. These new words and expressions give me a buzz. I'm flying high, literally. Drunk on words, on new ways of thinking. It doesn't take me long to discover that my thinking itself is different in English, and that the change brought about by these new ways of thinking is altering my perception of the world. I'm especially struck by the way in which English gives so much more agency to the self, so much more choice and responsibility.

For instance, if you're on your way to school and one of your books falls to the ground, here is what you would say in Spanish: "*Se me cayó el libro.*" It's hard to translate because English doesn't have reflexive verbs. In essence, what you're saying in Spanish amounts to a shirking of responsibility: "The book dropped itself from me." It's a way of thinking and speaking that is prone to fatalism and the creation of a victimized self. "Oh, damn, look at this: The book had the nerve to fall from me. Damn book. Damn gravity. Poor me. If only the laws of nature were different, I wouldn't be having this problem." In English, this is the only correct way of explaining what happened: "I dropped my book." Yes, I suppose one could say "The book fell." But that would be proper only if the book was not being held by you at all in the first place. What a contrast. It's your own damned fault in English: *You* dropped it because *you* weren't holding it tightly enough, or just simply because *you're* a doofus. Wise up. Straighten *yourself* out.

This difference stuns me. It's a totally new way of thinking: a big deal, bigger than any I've ever stumbled on to. Of course, at the time I can't explain it very clearly, if at all. My perception of this mind-bending difference is fuzzy at best, but it hits me hard and shifts my center of gravity. As I would discover much later, the deepest insights are often—if not always—beyond the radar of our conscious, rational selves. What we intuit at deeper levels is often—if not always—what shapes us most intensely.

If you don't want to think of intuition or of the transcendent dimension of tongues and brains as spiritual, that's fine with me. I understand. But I can't help but peer over the edge of the purely physical, as I run my tongue along my teeth, and encounter a realm that our ancestors once deemed "spiritual," which is linked to eternity rather than to the painfully fleeting here and now.

Tongues of flame didn't descend on me or Tony or any of the thousands of Cuban kids who were flowing into Florida. Unlike Christ's apostles at Pentecost, we weren't instantly blessed with xenoglossia or glossolalia, the ability to speak languages other than your own instantly or to speak in a heavenly tongue. We didn't get the gift of tongues, but at least we had nimble tongues of our own, which were capable of learning all sorts of new somersaults, cartwheels, and contortions. Our brains were still pristine, more or less, proverbial blank slates. Every word we learned, every new grammatical rule, didn't get filed away in an already crowded corner of our brains, but rather right next to the Spanish equivalents, in brand-new, easily accessible slots. We actually grew new neurons to handle the logistics of storage and retrieval. Our elders weren't so fortunate. Their brains were far less nimble and their tongues too set in their ways. To most of them, it was a titanic struggle to think and speak in English.

You can't teach an old tongue new tricks. You can sure as hell try. But you'd better be ready for plenty of frustration and disappointment. And very thick accents.

Our ancestors tended to think that words were one of our most direct links with the divine. They also accepted it as a fact that words were a curse. The Bible tells us that God got very, very angry when our ancient forebears aspired to reach his celestial realm by means of a skyscraper. King, architect, foreman, and bricklayer alike, they all spoke the same tongue at Babel, and the project flourished. And God put a stop to it by bending all their tongues, and twisting them in different directions, and by scrambling their brains. So, the profusion of tongues came about, a curse every bit as painful and beautiful as that leveled against us in the Garden of Eden.

And the half-built skyscraper was abandoned, and eventually it turned to dust, and its location was forgotten, along with that of all of Eve's poems, buried in haste, which were now incomprehensible to everyone. Gibberish, all of them.

Beautiful gibberish, but gibberish all the same.

Now, there's a beautiful word in English: *gibberish*. A billion, trillion times better than *turkey*.

Adjusting to both curses—those of Eden and Babel—has always been difficult, but never impossible. In fact, for children, that challenge has always been the greatest joy, the greatest gift of all.

Fershtay? Comprendes, coño?

Six

I've seen many a pool before, but none like this one. It's next door, just over the backyard fence. And these wonderful neighbors have told me that I can swim in it anytime.

If anyone has ever regretted saying anything, it must be this family. And they must rue their generosity deeply. I call nearly every day and ask, "May I come over and swim?"

At least I call first.

The beast in me chafes about having to pick up the phone. I just want to go over there anytime I feel like it. Fortunately, I'm sort of entitled to be a pest. I've become good friends with Mark, the boy next door, who's only one year older than me. Mark is one of the nicest guys I've ever met, and I'm actually surprised that he really exists. He seems more like a character in a novel than a real human being. Or an imaginary friend.

Mark seems nearly perfect, save for the fact that he's so much smarter than me and also smarter than anyone I've ever known. But you can't really fault a guy for being brilliant.

Mark has some sort of heart defect, however, that keeps him from being very active. Swimming is about all he can take, which is why his parents have installed an in-ground pool in their backyard. His curse, my blessing. Whenever I'm swimming with Mark, I fear for him. Norma has assured me that he's not in any imminent danger of having a heart attack or anything like that, but I can't help but think that Mark's always dangerously close to the edge.

Once, months after I first met him, he'd gotten very excited about the fact that it was raining in his front yard, but not in the backyard. Mark ran around his house, around and around, in and out of the rain, shouting loudly, "I can't believe this!" He ran out of breath, fell to the ground, and scared the hell out of me. That would be the very first time I'd ever see anyone so enraptured. Too bad that my worries about Mark's heart would keep me from seeing that mystical ecstasy for what it was.

I'd never known any other kid who constantly skated on thin ice with the grim reaper nipping at his heels. I tried not to put myself in his place, but I couldn't stop from thinking about how I would feel if I were him. *Coño, que mierda.* Mark would die while still a young man, and I'd only find out about it years after it happened.

I guess I had reason to worry about him, back then.

His pool becomes the center of my universe, especially after school lets out in early June. It's small, but its size doesn't really matter much. My chief interest when it comes to pools is not so much swimming in them as jumping into them. And this one has a diving board. I spend most of my time at that pool diving, finding ways of teasing gravity, and of proving to it that it really has no hold on me.

I dream of outrageously elaborate diving platforms and chutes, much like the ones now routinely found in water parks. Most of all, I long to free-fall from great heights, and to make the largest splash ever in the history of the human race. But Mark's diving board is only about four feet high.

Fortunately, I'm now in the land of infinite potential, where just about anything is possible and you really don't know from one day to the next how, exactly, opportunity is going to smack you right in the face, just like a giant bug on Alligator Alley as you're cruising along at sixty miles an hour.

One fine day, out of the blue, Norma and Lou are invited to some country club that has a giant pool in the shape of a *W*, and they bring me and Tony along. Of course, that letter figured prominently in the club's name, but I'll be damned if I can remember what that name was. The giant W pool is cool enough—it's four pools in one—but that's not the best thing about it. Its crowning glory is the tallest multi-level diving tower I've ever seen. I take one look and I know that my parents were absolutely right in sending me away.

I'll take exile any day and lose my family gladly for this thrill. That's my tower, the one I've been waiting for all my life. The top platform seems at least as tall as a five-story building, I guess, incorrectly. It's a ten-meter Olympic competition platform *only* about three stories above the surface of the water. I walk around it. I look up at it, and I resist the temptation to pray to it. This may be the closest I've come to something divine, I think. I peer into the water directly beneath it. It's beautifully deep, at least another five stories down to the bottom, I guess. It's not really that deep, but it sure looks like it. The color and transparency of the water remind me of the seashore at my Havana beach club. But this is better: There are no sea urchins, moray eels, or crabs at the bottom.

It's spiffy clean.

The only problem is that there's an enormously long line of kids waiting for their turn on this tower. From far away, the kids in line look like ants waiting their turn at a picnic basket. Up close, they're noisy, excited, and edgy. Most of them have trouble standing still. One by one they jump off at different levels. The line that moves the fastest is the one for the bottom springboard. The line for the top platform would probably be illegal nowadays. It's a continuous line from the pool deck all the way to the very top, and this means that there are dozens of kids clinging to a ladder that goes straight up about thirty feet. No safety rails or anything of the sort. It's a metal ladder and everyone has wet feet, and there's a lot of jostling and horsing around.

Tony and I split up immediately. He goes straight to the top platform and spends all of our time diving from there. Given the long lines, we don't cross paths at all. We're used to leading separate lives by now. So I nearly forget that he's there at all.

I take the lower springboard first, after a long wait in line. Hoo Weee. That was great. I do it a couple more times. Then I move to the middle level, the greatest height from which I've ever taken a leap. Hoo Weee. I do notice as I approach the edge and get ready to dive that an unexpected optical illusion makes the bottom of the pool seem very, very far down. It's a slight shock, but I don't let it disturb me.

I know I'm ready for the top platform.

I begin the long, slow climb. As I'm waiting in line, the kid behind me pokes fun at the religious medals hanging around my neck. They are my talismans, given to me by my parents. I never take them off. Ever. One of them—a medal of the Virgin Mary—has been in the family since the 1830s, and Louis XVI made a big deal of removing it from its display case and hanging it around my neck. In my mind, its sentimental value competes with its spiritual power.

Eventually, I'll end up losing this treasure at the Indiana Dunes, while swimming in Lake Michigan, seven years after King Louis gave it to me. I won't discover that it's fallen off its chain until I'm already back in Chicago, late at night. Of course, when something of that magnitude happens, God's not going to allow it to simply vanish from your conscience too easily. No way.

The very last time I spoke with my father on the phone, just a couple of months before he died, he had to ask, "Do you still have the medal?"

And I just had to lie to him: "Yes."

"Great, I'm so glad. Take good care of it."

Those were the last words he ever spoke to me. Sorry. Very sorry, Dad. *Lo siento muchísimo.* I wish I still had it with me.

"Hey, what are those dog tags?" asks the punk who's in line behind me.

"Holy medals. I'm Catholic."

"Oh, that's too bad. So sorry to hear that," he snorts.

I climb up the tall ladder, slowly. It's more like simply hanging on to the ladder than climbing it, the line moves so slowly. I pass the middle platform. The goal is near, finally, and now there's no turning back. With a long line behind you, there's no way to change your mind and go back down. And with each rung I climb I notice that the ground below me seems to be getting farther and farther away in a disproportionate measure.

How weird. This has never happened before. Of course, I've never been up this high before either, except inside a building.

The higher I climb, the stronger the vertigo gets. It's as if the earth is receding from me, sinking lower and lower, even when I'm not climbing. My head reels. I start to get woozy, and I feel as if my entrails are being sucked out of me by gravity. I look over my shoulder, to the line below, and I feel as if I've just been launched from Cape Canaveral. Hooooo. I'm in outer space, the ground seems so far down.

I think of Jimmy Stewart in Hitchcock's *Vertigo*, one of my favorite movies. I curse Hitchcock for not doing enough to convey a better sense of what it feels like to have the earth recede from you at the speed of light. All this time, I'd thought that Jimmy was just a little dizzy, and maybe something of a wimp.

So, this is it. This is vertigo. Hooooo.

When I finally reach the top platform, I get my bearings again. The ground stops pulling away from me, my guts rebound, and I'm able to look at the amazingly flat landscape around me without feeling woozy. Standing at the back of the platform is just like being inside a building: It gives you the sense of being enveloped by a structure. That awful feeling I had back there, on the ladder, ebbs. I take in the clouds, which look like a mountain range. I take in the sight of the people below, who look very small. I admire the big *W* of the pool, so turquoise, so perfectly carved into the landscape.

And everyone behind me starts yelling at me. "Huurry uuup!" "Juuump, already!"

I step up to the edge, out in the open. Nothing above but blue sky and ridiculously puffy clouds in all shades of white and gray, with hints of yellow; nothing below but the big turquoise *W* and the pool deck. Hooooo. What's this? The pool below recedes, nearly vanishes. Suddenly I'm a mile high, not ten meters. The bottom of the pool is so far down that I know I will surely die if I jump off. No one can survive this.

Yelling behind me. Lots of yelling. I've stalled the line. For all I know Tony is one of those yelling the loudest.

I know I can't go back down the ladder, and I know that if I jump, I'll die. This is it, I think: This is my last moment on earth.

I stare at the pool's bottom, a mile down. All of the open space around me and the vast abyss beneath close in on me. What a tight spot. I can't inconvenience those on the ladder, especially because they're all yelling at me. The politeness drummed into me since birth makes it necessary for me to jump. And I know if I just stand there, my wooziness will make me fall off. So I have no choice. I cross myself and leap into the crushing void. I fall and tumble, unable to steady my body as I plummet. I wanted to taunt gravity, and here I am, being sucked in like a bug on a lizard's tongue. The fall ends very quickly, and painfully. I hit the water hard, at an awkward angle.

Splat! Yeow! I've made the biggest splash ever, but, good God almighty, I feel as if I've hit the pool deck instead of the pool. The pain I feel and the water rushing up my nostrils are the only proof I have that I haven't died, because my eyes simply won't open. I let gravity have its say, and sink as far as it will take me. Then, slowly, I drift up, patting my chest with my hands to make sure I haven't lost my Mary medal; I break the surface, and swim to the pool's edge, my body throbbing from head to foot.

Many years later, while reading about Olympic divers, I'll discover that hitting the water flat from ten meters up can cause severe internal and external bruising, strains to the tissues that hold internal organs in place, and minor hemorrhaging in the lungs. *Splat!* Yeow!

No more diving for me that day, at the big *W* pool. No more dreams about colossal diving structures, either. None, ever again. My admiration for Jimmy Stewart—which was already very intense because of his access to Kim Novak's lips—increases tenfold, and now, more than ever, I set my sights on becoming Jimmy someday, or at least as close to Jimmy Stewart as any Cuban can hope to be.

I'm still unable to fully separate actors from the characters they play. But I've become an expert at separating my present life from my previous one. Charles has banished Carlos to the grave in which he belongs, a grave that is at least ten meters deep, on the planet Vertigo.

Yet, Carlos is summoned from the afterlife, much in the same way that spirits were summoned to the Ouija board by Louis XVI. Twice a week Norma and Lou summon Carlos's spirit to possess Charles, who then has no choice but to call Tony and talk to him. Once a week Carlos is also asked to move Charles's hand, as if it were a planchette on a Ouija board, and to pen letters to his parents, back in Plato's cave. On Sundays, no one has to summon Carlos. He simply shows up, takes over Charles, and makes him pedal all the way to St. Brendan's Church, where he suffers through the mass and exchanges a few words with his brother Tony.

That Sunday deal is weird, yes, but it feels all right.

The sole uncomfortable glitch in this new life is Freddy, the Cuban neighbor. Charles is forced to speak Spanish to Freddy, because Freddy is foolish enough to think that he's still the same person he was back in Cuba. Freddy refuses to accept the fact that Federico died, probably because his aunt and uncle keep invoking the dead boy's name, summoning him from the spirit world. Freddy is constantly possessed, and even more so in his house. Sometimes he manages to shake off Federico's spirit outdoors, or at my house, but the instant he gets within ten feet of his house, Federico rudely pushes Freddy out of his body and takes over.

This might be the chief reason behind our strained relationship. Federico is always looking for Carlos, and can't find him. Instead, he has to deal with Charles, who can sometimes be insufferably obtuse.

Mark is so much easier to get along with, not just because he's an easygoing guy and so smart, but also because Mark doesn't know that Carlos ever existed. Norma notices this, and observes this one day: "You and Mark get along so well, but you and Freddy are always fighting."

Sometimes we'd come to blows. But we'd always patch things up. We needed each other as much as we disliked each other. One time, however, Freddy tested our friendship to the utmost. Or maybe it was Federico. Or both of them together.

I'd developed a monster crush on a certain girl and was dumb enough to tell Freddy about it. I should have known better. Carlos was dead, but Charles still had all of his memories, intact. Back in the cave, in the old country, Carlos had been betrayed by a friend who'd been entrusted with the secret of Carlos's infatuation with a beautiful brown-haired girl. This Judas had told everyone else and arranged for a humiliating mating ritual in the school yard. So Carlos knew that Cubans shouldn't be trusted with love secrets and that Cubans also had a tendency to mock that most sacred of feelings and to embarrass the hell out of both parties in any love affair, whenever possible.

Charles owned that memory, but he made the mistake of ignoring it. Besides, this girl he'd fallen in love with was American. This was a totally different situation. New world, new life, new rules. Charles assumed that Freddy was on the same wavelength.

Jesus H. Judas-kissing Christ.

Freddy swam in Mark's pool very often because my free pass was extended to him too, and he hung out with me all the time. Normally, no females came anywhere near the pool, and the idea that some girl might end up swimming with us was simply inconceivable. Then, somehow, one magical day, unexpectedly, the object of my affections ended up at Mark's pool too. It was a miracle. I was so, so happy, and so fired up. If I'd been able to, I'd have jumped from a diving tower ten times higher than the one at the W pool, and not felt even a twinge of vertigo. Hell, I'd have jumped from the Telstar satellite, orbiting above the earth, into a wading pool. I'd have done anything to impress her. But the last thing I'd have done was to let her know how much I loved her.

For many, many years this totally moronic approach to romance governed my relationships with all of the females who beckoned me from eternity, not with words, but by simply being who they were. I'd never disclose my feelings, no matter how perfect they were, no matter how sublime their wrists or voices were, no matter how divine their presence. No way. It seemed like an imposition, some sort of rudeness, to let any female know how crazy I was for her. Or simply how crazy I was, period.

What I always wanted to say sounded odd to me, even though it made perfect sense.

"Hey, I've known you forever. Where have you been? I've missed you, so much."

Doctors Freud and Jung, please chime in at this point, if you feel like it. Too late now to help me with this problem, but I'd love to hear your take on it. My guess is that you won't attribute it all to brain chemistry, thanks be to God. But while you're at it, please also try to explain Freddy's behavior at the pool that day. I go nuts every time I think about it.

Freddy got his hands on a big black crayon, dove into the pool, and began to inscribe the walls of the pool—underwater—with very large hearts that contained my name and that of my soul mate. Heart after heartbreaking heart, all along the wall, round the entire perimeter, each about the size of a toilet seat.

Given that my attention was wholly focused on the girl in our midst, I didn't catch on to what Freddy was doing until it was far too late.

What's he doing? No. No. *Coño.* Dear God, no.

Unfortunately, by that point I couldn't do anything except to jump into the pool, grab him by the neck, and say through clenched teeth: *"Te voy a matar."* I'm going to kill you.

But I didn't kill him. I let him go, and he ran away, leaving the gate to the pool open. I stared at the pool walls, and at those offensive hearts and the names in them, which could be read clearly enough through the ripples. I wanted to shrink and disappear, to be swallowed whole by the earth. It was a very different kind of vertigo from the kind I'd felt on top of the diving platform, but vertigo all the same. Everything pulled away from me at the speed of light, including that wondrous girl, whose face I couldn't dare to look at.

She left, quickly, and never spoke to me again, ever.

I apologized to Mark, assuming responsibility for Freddy's dumb-ass stunt, simply because if it hadn't been for me, he wouldn't have been there in the first place. Mark shrugged it off. The next time I came over, the hearts were gone, totally wiped out, as if they'd never been there. Mark's parents were nice enough never to say anything about it, and I was far too embarrassed to bring up the subject. At that age, you always hope and pray that bad stuff will go away on its own, thinking that if you don't acknowledge its existence the nasty stuff will simply vanish, as if it had never taken place. And that's exactly what had happened here. No way I was going to bring it up.

God only knows how long they had to scrub the walls in order to get rid of those hearts, or how much they had to pay someone to do it.

I couldn't decide what upset me the most: the fact that Freddy had totally ruined my chances with this girl, or the fact that a fellow Cuban had defaced a very generous neighbor's pool. Charles was befuddled, ashamed of what Federico had done. It had to be Federico, not Freddy. Those dead Cuban boys could sure get you into a heap of trouble, much against your will. And they could also make you feel very ashamed of once having been Cuban.

That pool never felt the same afterward. I couldn't swim in it or jump into it without feeling a twinge of guilt and vertigo. Poor Charles was very, very confused by all this unpleasantness, which had been caused by a Cuban. And even if Carlos was buried ten meters deep on the planet Vertigo, Charles knew very well that there was still a link between him and that dead boy, and—through him—to every other Cuban.

Whatever one lone Cuban might do is a reflection of what any Cuban is capable of doing. One jerk, two jerks, six million jerks. It's a geometric progression unlike any other on earth: One bad Cuban makes all Cubans look bad, especially on foreign soil.

"*Coño, que mierda,*" shouted Carlos from his grave, not even caring that one single utterance of the word *coño* was enough to transport him from the planet Vertigo to hell, forever and ever.

When your own people betray you, the only right thing to do is to spew forth the worst words of all, even to shout them as loudly as possible, again and again, until the sound of them fills the whole earth and makes the mountains crumble. When your own body betrays you, it's one thing. A big nose, or buck teeth, or vertigo are not your fault. You can chalk it up to biology and a crummy set of genes. But when your own people betray you, it's a whole different ball game, because they make you hate yourself with a passion, simply for being one of *them.* It's not a fully rational response, but then again, reason can take you only so far.

What matters most is always totally unreasonable. Totally.

Like the shape of a girl's wrist, or the way her hair brushes against her cheek.

Seven

J uan Becquer has come to pick me up. Tony's already in Juan's beat-up car. Some sort of Plymouth, but a lot newer than the one my dad owned back in Havana. He's come to take us to his house so we can spend the weekend with him and his family.

He thinks we need this.

Truth be told: Charles doesn't think he needs any time away from the Chait household, or from the United States of America. Going for a weekend at the Becquers' will be a lot like leaving the country. Even though I've never been to their house, I know it'll be very Cuban, and I'd rather forget about all that Cuban stuff.

We drive for a long, long time, and we end up in a neighborhood that doesn't look at all like Miami. At least not the Miami I've come to know. This place is all run-down and full of old ugly houses and lousy old cars, some worse than Juan Becquer's. The trees are old, and huge, and they smother everything with a very dense choking shade. For the first time since I left Cuba, I'm in a place that might be full of ghosts.

Is this the same country I've been living in?

Shotgun shack. That's what they live in. A long narrow house that feels more like a railroad car than a house. But there's no hallway. To get from the front room to the back, you walk through room after room. Somewhere in there, a few rooms back, there's a kitchen and a bath-room. If all of the doors were to be opened at the same time, you could blast away with a shotgun from the front room—which is a porch of sorts—and the pellets would come out of the back door.

This is not how it was for the Becquers in the old country. Far from it. Their house was nicer than ours. Much nicer. In fact, it was nicer than any house I've been to in Miami thus far: more like the houses in Coral Gables—that nearly exact replica of my native Miramar—or those houses on those small islands between Miami and Miami Beach. Six people live in this wooden shack: Mr. and Mrs. Becquer, their two small children, and Mrs. Becquer's parents. The old folks are in double exile: They're Spaniards who fled to Cuba back when it was part of the civilized world.

Tony and I are going to sleep in the front room, which is practically all windows. And that's just fine because this house doesn't have any air-conditioning or fans.

It's good to see the Becquers again, and eat Cuban food. I begin to feel my split personality surface, intensely. I'm no longer just "me," but Charles *and* Carlos.

Charles had forgotten how good Cuban food could be and had steadfastly refused to admit to himself that American food was far inferior. So tasteless, for the most part, and so unimaginative. A piece of animal flesh. A vegetable. A starch of some sort, usually potatoes. Salt and pepper. Some bottled sauce of some sort for the meat. God forbid that any of these basic elements ever be mixed, or spiced up.

Here, in this shack, it's impossible to deny the inferiority of American cuisine. The fried plantains, especially, are out of this world. In the western end of Cuba they were called *chatinos*; in the eastern end they were *tostones*. Carlos always called them *chatinos*.

Charles had forgotten about them. Tony has not. Tony has barely forgotten anything. In fact, Tony refuses to accept his death and stubbornly clings to the illusion that he's still the same boy who climbed onto the KLM flight back in Havana, with his beautiful dark abyss in tow. Maybe it's that abyss he carries inside that prevents him from seeing things as they really are. It's so deep, and so dark, it affects his judgment.

These are green plantains, nice and green, the very essence of tartness and crunchiness. Charles smothers the *chatinos* in salt and he relishes that they're not made from ripe plantains. *Chatinos* made from ripe plantains come out all mushy and are way too sweet. Carlos hated them, and so does Charles.

My, how these folks have tumbled from their high perch, Charles observes, relying on Carlos's memory. Juan Becquer was a successful attorney back in Havana. His wife was also a professional of some sort. Charles doesn't know and really doesn't care what she did. All he cares about is how good these *chatinos* are.

The food unnerves Charles, little by little. He feels Carlos taking over, being pushy, claiming his entire body. Charles resists, even when he hears the two Spanish oldsters speak in their thick accents from the northern coast of Spain. They remind him so much of his grandparents, back in Havana, whom he does not want to miss. Better not to remember them, those Gallegos, for it's too painful. God only knows what might happen if that door gets opened, the door to the Vault of Oblivion. It's the scariest place in the universe, and possibly the lair in which the Void hides out.

The house is neat and clean inside, but there's no hiding the squalor: secondhand furniture, all scuffed, stained, and time-worn; bare walls full of cracks, peeling paint.

Charles gives no thought to the fact that this family is sacrificing a great deal by merely feeding him and his brother, and by spending so much money on gasoline. There's a lot of Miami to cross in order to get here: They don't exactly live next door to the Chaits and Rubins.

It's a long weekend, very long. That house is nothing but a vortex of pain and sadness, and of constant talk about what's been lost and how difficult life is in Miami. Even the little kids look depressed. There's also plenty of storytelling and reminiscing about good times, long ago. Charles begins to feel oddly at peace with Carlos and allows him in. In a weird and unexpected way, this hard-luck family has made both Charles and Carlos feel at home.

The couch in the front room makes for a nice bed. Cozy and cool, under all those jalousie windows. The huge trees outside make the shotgun shack feel like a cottage in the Black Forest, that fabled place Carlos read about long ago, before he died.

Juan Becquer works hard during the week, at Sid Rubin's warehouse. He's a tough character: medium in height, well muscled, something of a bulldog in human form. Nothing seems to get him down. And he's got a tender, fatherly air to him. He tells Charles and Tony that everything will be all right, that the losses will be recovered, somehow, and advises them never, ever to despair. Tony knows what he's talking about, but Charles doesn't have much of a clue. Despair? Come again? Why? Life in the United States of America is just peachy keen.

Juan Becquer and his wife Marta will eventually reinvent themselves, earn PhD's, and become college professors in Michigan. Charles has no way of intuiting at that moment, in that shotgun shack, that the good folks who are trying so hard to comfort him, at great expense, have also died. Grown-ups, he thinks, come over here in one piece, unchanged. They're grown-ups, after all. Nothing affects them. He also has no clue that there are hundreds of thousands of Cuban families like the Becquers in the United States, and especially in Miami, who have willingly embraced poverty for the sake of freedom and consider it a blessing of sorts to find themselves at the bottom of the heap, and an even greater blessing to know that they will climb their way back to the top, no matter what.

Whatever losses Charles has experienced are all emotional, not material. Yes, he misses his family whenever he dares to think about them, and he misses his childhood friends too, but he's gained more than he's lost when it comes to creature comforts. He has his own room, a transistor radio, a baseball glove, a bicycle, plenty of food, a pool next door, a weekly allowance, and loving foster parents. Norma is so wise and funny. Lou is a funny guy too, and cool. He plays the saxophone, for heaven's sake, and sometimes takes Charles to jam sessions, or out on boats to fish in Biscayne Bay. So Charles is very, very happy in his fool's paradise, his comfortable cocoon, out there in Westchester, where there's no squalor whatsoever, and no one ever talks about Cuba.

Idiot. *Imbécil.*

I should have been reading the only book the Cuban authorities had allowed me to bring along on my journey, the awful book chosen by my parents: *The Imitation of Christ*, written by Thomas à Kempis in the fifteenth century and translated into Spanish by Juan Eusebio Nieremberg in the seventeenth. But I couldn't read that depressing book any more than I could have pounded nails into my own hands and feet or rammed a crown of thorns onto my head.

Good God. Jesus H. Inimitable Christ.

My parents had told me that the book would always answer whatever questions I had, especially those that had to deal with which path to take. It was an old Spanish superstition, similar to the English Protestant one about the Bible. Ask your question, open the book at random, and there you'll find your answer, somewhere on those two pages. Search through them; the Spirit will lead you to the right passage.

I'd already tried that several times, but the book never spoke to me in a good way. Instead, it scared me half to death. Every page was filled with instructions on how to empty yourself and gain detachment from the world. Set your sights on heaven, not earth. Forsake the world. The light is above, always above, not down here. True love is selflessness, endless giving of yourself to others, endless suffering that will be amazingly transformed into the ultimate joy. Avoid loving this world with your heart of clay, forget about girls' ankles, fast cars, baseball games, even your transistor radio; forget anything and everyone in this world, including your entire family.

Forget it all. Let go. This is all like a bad dream that seems real. The real life is elsewhere. What you're really pining for with every fiber of your being is not here.

Not exactly what an eleven-year-old boy wants to hear. Or anyone else of any age, for that matter. It's the most depressing book ever written by any human being, in all of human history.

Oddly enough, I was as attached to that accursed book as I was to the Mary medal that Louis XVI had given me, and which I'd eventually lose. It was my only physical contact with my loved ones, those whom I didn't want to admit that I missed. I kept it close at hand, as a talisman or a holy relic, even though I couldn't abide what it had to say. I wasn't ready for it. No way, no how. So I clung to the book that told me not to cling to anything on earth.

If my life was a dream, it was a good one, I told myself. Damn good. Little did I know how quickly I'd wake up, and how much I would need that book's advice. Eventually, it would save me from myself.

While I wasn't looking, and while no one else in the world was looking, the Soviet Union was filling up Cuba with nuclear missiles. Some Cubans knew about it, of course, and many of them tried to tell the world. Some went straight to those very, very intelligent folks in Washington, D.C., who worked for President Kennedy, but their reports were dismissed as fables, or mere rumors. "Crazy Cuban exiles," they said in Washington. And as Cuba filled up with enough nuclear weapons to wipe out the entire East Coast of the United States and most of the Midwest, my clock began to tick loudly, even though I couldn't hear it at all.

Soon enough, I'd lose everything, again, in an instant. Those missiles would never be fired, but they'd kill me nonetheless, and also every other airlift kid whose parents were still stuck in Cuba.

I went back to the Chaits' after that weekend at the Becquers' shack feeling odd, less sure of who I really was. Carlos had taken over Charles a bit too intensely. Charles had also realized that maybe there's a level of comfort among your own that can't be duplicated among foreigners, no matter how nice they are to you. Squalor has its charms, under the right circumstances, with the right folks.

While I was with the Becquers, I couldn't help but wonder where my uncle Amado was, and why Tony and I never heard from him. Being with Cubans who weren't related to me made me think of Amado. I had family here, after all. But where was he?

Uncle Amado was my father's older brother. He'd left Cuba just a few months before Tony and me, and he lived in Miami. But it was as if he'd disappeared into thin air. At the time I had no way of understanding why. Now I do, of course.

The man was sixty-two years old, and he had a wife and two daughters to take care of. And one of his daughters had special needs, as we say nowadays. She'd always been a bit slow and physically challenged. Amado had been a successful architect back in Havana, head of his own firm. And here he was in a new country, penniless. At an age when most men began to prepare for retirement, he had to start all over again. As if this weren't bad enough, there was no work for him in Miami. The city was flooded with Cuban refugees, many of them professionals of all sorts, and there weren't enough jobs to go around, not even menial ones. Juan Becquer was one of the lucky ones, having landed a job as a janitor.

God knows what Amado, his wife, and two daughters were doing, or where they were living. But you can bet that they weren't too happy or comfortable. And you can bet that Amado had more on his hands than he could handle. Hell, I'm surprised that he didn't simply melt away. If I had to toss my profession aside, give up everything I owned, and move to a foreign land right now with a handicapped child in tow—at the age of fifty-nine—I'd probably dissolve into a puddle. The last thing I'd want to do is to add two snot-faced boys to my household, or even to check up on them.

I have to be honest with myself, and with you.

One fine day, however, Amado finally showed up. The whole gang came to visit us, at the Rubins' house: Uncle Amado, Aunt Alejandra, and cousins Marisol and Alejandrita. They came to say good-bye, even though they hadn't yet come to say hello. Amado was being relocated to a small town in Illinois, one of those northern states. Like thousands of other Cubans in Miami, and like all of the airlift kids, he was being booted from Miami, where there was no place for him.

They knew nothing about their destination or what might be waiting for them, other than the fact that Amado had been hired by an architectural firm as a draftsman, for a whopping ninety dollars a week, before taxes. This was an offer he couldn't refuse. It was all part of a federal program that relocated Cubans all over the United States. Scatter them all, get them out of Miami, as quickly as possible, and as far away as possible. Give employers a bonus for hiring a Cuban, tell the Cubans that if they don't take the job they'll be completely on their own in Miami. No welfare checks, no food stamps, no medical care. Nothing. *Nada.* Take the job, or else.

So Amado had taken the job in Bloomington, Illinois, hometown of former presidential candidate Adlai Stevenson, and also home to State Farm Insurance, Eureka vacuum cleaners, and Beer Nuts, the preferred snack at many an American bar. Also where Abraham Lincoln had once given a remarkable speech that no one wrote down, a soul-stirring oration, the words of which no one could remember. It's simply known as his "Lost Speech." Of course, Amado and his family knew nothing of this. All they knew was that this was the only choice they had, which is the same thing as having no choice at all. The architect was now going to work as a draftsman. It was better than working as a janitor.

It was strange to see my relatives at the Rubins' house. Matter out of place. Wait a minute. This is my family. My flesh and blood. What? I have relatives? And here they are, saying hello and good-bye at the same time. I'd gotten so used to having no blood relations. Now, many years later, what I think is the weirdest thing of all is that I didn't bother to ask how they'd gotten there. They had no car, and no money to pay for a taxicab ride to the very edge of the city.

As usual, Uncle Amado was wearing a suit and tie—the only one he'd been allowed to bring from Cuba—and he seemed stiff and uncomfortable and couldn't really move the conversation along in his heavily accented English. His wife Alejandra saved the day, though she spoke no English. She had the gift of gab and could put you at ease right away, even through an interpreter. My cousins seemed uneasy and awkward. Tony and I did our best to make this seem like a normal situation, but it was hard going. The whole setup was too weird. I had to do most of the translating, for Tony was still struggling with his English.

All I can remember is that we went out to the backyard, and little Philip Chait, who was then about twenty months old, walked barefoot on the grass, and this amazed my aunt.

"Ay, mira eso!" Look, he's barefoot on the grass!

Being barefoot in Cuba is dangerous. You can pick up parasites that way. It's every mother's worst nightmare, to see a child venture into the outdoors barefoot. Maybe worse than getting an eye poked out. Back then, before Cuba went Neolithic, going barefoot was practically the same thing as going naked. It could only mean two things: You were either destitute or debauched, or both. Letting your children go barefoot in public was akin to hanging a sign around their necks that said "Look, I'm neglected; my parents are the lowest of the low."

To this day I avoid going barefoot even inside my own house. Sandals? *No me jodas.* Only *maricones* or women wear sandals.

That was that for their visit, anyway. They came and went. Good-bye. *Hasta la vista!* Hope to see you again sometime. Good luck.

Zip, they were gone. We'd see them again, but we had no way of knowing that. More than that, they'd end up rescuing us in the end, after our artificially safe and comfortable life was vaporized, like a test dummy at ground zero in a nuclear blast. And the Becquers would also end up doing a lot for us, acting as family even though we weren't related to them. So, in the long run, it would be our strange relatives and some strange outsiders who would come to our rescue when we needed rescuing most intensely.

You never know how things will turn out. Or who your real family might be.

Flash forward, eighteen years.

I'm in Spain, in Galicia. Cool, green, craggy Galicia, where the native Celts and their barbarian German overlords, the Sueves, held out against the Muslim invaders from North Africa back in the year 711. It's the only corner of the Iberian Peninsula that wasn't conquered by the Moors, the tiny sliver of land from which the Reconquest was launched, under the spiritual leadership of Santiago—St. James the Apostle—who was buried there, at Compostela. These people were too rude and savage to allow anyone to steal their land, and the Moors knew better than to mess with them. They were so tough and hardheaded that they made the Visigoths look like wimps. My corner of the world. My ancestral homeland, on my mother's side of the family, and also, in part, on my father's.

I'd just spent a month traveling in Europe, living on trains and in train stations, with hardly any money to spend. Most of my travel budget had been consumed by airfare and a Eurail pass. Hostels and restaurants were out of the question, most of the time. A successful day was one in which I spent no money at all, surviving on whatever food was left in my backpack from the previous day. The markets were great places to pick up cheap food: mostly cheese, bread, and fruit. My greatest expense sometimes was bottled water. A bad day was one in which I'd have to spring for a shower, somewhere. I'd already dropped about twenty-five pounds and my jeans were falling off. I had no notches left to tighten on my belt, so I poked a few more into it with the only luxury I had allowed myself: a Swiss Army knife, purchased in Geneva.

I'd never been happier and seriously considered making this lifestyle my profession. Moving from place to place constantly, living by train schedules, figuring out where to wake up the next morning, discovering new places day after day, with only a duffel bag to weigh me down. Living like the birds and the lilies of the field, with no interest in buying, owning, or being number one at anything. My sole interest was to see all the places I'd read about, to touch the distant past, and to dodge the Void.

This must be the best way to follow *The Imitation of Christ*, I joked to myself.

I'd already covered every country in Western Europe, save for the British Isles, and had finally made it to Spain, where I knew I could mooch off my relatives. After all, I had more family there than anywhere else on earth.

So, I've made it up to Galicia, and I'm staying with family, in the house where my grandmother was born, and her grandmother, and her grandmother, and her grandmother, and so on, God only knows how far back. The place looks and feels older than the Colosseum. It's a house made of stone, and it's cold inside, even in June. It's a farm, and there are livestock in the room directly below mine. This part of the house is really the top floor of a barn. Back in the old days, that's how most farmhouses were built in Europe. The body heat from the livestock helped to warm up the living quarters above for the humans.

I open what I think is a closet, looking for a place to hang my shirts, and I'm surprised by three hams, hanging from hooks. It's the whole leg, really, not just that squat, round piece of meat that we call *ham* in America. These are pig legs I'm looking at, from the hip down, hoof and all: smoked hams, cured by my family. It's *jamón serrano*, the staple of every bar in Spain. The rafters in the kitchen are full of them too. They just hang there, these hams. One of them is always smaller than the others. When you want some, you just pull that one down and slice yourself off a piece. Then you hang it back up.

I've come to Spain in search of my roots. I need to find out who I really am. I need to come home, I tell myself. Cuba is not my real home, and never was. It's a hopeless mess, that odious island, beyond fixing. I'd spent years poring over maps, looking for this spot, longing for it. Not just when I was a small child, but for years and years, even as I was writing my doctoral dissertation, reading German texts all day long.

I'm not the only Cuban there. Sort of. My grandmother's youngest brother, Ramiro, now in his late seventies, had once lived in Cuba. Like many other Gallegos, he returned home after a while, with lots of money in his pockets, and bought up acres and acres of land. Incredible as it may seem, Cuba was once a prosperous place where Europeans went to get rich. Although Uncle Ramiro was born to a family of tenant farmers, he now owns land as far as the eye can see. He opens a window and says to me: "Everything you see here, all the way to the horizon, is mine." Ramiro chops firewood as if he were my age and mows the hay vigorously, with a sickle identical to that of the Grim Reaper. He's one tough guy. Ice-blue eyes bluer than the sky, cheeks so red that they look as if they're on fire. His son Arturo and his grandson Alberto, my cousins, look just like him.

I feel so much at home, and so much like an alien, all at once. This place is in my blood, and it feels right, but in a strange way. It also feels like another planet. For one thing, I've never spent time at a farm before, or pressed my nose against the food chain so intensely. I've just had to select the rabbit we slaughtered for dinner. This is more than a farm: It's more like a survivalist camp, or a hippie compound gone insane for organic food and total sustainability. My family grows and prepares absolutely everything they consume, and they use only natural fertilizers. The only store they visit, I think, is the one that sells parts for their farm equipment. They buy gasoline too, of course, but if they could drill for oil and tap petroleum, I'm sure they'd refine their own fuel too.

Even the grasshoppers are put to use. Cousin Arturo shows me how he catches them and uses them for bait. There are some nice, clear streams flowing nearby, full of fish.

Cousin Arturo takes me into a barn, jug in hand. Inside the barn there's an oak barrel, about six feet in diameter. He turns the spigot and fills the jug with red wine. "We make this ourselves, from our grapes," he says. "Taste it." *Pruébalo*. Oh, man, this is good wine, I say. *Buenísimo*. It's one of the finest wines I've ever tasted, way up there with any great Beaujolais Nouveau.

Any time they want some wine, my relatives just go into that barn and fill up a jug. They bake their own bread too, which is made from the wheat they grow and mill. It's round, dark, and grainy, and it tastes great. They take slices from it with the same big knife that they use on the hams. "Why eat that crap they sell at the store? It's not really bread," says Arturo.

The amount of work they do in order to live like this is incredible. They're up before dawn and they keep going until ten at night, when they finally sit down for dinner, which, when you come right down to it, seems to be the sole purpose for their existence on earth.

So, I tell myself, this is who I really am. This is who I am supposed to be; this is what my blood should compel me to do. I should stop reading. I should give up on being a vagrant for the rest of my life, or a college professor.

Ramiro tells me one night, "You know, when I was a little boy, living in this house, the animals had a nicer life than we did." I begin to understand the whole migration deal, the search for greener and warmer pastures in the Caribbean.

In my first three days there, I spend all of my time with Ramiro and his family: my grandmother's side of the family. I have yet to meet my grandfather's side. Arturo tells me that I'll meet them soon enough.

As I'm walking down the road with Arturo on day four, a tractor passes us. The guy behind the wheel is about my age, and he looks awfully familiar. He's a younger version of my grandfather. The resemblance is shocking. I notice that the tractor has my surname, *Eire*, inscribed on its side. Arturo says to my grandfather's replica: "Hey, look, I've got one of your relatives." We have a brief conversation, and he takes off with his tractor. Just like my *abuelo*: a man of few words.

That night, as I'm sitting at the kitchen table with Ramiro and family, slicing up a ham and drinking wine, two young women show up, suddenly.

"We hear that you've kidnapped one of our cousins," they say.

The next thing I know, I'm being driven somewhere by these women. They drive fast, very fast, and the driver takes her eyes off the road constantly, to engage in conversation the only way that the Spanish find acceptable: by looking at you. The women, Teresa and Dolores, are about my age, and I can't quite figure out what sort of cousins they are. All I know is that they're from my grandfather's side of the family. They'd been alerted to my presence by the guy on the tractor.

Five years later, one of these lovely women will die in a head-on collision with a truck while passing another car on a sharp curve.

We end up at a huge wall with a large gateway and drive into a courtyard. It's a moonless, pitch-black night, but I can tell that we've arrived at a substantial house with a chapel beside it. An older woman hugs me the instant I emerge from the car. She was waiting there to pounce on me.

"Let me look at you," she says. Her name is Carmen, and she looks a lot like my mother. She runs her hands along my face. "Oh, it's so good to have you here." I walk into the house and am taken to a huge kitchen with a gargantuan fireplace, next to which is a long table. I feel as if I've entered a medieval banquet hall, and, in fact, I have. This is one of the estates owned by my grandfather's side of the family, who, I find out that night, were once the feudal lords of this area. Like many such baronial houses, it was built piecemeal. This kitchen seems to be the oldest room in the house. The rest of it—the "new" part—dates from the early eighteenth century.

One by one the members of this household show up. I can't keep their names straight. But I recognize each and every one of them as someone I've seen before. They all look like one another, and like me. Much more so than Ramiro and his clan. My grandmother's relatives are all of slight build. These cousins are all tall, except for one named Paco. And there's a remarkable consistency to the faces, both male and female. If you stood all of us together in a police line-up after a crime, people would have trouble telling us apart.

"Now, tell us, which one of these snatched your purse?"

"It's all of them," the victim would have to say.

In walks Julio, whose name I'll have no trouble remembering. He's a poet, and he has no legs. Like my own mother, he was stricken with polio as an infant, back in the 1920s. His parents did all they could to straighten out his useless twisted legs, but as soon as he was old enough to get his way, he simply said, "Hack them off; they're a nuisance." He cracks joke after joke, and all of them are funny. Spontaneous humor, not prepackaged jokes. He seems to have a way of finding humor in everything, and especially in his own condition. "I proved to be too much of a challenge to Our Lady at Lourdes," he says about a pilgrimage he was forced to undertake years ago. "I asked her not just for new legs, but for very pretty ones."

The last relative to walk in is Alec Guinness. Or so I think. I'm dumbstruck. What's Alec Guinness doing here? Obi-Wan Kenobi?

"Meet Camilo, your grandfather's youngest brother."

Camilo is in his late seventies. It was his birth that killed my great-grandmother. He was her tenth child, and the last. I can only imagine what medical care must have been like back then, at the turn of the century, in this part of Galicia. I'd been hearing about Camilo all my life, but all I knew about him was this one horrible thing: He'd killed my grandfather's mother, and after that the family fell apart.

"Are you married?" he asks me.

"Not at the moment," I say.

"Neither am I. So I guess this makes us the two most eligible bachelors in the world," he says, deadpan.

I find out that Camilo doesn't live there, but on the other large family estate, which has fallen to ruin. The one I was supposed to inherit part of, but never did and never will.

They bring out the *aguardiente*, the firewater, which is about eighty percent pure alcohol. They make a *queimada* by pouring the firewater into a large shallow silver tray and setting it on fire, after all of the lights in the room have been extinguished. The flames light up the room, and we drink up what the fire leaves behind, along with what is still in the bottle. We all have a wonderful time getting to know one another.

As the home-brewed firewater starts to work its magic, and as I look around the table, I begin to feel happier than I've been in a long time. Then I'm not just happy. I'm more than that. I am who I am, finally.

Bonk. I'm out of my body. I'm one with all of my relatives at that table. I have no body of my own. I'm part of a much larger package deal. All of us at that table aren't simply linked, we're one. I look at my hands and all the other hands around the table. It's the same hand. I look at the eyebrows. It's the same ridiculously large pair of eyebrows, unfortunately. I look at Julio's legs, which are just two stumps. I look at his beaming, smiling face, which looks so much like my grandfather's and mine, but has an almost beatific glow to it. I see, somehow, that Julio is not a broken man, but just the opposite: Of all of us sitting around that table, he's the one who's lacking nothing, the only one who seems to be living in a resurrected body. A perfect body.

Bonk. The veil begins to part between this world and that other one—the eternal one. I catch a fleeting glimpse of the divine spark in each of our souls, and of the way in which our bodies in that room are but an extension of that spark, every bit as eternal, as totally indestructible. I intuit, for the first time in my life, how much of what we call "real" is but one tiny sliver of an immensely complex whole that our brains have trouble processing, a dimension beyond paradoxes in which amputated legs are at once horrible little stumps and gloriously beautiful, eternally intact limbs; and in which we are each at once unique and mere extensions of those to whom we are bound by blood.

Damn. Just as it all starts to make sense, the veil descends again, gradually, and I return to my body, and, eventually, to Ramiro's stone house, and back to the United States and desolate Minnesota, where the Void stalks me relentlessly.

But I'll never be the same again. Ever.

I'll never again have any trouble holding contradictory thoughts in my mind, especially about my own identity, and that of those I could call family. I'll also have no further trouble understanding how it was that those teachings in *The Imitation of Christ* that once scared me half to death eventually saved me from the pain that Charles refused to recognize and Carlos had to bear.

The blessed pain of learning how to die.

Eight

I f bowling can't turn you into an American, then nothing can. Or so I thought. Is there anything on earth more perfect than a bowling alley, or more American?

I'd seen a small bowling alley at a beach club in Havana once, but it was nothing like this one.

This bowling alley was like the vestibule to heaven. It was huge, subtly lit, and cooler than any movie theater. Lane after lane after lane. It seemed to go on forever. The pins at the end of every alley, all perfectly lined up, and all lit up, like idols in their own niches, taunting you, just begging to be mowed down, toppled. The balls, such perfect projectiles. Cannonballs for you to launch, with holes drilled into them, into which you stuck your fingers. The mechanical equipment couldn't have been more amazing, or a better summation of American ingenuity. Surely a Nobel Prize must have gone to the genius who designed the contraption that picked up the pins that you left standing and swept away the ones that were still loitering about on their sides, sprawled on the floor, defeated. It not only laid the upright ones back in their places, but also knew how to distinguish between your first and second frames. After your second try, it would sweep everything away, like the Grim Reaper, and then install a pristine set of tenpins, all resurrected. The ball return was as much a marvel as any Mercury spacecraft. You'd see your ball for an instant as it sped out of the back of the alley into that long chute that fed the ball return, and seconds later it would emerge at that console, just like the cannonball it was, super-fast, and then it would be slowed down by a reverse-spinning wheel, and gently roll onto a trough, harm-lessly, and make the nicest *clunk* as it hit the other balls in the return tray. And that dull *clunk* was just a teaser. The sound of the alley was sublime. It was just about the sweetest I'd ever heard indoors, anywhere. The thudding, sliding, and rolling of the balls. So hushed, so muffled. Con-trolled thunder on a human scale. The crashing. *Ka-blam*. Crash after crash, each and every pin letting out its own sweet scream, all achieving the most perfect harmony.

They sang of surrender, tirelessly and joyfully, like some celestial choir.

Irenaeus of Lyons, a second-century Christian bishop, once said that in the world to come, the fruits and vegetables will all beg to be picked and eaten, and actually try to outshout one another, all crying in unison, "Pick me, eat me, eat me." The first time I ever read that passage in Ire-naeus, years later, I thought of the sound made by bowling pins when they're struck by a fast-rolling ball.

"Knock us down, hit us as hard as possible. Kill us, reduce us to splin-ters."

And could there be any sight sweeter than those pins scattering in all directions?

Controlled violence. Deconstruction of the highest sort: the kind that doesn't get you in trouble because it's never permanent and it's been turned into a game.

But those ridiculous bowling shoes. They put a damper on things. They belonged on clowns, not on normal people.

Tony and I had been enrolled in bowling lessons by our foster par-ents, and we were driven to the alley twice a week for what seemed to be a good part of that summer but might have only been a few weeks. We'd never taken lessons in any sport or game, much less in one so well designed to harness our destructive instincts. Wearing those stupid shoes was a small price to pay for the privilege of bowling.

We were the only Cubans in that alley.

"One, two, three, slide, release . . ." Keep your eyes on those small arrows inlaid into the gleaming, thickly varnished wooden boards. It all seemed so easy, and so much fun. But it was harder than it looked. Gutter balls are one of the saddest sights on earth, and so much easier to achieve than strikes. The inescapable down that comes with every up, the funeral that's at the other end of every baby shower, the divorce that no one wants to imagine on their wedding day.

Coño, que mierda.

I didn't do so well in my first full game. I scored a sixty-eight, but I didn't really care. The real challenge was not scoring higher than others, but topping that score in the days to come and keeping the ball out of the gutter, forever more.

The bowling was just a bonus surprise during that great summer of 1962. If I wasn't swimming, I was having fun some other way. Lots of it. Yes, Miami was much hotter than Cuba, but I didn't let that stop me. Living in an air-conditioned house allowed me to scoff at the heat, which was unlike any I'd experienced up until then. The scorching sun was manageable too. After one severe sunburn that laid me out for about three days, I was fully protected from the killer sun by a nice tan.

I kept getting letters from my parents every week that told me everything was all right at their end, and I kept sending them six-page letters like clockwork, in which I detailed all my adventures. I know my dad saved them all. He saved everything. But God only knows what happened to the letters after he died.

How I'd love to get my hands on them now. Especially the one where I described the first time I crossed the causeway into Miami Beach at night. I'd never seen anything so unearthly, so ethereal, so hard to describe.

Miami had this one advantage over Havana: You could drive out into the sea, and look back at its skyline while you were also looking ahead to other islands and their own skylines. Two for the price of one, like everything else in America. Excess taken beyond its limits. All that was lacking were a few city gates made of precious stones, gold, or silver.

If the New Jerusalem were to descend from heaven onto some spot in America, there would have to be at least two of them, at minimum, and they'd both have to be equally outlandish and way over-the-top.

My mom kept getting ever closer to her goal of leaving the accursed island Tony and I had left behind. Her visa and exit permit were just over the horizon, she kept telling me. It was only a matter of weeks before she'd be able to join us in Miami. Carlos loved that, but Charles always had questions. What would Marie Antoinette do in Miami? How would we live? Would we end up in a shotgun shack, like the Becquers? And what about Louis XVI, who'd be staying behind? What would it be like not to have a father, or a swimming pool next door?

I had better things to do than to worry about the future, however. Who cares? The present was mighty fine, and getting better and better.

Sometime during that summer I was lucky enough to break my glasses. It was an accident, I swear. I didn't do it on purpose, although the thought of breaking them intentionally had crossed my mind. I hit a bump while riding my bike and flew off my seat. Really, really. Cross my heart and hope to die. The landing proved too much for my Cuban *espejuelos*: Both lenses and the tortoiseshell frame were crushed. So I ended up with some scrapes and bruises and new American eyewear: a plastic frame with round lenses, which was dark gray on the top and perfectly clear on the bottom. So new and cool, then. So 1962.

"You look much better now," said Norma. "Now you look like all the other boys."

Yes, I thought so too.

My English had improved enough to take its place right alongside my native tongue and to constantly elbow it out of the way. Every now and then I'd have to look up some word in the dictionary, but quite often they were words any eleven-year-old native speaker of English might have had to look up too. Like *curmudgeon*.

I'd grown fond of Norma and Lou, and also of their two boys, Philip and Eric. I loved my foster parents and I loved playing with their kids—something I had to learn how to do. Never before had I dealt with babies in diapers, or played their sorts of games. Philip was learning to speak; Eric was starting to walk. All I remember is that it felt good to hold them, to act like an older brother. Victor the dog was a lot of fun to have around too. And that summer I stopped speaking to him in Spanish, as I'd been doing since my arrival. Dogs can understand any language, you know, but the one they understand the best is the one you're most comfortable with.

Fairly often, we'd go out to eat, something my family tended not to do in Havana. Louis XVI didn't like restaurants because everything they had to offer paled in comparison to the cuisine at Versailles. My favorite restaurant in Miami was an Italian one, where they'd serve you a plate of spaghetti and meatballs larger than you could possibly eat. I'd always manage to put it away, though, and to walk out of the restaurant feeling as if I'd swallowed one of the balls at the bowling alley. Another favorite of mine was a place on Coral Way that served foot-long hot dogs. They weren't as good as those that the Chinese hot dog man used to cook up in Havana, but they were longer, and that made them better. All of the stuff they brought to the table made up for the fact that they were boiled rather than fried: relish, onions, mustard, sauerkraut, ketchup that you could pile on the hot dog so thickly that it would all come squirting out the sides of the roll every time you took a bite. Then there was the International House of Pancakes. I'd go nuts in there trying to make up my mind about which kind of pancakes to order and what kind of syrup to use. It was so bewildering, all this choice, and so exhilarating, so totally American.

Every time I go back to Miami I try to make my way down to that International House of Pancakes, which has remained firmly fixed in the same spot, by the Westchester Shopping Center. I don't go there to eat. No way. I just like to drive by and make sure it's still there. No other building in the United States brings me as close to my childhood, and the pure joy that a child can feel over the simplest things, like eight different jars of syrup.

The International House of Pancakes was my antidote to *The Imitation of Christ*, proof positive that this world was not so bad, or so worthy of scorn.

Sauerkraut was also a great secondary antidote. Man, that stuff was charged up with a heavenly essence that convinced me of the presence of the divine in creation. Sauerkraut, of all things, was strong evidence for the existence of God.

We didn't go to movies very often, though, and for me that was a serious problem. But it was no more irritating than bowling shoes. I could put up with this problem, as long as I could be distracted from it. There were so many other things going right. Films had been an essential part of my life up until then. I lived through films, even used them to interpret my own life and put everything into perspective. But my life now was a film of sorts. I was living out a great movie script, in the land where all of the best films were made.

I missed the movie theaters, though. A real landscape had to be filled with theaters, and I hardly ever saw any, out where I lived. I also didn't get to go into any of the ones I saw on my brief forays into downtown Miami and Coral Gables. They beckoned, but I had no way of gaining access to them.

I remember going to only one movie, the entire time I lived with the Chaits. As divine providence would have it, the film was none other than *The Vikings*, my favorite, the most important film of my entire childhood, which was rereleased in 1962, and played at some theater in Coral Gables.

It was so much better than I remembered, especially because this time around I didn't have to read subtitles. I could focus entirely on the images on the screen, and I could understand everything that was being said, and even perceive the difference between the British and American accents. I was one with the actors on-screen, with no filter between me and them. Janet Leigh was more beautiful this time around, somehow. Before, I'd had a hard time understanding why men might fight over her, even kill and maim each other, but this time it made perfect sense. The final battle scene, and the duel to the death between Kirk Douglas and Tony Curtis, all fell into perspective, in a new way, given my increased appreciation for Janet Leigh's eyes.

I'd made it. I was so much closer to turning Viking. After all, in this movie, all of the Vikings spoke English with American accents. And Tony Curtis not only looked a lot like Lou, my foster father, but actually spoke like him.

The Nordic setting seemed not so alien anymore, not so far away, even though I was still surrounded by palm trees and lizards rather than by fjords. I was a few inches closer to Norway on the map, and to a cold climate where everything was better. The fact that Florida was connected on the map to other states where it snowed lent an air of redemption to the place. It wasn't as bad as Cuba, it just couldn't be. No way. The divine grace found in snow reached beyond state boundaries.

I remained convinced that what made Europe and North America so superior to the rest of the world was their climates. Now that I was north of the Tropic of Capricorn, I felt far less inferior, and seeing *The Vikings* again, at this latitude, made me feel better about exile. Much, much better. Being this close to snow was a lot like being nearly redeemed.

Much as I hated to admit it, though, something kept my life from being perfect. It was something totally irrational: that feeling I'd first experienced on my first morning at the camp in Florida City. The feeling of being utterly alone and abandoned forever, of being stuck with no one but myself for eternity. The Void.

It pursued me, hidden from view.

I could ignore it most of the time because the Chait household was normally a busy place, full of people. Norma and Lou didn't go out much, as is often the case with the parents of small children.

But they were normal folks, and every now and then they went out. And that's when the Void would strike without hesitation or mercy.

It first attacked me one day that summer when I came home, and the house was empty. Lou was at work, and Norma had gone somewhere with the babies. As soon as no one but the dog responded to my "Hello," I knew I was in trouble. Whoa, what is this? *Ay.* In a flash, the house itself was gone, and the dog with it too. I was alone, totally alone in one vast Nothingness. Alone forever and ever. Stuck with myself and no one but myself. The pain was unbearable.

Fortunately, within a few minutes Norma and the kids came home, and the pain vanished instantly. But this left me feeling more than a little spooked.

Where had this come from? Could it attack me again?

I had no clue what this was, but I recognized it immediately and I knew one thing for certain: This did not come *from within* me. It wasn't something I could control. No way. This was much bigger and much more powerful than me, and it definitely came *from without*. It was a presence, even though its very essence was Absence.

Much to my dismay, it happened two or three times again, in exactly the same way, when I came home to an empty house. Damn. But at least these attacks didn't last very long. As had happened the first time, the house filled up right away and the Void vanished, like a demon driven out by an exorcist.

I cruised along in between these attacks, pretending that they were stupid aberrations, something that would stop happening. Then, one fateful Saturday evening, Norma and Lou decided to go out to dinner at someone's house and leave me with Philip and Eric. "You're old enough to watch them," they said. I'd already learned one of the stupidest nouns in the English language—*babysitter*—but it hadn't crossed my mind that I'd end up as one.

All right, I thought: I can handle this. No problem. This is like taking out the trash: a nice assignment, a sign that I'm responsible and American. So what if Norma and Lou aren't home for a while? The house will have other human beings in it. So what if they're babies? Besides, I've gotten over those other attacks, and nothing like that can happen again, no matter what. I can handle this, yes.

Sure. No problem. At first, everything was fine. I put Philip and Eric to bed and checked on them a few times to make sure they'd gone to sleep. Philip always took his time, so this kept me busy. Check and check again. The television shows were all right. The NBC channel always had movies on Saturdays, in living color. Not crappy B movies, like you'd get in the afternoons, but really good ones that had been box office hits in theaters.

Could I have lucked out more than this? The movie tonight is *River of No Return*, starring Marilyn Monroe and Robert Mitchum. Marilyn! How did this movie ever get past me? I'd never heard of it. It's action-packed and set in the Old West during the Gold Rush. Marilyn and that bonehead Mitchum are stuck with each other on a raft, and they face all the dangers one can expect in a fast-flowing river in the Western wilderness, back when the natives outnumbered the white settlers. Mitchum is a total idiot, as is every man who is paired up with Marilyn on-screen, and every man linked to any woman who has made her way into your heart. But Marilyn is Marilyn. I don't care what she says or does. I just like to look at her.

I figure Norma and Lou will be back before the movie is over at eleven.

Victor keeps me company. He lies down at my feet and stays there as I spend time with Marilyn. He's my watchdog, my friend, better than any guardian angel. Ten o'clock. Ten thirty. I start to feel a little shaky. Where are they? That feeling hovers over me. I have no name for it, but I recognize it immediately.

Eleven o'clock. The movie ends. No more Marilyn. No one returns home. The local news show begins.

Whoa, Lord have mercy! I'm ambushed as never before. It's fierce this time. I thought the first attack was bad, at Florida City, but this one makes that one look like child's play. The Nothingness, the Absence, the utter despair is unbearable. I'm being torn to shreds. I think that I'll surely die if this feeling doesn't go away. I keep telling myself, again and again, that Norma and Lou will be back very soon and the pain will vanish as quickly as it showed up.

Eleven thirty. Where can they be? Why haven't they come home yet? I don't worry about them being in an accident or anything like that. In fact, I don't worry at all. This is not about worrying. When you worry it's because there's some uncertainty to deal with. I have no uncertainties of any kind whatsoever. I know for certain that I am utterly alone and will forever be utterly abandoned, adrift in Nothingness all by myself for all eternity.

Midnight. By now I'm pacing up and down in the living room, frantically, and checking on Philip and Eric constantly. Victor senses my pain and stays close to me, following me around like the good shepherd that he is. But he seems more like an illusion than a real dog.

No pets allowed in the Void. No pets in Hell.

I've had a lifesaver in my pocket all along, a telephone number I don't dare use, the one where I can reach Lou and Norma in case of an emergency. I've been wanting to call them since eleven, but haven't dared. What can I tell them? Please come home because I've been suddenly transported to Hell? Yeah, sure.

They'll just think I'm a wimp, and they'll be mad at me for spoiling their evening.

I surprise myself. I can actually think this through as I writhe. I have a job to do, and I'm old enough to do it. I tell myself they'll be home any minute, anyway.

But as always happens with real pain, there comes a point when you can't stand it anymore, and something in you gives way, and you have to moan or scream. You don't want to, but the sound comes out of your mouth and it's weird and alien, but it helps you deal with the pain. Or you pass out, and regain consciousness moaning, hearing your own noises but refusing to accept them as yours. Or, as happens with nausea, there comes a point when your body says, Okay, enough, out with it. And you can't hold back what your gut doesn't want to keep.

I break down and call them. I make up some story about a horrible nightmare that has frightened me out of my wits. I figure they'll understand that. I also don't care at this point what they think, or whether they'll be mad at me.

Within ten minutes, they're home. The Void vanishes, instantly, but the pain lingers for quite some time. For days, in fact. I do my best to explain my "bad dream," but fail miserably. I tell Lou and Norma that I dreamed that I'd been taken to the top of a very tall mountain and that from there I was hurled across the Florida Straits back to Cuba. I break down and cry, just as I did on that day when I first came to visit this house and this family.

How the hell did I come up with that one?

Norma tells me not to worry, that the highest point in the state of Florida is only around three hundred feet above sea level, and that it's way up north, hundreds of miles away. There's no mountain anywhere within sight that I can be taken to, and besides, she wouldn't let anyone send me back to Cuba. And she hugs me, of course.

Thank you, Norma.

My adversary had won. No doubt about it. Knockout in the first three seconds of the first round. To top it off, without the Marquess of Queensberry rules, I was screwed from the get-go. My opponent just wouldn't quit. The *sónomambíche* kept pummeling and kicking me while I was down and out, grinding me to a pulp.

After that night, I knew I couldn't face this opponent again. The only advantage I had over it was that I knew it could attack me only when I was alone. It was fairly easy to figure out how to avoid it, but telling Norma and Lou that they shouldn't ever leave me alone wasn't easy. I dawdled, and hoped they'd never go out again, in that way that kids hope against all hope, thinking that if they want something to be a certain way, all they have to do is wish for it hard enough. So I got waylaid a couple more times, when I came home and found the house empty. Then, another fine Saturday evening, they announced that they were going out again, and that I'd be babysitting.

That was it. Meltdown time. I broke down again and told them I couldn't stay alone again. Never again. I couldn't find the right words, but tried to explain my fear anyway. All they could hear was that I was afraid. I suppose it was all they could understand. No one could understand this. I didn't quite understand it myself.

From that point forward, any time they went out they hired a babysitter. And Norma made it clear to me that she wasn't too happy about that. An eleven-year-old boy shouldn't need a babysitter of his own, she told me in no uncertain terms. Something was lacking in me, something important.

I couldn't have agreed more.

Oddly enough, the goddamned babysitter from across the street, who was only a couple of years older than me, kept the Void at bay. I didn't know why, exactly, but she did. All I could intuit was that she embodied their presence, somehow, simply because they'd hired her, and because I knew they'd have to come home to pay her and allow her to go back to her house.

Through a haze, I figured out that, somehow, they'd come back for her, but not for me, or Philip, or Eric, or Victor. Parents and relatives had a way of disappearing, but neighbors and friends did not.

It was crazy. But then again, I was crazy. What else could one expect?

Knowing I was nuts didn't keep me from moving on with my life or from having fun. No way, no how. I told myself I was only insane about one thing, and that in America, the land of excess, it was perfectly acceptable to have a quirk like mine. So, armed with much better English than I'd had back in June—and outfitted with new American eyeglasses— I went back to Everglades Elementary School in September, ready to begin sixth grade, finally, a year behind. No more outcast classroom hut on stilts for me: I went straight into a regular class for American kids, in which there were only two other Cubans.

I didn't feel like an outsider as I rode my bike to school that first day.

Me? I'm just like you. Look at me. Do I look any different? Listen to me speak. Do you hear anything odd, anything close to Desi Arnaz? Do ya? Watch me perform in the classroom. Betcha I'll not only keep up with you, but lead the way. Football? Yeah, I can do that. Hike! Ask me about any movie or television show. I know 'em all. Come on, I won't wait for you to test me, I'll test you: Tell me, what's on the tube on Tuesdays at eight thirty? Music? Yeah, I know all the top songs, including that new one by The Four Seasons, with the freak who sings like a girl, "*Sherry, Sherry baby . . .*" Just don't ask me to dance; I'm a bit self-conscious when it comes to that, even if it no longer involves dancing with a partner, thanks to Chubby Checker and the Twist. Come over to my house, you'll see how normal everything is, how perfectly American.

Totally *Leave It to Beaver,* my life. Better believe it.

Oh, yeah. One more thing. Wanna go bowlin'?

Nine

"Teach me how to swear in Spanish."

I can't add up how many times I've had this request already. Everyone wants to learn all the bad words in Spanish, even the girls. This puts me in a tight spot, for uttering bad words is against the First Commandment and an entry ticket to hell. So, if I teach bad words to anyone, I'm endangering not only my eternal fate but also theirs, and that makes my sin doubly worse. And if I say nothing, they'll just keep pestering me.

I tried that, and I know that silence won't work. Plus, if I refuse I'll be totally uncool, worse than a nerd. What's a boy to do? Toss them a bone, maybe.

"*Remolacha,*" I say.

"What's that?"

"It's the Spanish word for *sex,* you know, the really dirty word with the *f.*"

"Gimme more."

"Okay, how about '*Méteme una patada en las nalgas.*'"

"What's that?"

"It means 'Go have sex with yourself,' you know, another version of the big bad f-word."

"Thanks, Charles. Thanks a lot. This is great."

I don't tell him that what I've just taught him to say is *beet* and *kick my buttocks.*

The Monty Python guys would steal this trick from me a few years later, in their "Dirty Hungarian Phrasebook" skit. How they did it, I'll never know.

John Cleese: "Drop your panties, Sir William; I cannot wait 'til lunchtime."

Eric Idle: "Here, I don't think you're using that thing right."

Giving foreigners the wrong information about swear words is the ultimate revenge, the surefire way to undermine their civilization and to escape hell, all in one fell swoop.

Monty Python, you thieves: "The Hungarian phrase meaning 'Can you direct me to the station?' is translated by the English phrase, 'Please fondle my bum.'"

John Cleese, Eric Idle, both of you owe me, big-time.

Thousands of Cuban soldiers would end up in Ethiopia in the 1970s, doing the fighting that the Soviets couldn't take on openly. Had I stayed in Cuba, I'd have been among them, for sure, if I hadn't yet ended up in Angola, or in prison, or executed. And maybe I'd be dead, and you wouldn't be reading this. But what matters the most is that they too stole my trick. Their sweet revenge on the locals was to teach them to say "Go screw your mother," and make them think that they were saying "Have a nice day."

I know one Cuban who was there in Ethiopia, with the troops, and he was shocked to find Ethiopian after Ethiopian who greeted him on his first day by saying—with a huge smile—"Go screw your mother." Of course, this phrase included the *f* equivalent of the more polite *screw*.

They all owe me too, big-time.

Everyone knows I'm Cuban, here in the sixth grade at Everglades Elementary School. Damn. How do they know? It's my tongue, of course, but I refuse to accept the fact that I haven't surpassed Desi Arnaz yet. I thought my English pronunciation was perfect. I'm in a total state of denial.

Then, one day during that first week of school, I raise my hand to answer one of the teacher's questions, and he calls on me.

"That's easy," I say.

The entire classroom erupts into laughter. Belly laughs, not mere snickering. Prolonged outright laughter.

Before I can ask myself what's wrong, the whole class starts repeating what I've just said, again and again. And it sounds so wrong.

"Eassssy, eassssy, eassssy!" Ha! How funny! Ha, ha, ha!

Not "eazy," which is what I thought I'd said.

The laughing seems to last forever. From that day forward I'm called "eassssy boy." One girl loves to say "eassssy" again and again every time she sees me.

I resolve at that moment, as they're all laughing so hard, to dedicate myself one hundred percent to losing whatever accent is left in me.

"They'll never laugh at me again, ever," I vow.

And what's this crap? What's wrong with these books?

My geography and history books have chapters on Cuba, and also on other Latin American countries. What I find in them is shocking. According to these books, every country in Latin America is just about the same as all the others: All of them are very, very poor, and terribly backward. All of them are ruled by a tiny number of rich, nearly white but not really white people who exploit the darker-skinned poor folk and suck their blood. The photographs in the books speak volumes: starving barefoot peasants behind ox-drawn plows, half-naked children in straw skirts. All that's missing are bones in their noses. But wait! Here's one with a bone through his nose! And he's holding a bow and arrow too! Damn, I didn't know I was a savage. My geography book has only one photograph of Cuba, and it's of a grass hut and half-naked, barefoot black kids standing at its door, looking hapless and helpless (two new fiendishly similar English words I just learned). My history book says that Cuba, like all Latin American countries, is too backward to handle democracy or genuine civilization, and that whatever little progress it has made is due to the help that the United States has offered since it freed the island from Spain's grip in 1898. I also learn that the real hero of the Cuban war of independence was Teddy Roosevelt.

Jesus H. Textbook-shredding Christ!

No wonder I get these questions all the time:

"What was it like to wear shoes for the first time when you got to America?"

"You had toilets in Cuba? Televisions? Hospitals? Cars? Pants?"

"What's it like to ride on donkeys all the time?"

"How'd you learn to read so quickly, if you just got here?"

And so on. I might as well stick a bone through my nose and show up barefoot, to confirm their worst suspicions about me. Maybe I should grunt a lot too.

The most annoying question of all is "Why aren't you dark?"

My blond hair throws everyone for a loop.

"My ancestors were barbarians, just like yours," I say.

"Oh."

"Hey," I say, "wanna learn another dirty Spanish phrase? Here you go: 'Soy un comemierda.'"

"What's that?"

"Kiss my butt, you know, with the a-word."

Someday they'll find out I just taught them to say "I'm a shit-eater," which is the same as saying "I'm a total idiot." Somehow, the word *comemierda* is not against the First Commandment. I use it all the time. It's only a venial sin.

Welcome to America, Charles. By the way, could you tell me, please, why all Cubans have big lips?

That's a question some boy asked me in the bathroom at school. I'd never thought of my lips as big before. I still don't think of them that way, especially nowadays, when so many women who can afford cosmetic surgery have their lips blown up to look like blimps.

"I guess those Mambo lips make all of you really good kissers," says the boy in the bathroom.

Prejudice dogs me, everywhere I go. It's inescapable. There aren't any Negro kids to pick on at this school. It's 1962, and Florida schools are still segregated. Why we Cubans weren't sent to the Negro schools still puzzles me to this day. After all, we weren't considered white then, same as now. But given what the textbooks have to say about me and those of my ilk, you can't really blame anyone for thinking of me as inferior.

I want to be a crossing guard. They're so cool, these kids. They get a really nifty belt from Triple-A, the American Automobile Association, one that goes around their waist and also up and around their right shoulder, with a shiny AAA badge on it. They can stop traffic and control the flow of pedestrians and bicycles. Some of them wield these flags on long poles. They're almost like cops, for heaven's sake, or like soldiers.

They have real power, and prestige. They keep their AAA belts on top of their desks all during class, so you can admire them all day long.

I'm not allowed to join the crossing guard patrol. Something about my English. It's not quite right, you know. I have trouble with the letter *S*.

One day, mysteriously, my bike gets torn apart. I come out to unlock it from the bicycle rack, and it looks as if a truck had crushed it while one of the AAA crossing guards was asleep. What's this? How did this happen? My wheels look like pretzels, those wonderful twisted crunchy snacks. The only thing missing is the salt. Pretzels are up there with sauerkraut on my list of new wondrous things found only in America. But damn, the seat is sliced up too. Nice job: Jack the Ripper would be proud of you, whoever you are. The chain is gone, and so is the gearbox. Vanished. And the brake and gear cables have been diced and sliced, like salad fixings. But all is not lost. The handlebars, the pedals, and the frame are still in one piece. Oh, but damn, my handlebar grips are gone too.

I have a hard time explaining the bike to Norma and Lou. I expected them to be furious and to call me irresponsible. But they're nice enough to buy me another one, that same afternoon.

"Nice new bike," say a couple of guys as I lock it to the rack the next day. "I hope you have better luck with this one than the last one." I stop riding my bike to school. It's not a very long walk, after all.

I make a friend in class, a really nice Jewish guy named Toby. He reminds me a lot of some of my friends back in the old country, Plato's cave. He and I get along well, and he even invites me to his house one afternoon after school.

"Stay away from Toby," says another guy in my class the next day, a guy whose skin is about ten shades darker than mine and whose hair is jet black. His face is burned into my memory as clearly as Christ's is on the Shroud of Turin.

"What do you mean?"

"You know what I mean."

"No, I don't."

"Yes, you do. Don't play stupid. I know what you're up to, and if you don't stay away from Toby, there'll be lots of trouble for you."

I'm so dumbstruck I have no more replies, or questions. And I have to refrain from punching him in the face. Every cell in my body screams out, but my brain steps in. The beast in me wants to hit him as hard as possible, and to keep pounding on his face until nothing is left of it. Contemplating an image of his mug, all bloodied, gives me great pleasure, but some part of my brain says, "Let it go, you're way outnumbered."

The same threats continue to issue for a few more days from the same guy. I stop all after-school and playground fraternizing with Toby. We remain good friends in class, but all of the extracurricular socializing comes to an abrupt end.

I don't know what the swarthy dark-haired guy thinks I'm doing to Toby, or what he means to do to me, but I don't want to find out. By now, I'm seeing a pattern, and it's not a very pretty one.

In the lunchroom, a boy named Curtis tells me not to come anywhere near him and to keep my "stinkin' mitts" off his tray. Well, the word isn't really *stinkin'*, it's that f-word that I translate as *remolacha*, or *beet*, for those who beg me for cussing lessons in Spanish.

Curtis is big and burly, with red hair and freckles, and loves to call me a spic. He looks like an overgrown Howdy Doody, and he hasn't discovered the charm of underarm deodorants yet, like I did three years ago, back in my grass hut. Yeah, my grass hut.

I'm doing fine in class, though. My grades aren't anywhere near what I'm used to getting, especially in math, but I chalk it up to the fact that I missed a whole year of school back in Cuba. I do a class report on the country of Turkey, and it's a winner. I spend hours on the map, and it ends up being so detailed that the teacher expresses no small measure of amazement.

"Not bad for a Cuban."

Freddy and I become better friends than ever. Somehow, I don't mind it much anymore when Federico takes over his body. We spend time together after school and on weekends.

And we had a blast on Halloween. It was my first, ever, and his second. He was a veteran. We didn't have Halloween in Cuba. I'd once seen some American kids in costumes walking down Quinta Avenida in Miramar, doing their trick-or-treating, headed for certain frustration, and I'd been enraptured by their appearance and their quest. Louis

XVI explained it all to me, back then, before the earth got sucked into another dimension.

"In the United States children celebrate the day before the Day of All Saints by dressing up in costumes and going door to door, begging for candy."

"You're pulling my leg again."

"No, seriously, this is what they do. Take a look at those kids: That's what they're doing right now."

"But we don't do that here."

"No, we don't. And those poor kids are in for a big letdown."

But I wasn't in for a disappointment, here, living with the Chaits in Miami. No way. This was the United States of America, and Halloween was guaranteed by the Constitution. It was in the Bill of Rights, or something like that.

I got all fired up about Halloween as early as September, when the decorations began to show up in stores. Pumpkins. Scarecrows. Cornstalks. Red, orange, and yellow leaves. Witches. Spiderwebs. Skulls. Skeletons. All sorts of spooky stuff that belonged up north, where it snowed, rather than down here in Florida. I couldn't wait, and I counted the days. This was going to be better than Christmas, I told myself. Bigger than any birthday. Imagine going from door to door and getting candy. Imagine being able to vandalize people's homes with impunity if they have no candy for you.

Louis XVI hadn't told me about that last part. And that was the best thing of all. The right to vandalize, guaranteed by law.

"You know, you're a little too old to go out on Halloween," said Norma one day, close to the magical date.

"Am I?"

"Almost, but not quite. I think it's all right if you go out trick-or-treating, but this will be your last chance. Next year you'll be too old for that."

All the more reason to enjoy this as much as possible, I told myself. This will be one total blowout. I could barely contain myself as the day approached.

I couldn't even bother to pay attention to the Cuban Missile Crisis, which unfolded in the week just before Halloween. Nuclear warfare? No, it can't happen, at least before Halloween. No way. Khrushchev, Kennedy, and Fidel will work all of this out. What's the big deal? Those missiles have been there for such a long time already. So what if the geniuses at the Pentagon finally convinced John Kennedy of the threat that Cubans have known about for so long?

Finally, the magic day arrived, as I'd predicted, without a nuclear holocaust. I didn't have a costume, so Norma helped me improvise. I went out as a hobo, with black crayon smudges on my face and a flannel shirt untucked. Back then no one dared not to tuck their shirt into their pants. Just enough of a disheveled look to let people know that I was wearing something close to a costume. Freddy ended up with more or less the same disguise. We didn't care what we looked like. We just wanted to collect candy and destroy the neighborhood, like all American kids.

"You know," Freddy told me, "if no one comes to the door, or if they have nothing to give you, then you're entitled to wreck their house any way you want."

"Are you sure?"

"You bet."

So, armed with paper shopping bags we ventured out into the tropical night. It was even better than I'd expected. Most of the houses were decorated with Halloween stuff, and all of their lights were on. The pumpkins were all angels in disguise, I was sure. Seraphim or archangels, to boot, not some lackeys from the lower ranks of the celestial hierarchy. We went from door to door and scored big everywhere. I couldn't believe this was really happening. It felt as if I'd gone inside a movie screen and become part of a movie—part of that world that was even more real than the United States itself—or that I was simply having the best dream I'd ever had.

"Trick or treat."

The ritual was sublime. I think the incantation that came out of my mouth wasn't pronounced correctly, but it didn't matter. All the grownups who came to the door knew why Freddy and I were there.

"Let me guess what you are," a few of the talkative ones would ask.

"We're in disguise," I'd say. It probably sounded more like "diss-guy," but no one seemed to care. That night, it didn't matter to anyone that Freddy and I were Cubans.

On Halloween all children magically turn into goblins, and no one cares if Goblinland is American or not.

Candy bars. Whole candy bars. Good God in heaven. Hershey's, Nestlé, 3 Musketeers, Almond Joy, Mars, Mounds, Baby Ruth. You name it, we got some. Bags of M&M's. Peanuts. Jordan almonds. Licorice. Junior Mints. Hershey's Kisses. Chewing gum, lots of it. One guy gave us donuts. Donuts, imagine that. Then there were the sorry-ass houses where they gave you apples, or where all they had was this cruel hoax called candy corn, which was awful but still counted as candy and therefore didn't allow you to vandalize the hell out of the place.

"Are you sure that this crap counts as a treat?" I asked Freddy.

"Sadly, yes." *Es una lastima.* "It's a pity," said the expert.

We did hit a few houses where no one was home. Hooo Weeee. Trick time. We exacted vengeance, as required by law, in all sorts of creative ways. I can't divulge most of our reprisals, not knowing what the statute of limitations might be on the crimes we committed. Just let it go at this: We were very creative. Sticking chewing gum into keyholes was our least imaginative effort.

The thrill of making life miserable for someone else was unbearably exhilarating. Nothing had ever felt so right, so virtuous. We attacked the skinflints and scrooges with all the zeal of Crusaders, certain that ours was a holy venture.

Doing wrong can feel so right, so very right, and so totally fulfilling. Yes.

And it's even more satisfying to be a cretin when you get to go home with a bag that's about to rip open because of the weight of the treats in it. I had enough candy at the end of that blessed night to keep me going for the next two months. Of course, it was all gone in less than a week.

Finally, I'm wholly and truly American, I told myself. Forget the accent and all the harassment at school. I don't care. Now that I've done this, I'm the real thing. Hooo Weeee. It's like I've died and gone to heaven. I'm living out the life I've always wanted to have. I'm just like those superior American children I saw on Quinta Avenida back in Havana, years ago, who were headed for certain disappointment in my inferior homeland. Heck, I'm better off than they were, for I'm here, where there's a real Halloween.

Now all I need to become a really real American is to become Jewish and have a Bar Mitzvah.

It's what I thought was normal. What else could I think, living with a Jewish family? All around me, boys my age were preparing for their entry into manhood, and I was just floundering, pedaling my bike to St. Brendan's on Sunday.

I'd gone to a couple of Bar Mitzvahs already. It seemed like such a reasonable religion, and so un-scary. Yeah, the Hebrew was a drag, but then again, so was Latin. Well, maybe Latin was a little less extreme. But going through a ritual that turned you into a man seemed like a great thing to me, worth even having to learn that strange tongue. *Baruch* this, *baruch* that, and *Adonai* to you too. And *Eloheinu* while you're at it, and *melech ha-olam* on top of that.

Yeah. Why not? *Dominus vobiscum. Et cum spiritu tuo. Oremus.* What's the difference?

Jesus was a Jew, after all. And he had a Bar Mitzvah. I knew that. The Virgin Mary was Jewish too, and St. Joseph, and every single one of the twelve apostles, including St. Peter, the first Pope, who now guards the gates of heaven. Jews, all of them. And we prayed to them. *Ora pro nobis,* yes, please. Chosen People, all of them. Chosen, like my foster parents and Tony's. Exiles, since day one. Always on the move. Always chased out, always stripped of everything they've worked for. Always ridiculed. Always vandalized and threatened. Always chosen as scape-goats for this and that. Sacrificial offerings.

Refugees of the highest order. I don't even come close, nor do my people.

My twelfth birthday is approaching, less than a month after Hallow-een. I know I won't get a Bar Mitzvah, but I'd sure like to have one about a year from now.

That would make everything all right, even if I have to wear one of those stupid little caps that refuse to stay put on the back of your head. This ritual might even cure me of my accent, and give me one more chance to go out on Halloween. Next year, at this time, I won't be a man yet. No.

I'll still be a boy, barely, but a boy nonetheless, with three weeks to spare.

A very lucky boy, mambo lips and all, with no bones through his nose, who can teach curious American kids how to cuss incorrectly in Spanish as he pines for fjords and Bar Mitzvahs, with no concern whatsoever for the pain that comes with circumcision or with finding your front door keyhole has been carefully jammed up with Bazooka bubble gum.

"Hey, Charles, what's the bad word of the day? Give me a really bad one this time. Really, really bad."

"*Berenjenas.*" Eggplants.

"What's that?"

"It's a very nasty way of saying *breasts.*"

"Yeow. How about one more?"

"*Me encantaría saborear tu flema.*" I'd love to savor your phlegm.

"That sounds even worse. What is it?"

"It's a very bad way of saying 'I'd love to kiss you all over.'"

"Thanks, Charles. You Cubans have such dirty minds. Thanks."

"You bet. It's eassssy for us. It's all we can do in our grass huts, you know."

"What?"

"*Vete al carajo, cabrón.*" Go to hell, you bastard.

"Say what?"

"Nothing. Never mind."

I know that I've just bought myself an entry ticket to hell, especially since I've stopped going to confession, but I don't give a damn. Hell, I don't give a flying *remolacha.* Somehow, in some half-assed way, I've figured out that heaven and hell intersect all the time here in Miami.

Coño, que mierda.

Ten

"Y ou'd better take a look at this," says Norma as she hands me *The Miami Herald*.

I know something must be wrong, not just because of the look on her face, but also because she's never ordered me to read the newspaper before.

"Here, read this article." She points to it.

So, I take the paper and, in an instant, the world starts spinning in the opposite direction.

Whoa.

The article in question says that due to the missile crisis, Castrolandia has shut the door on all emigration, indefinitely. I read the article several times, to make sure I have all the details straight. Unfortunately, it's not that hard to get to the bottom of it all: No one can leave Castrolandia. No one.

My mother was holding an exit permit for mid-November, just before my birthday. She was all set to go.

Now she can't leave.

Norma looks very upset. I guess I do too, but I try not to show it.

I feel the Void snarling, feel it tensing up, getting ready to pounce.

Halloween still has me all pumped up, however, so I'm able to put my nearly superhuman powers of denial to work.

"Oh," I say to Norma, "this is just temporary; it will change soon."

"I'm afraid not," she replies. She looks really, really upset.

Just a little bit of fallout from the nuclear holocaust that never took place. Fidel Castro is pissed as all hell because Nikita Khrushchev wouldn't let him vaporize New York, Miami, and Washington, D.C., so he slams shut all doors that lead out of the island for Cubans.

"You're stuck here, with me," he says to my mom and to the parents of more than ten thousand airlifted children, and millions of other Cubans. "Nobody gets to leave now."

Having been exposed to the world as a mere puppet of Moscow, Fidel throws a fit unlike any he'd thrown before. His rage knows no bounds. He had so, so desperately wanted to be seen as a major world leader, one of the few able to push a button and kill tens of millions of human beings. He'd actually told Nikita that he was ready to nuke New York, and Nikita had reminded Fidel that this would mean the end of Cuba. "You'll be wiped off the map," said the Russian. But Cuba's annihilation didn't bother Fidel. He was itching to press the button, regardless of the consequences, and he told Nikita to mind his own business. And this is what made Nikita blink in his face-off with John F. Kennedy. Knowing that he was dealing with a maniac changed the game completely for Nikita.

The missiles are withdrawn from Cuba by the Soviets, or so they say. I see images of the Soviet ships on television, loaded with "missiles" on their way back to the U.S.S.R. In exchange, President Kennedy assures Nikita and Fidel that the United States will keep a close eye on all Cuban exiles and never again let them lift so much as a finger against Castrolandia.

Now that everyone knows that the button was never his to push, Fidel has to find an outlet for his frustration. I've seen my cats act in exactly the same way, many times. If they're frustrated about anything, they'll attack one of the other cats in the house, especially those that are just lying there, sleeping or minding their own business.

So now Fidel will show the world who's really in charge of Cuba. Yeah.

It takes a few days for me to hear from my mom, but when I finally get a letter it confirms all of my worst suspicions, and those of Norma and Lou: The door has been shut tightly and there is no way out for any

Cuban. No way whatsoever. Somewhere, in one of his many mansions, Fidel pats himself on the back.

"So sorry," says Marie Antoinette. "So, so sorry. I can't leave. But I'll find some way out, I promise. I'll dig a tunnel under the Florida Straits if I have to." Of course, she has no way of knowing it will take her another three years to find a way out, and that digging that tunnel might have been faster than trying to fly out. No one knows what to expect at that point.

Except for Norma and Lou. They know that the boy they'd taken in for just a few months has suddenly turned into a boy who might be with them indefinitely, maybe forever.

What the hell are they supposed to do now?

Of course, at that time, all I can think of is myself. Poor me. It never crosses my mind that this is a much, much larger problem than I can imagine.

Fortunately, my powers of denial have increased dramatically, and this sudden surge of willful blindness is fueled by the crisis itself. It's a strikingly beautiful vicious cycle. As the pain ratchets up, so does my ability to deny it. I'm cooler than a dead fish that's been frozen for twelve years. And my eyes probably look just about the same as those of any such fish.

I just can't notice when I look in the mirror. I refuse to notice it.

One thought and one thought alone keeps bouncing off my protective force field: "I will never, ever see my parents again." I notice it, of course, the way one does a neighbor's barking dog, but I'm able to dismiss it.

Who cares? My birthday is coming up, and so is another great American holiday: Thanksgiving. And we're in the thick of football season and I'm all fired up about this new game—the ultimate in violence—that I'm learning to play. I envision monster bruises, maybe a broken bone or two. Lou has promised to take me to a Hurricanes game at the Orange Bowl.

I don't care at all that Thanksgiving meals involve turkeys. Norma and I have an agreement. I can pass up on the big disgusting bird, and so can Tony.

Tony and I have birthdays that are only two days apart, on the twenty-third and twenty-fifth of November. So the Chaits and the Rubins decide to celebrate both of our birthdays on Thanksgiving Day, at the Rubins' house.

Damn. I'll forget most of what happened at this event and hit a blank spot every time I try to recall it. Except for one weird thing. One of my gifts is a football, something I've been hankering for. I stare at this beautiful oval brown thing, and its perfect white laces. I admire the texture of the pigskin, and run my fingers over it. I pick it up and feel its perfect heft. I smell it. Sweet vapors, almost as perfect as DDT or bus exhaust. Maybe even better.

Damn. Damn. Damn. What the hell is wrong with me?

Why am I sobbing like a girl? Where the hell did these sobs come from? I'm not doing this. No. No way, no how. Not again. These sobs aren't mine, and neither are these white-hot tears, streaming down my cheeks. What kind of moron am I? Why am I feeling the presence of my parents so much? Or is it their absence I feel? Crap.

Black out.

Years later I'm told by several people who were there on November 22, 1962, that Sid Rubin put his hand on the back of my head and pushed my face into the birthday cake at that point. I'm also told that this was all captured on eight-millimeter film, and that many people have seen this silent family movie over the years.

I have no reason to doubt these reports. But, much like someone who's been knocked out by anesthesia for surgery, or someone who's been shot in the head, I have no memory of any of this, whatsoever.

I'm also told that everyone started laughing and that I, too, emerged from the cake laughing, my face smeared with frosting, like one of the Three Stooges.

Some day, I'd love to see this film, taken with the same kind of camera that Abraham Zapruder would use exactly one year later, on November 22, 1963, to capture images of President John Kennedy's brains being blown out in Dallas by an assassin's perfectly aimed bullet.

Eight millimeter film is so reliable, so godlike. And the whirr of the projector is so comforting, such perfectly sacred background music.

All the more reason to wish that the Chaits would have filmed the next three weeks, every single goddamned minute, in living color. I remember next to nothing, save for the most exquisite pain, and a very sudden transformation, much more surprising than the one Tony and I had undergone when we'd boarded our KLM flight in Havana seven months earlier.

It was the burning silence again, the awesome transfiguration that reduces you to nothing, even less than nothing. The sweet flame, again, now slightly familiar, reminiscent of eternity, and of nothingness, all at once.

Sweet death.

This time around it took us longer to die. In Havana, it had taken only a few minutes, inside that airplane, and we'd hardly been aware of what was happening. This time, it took about three weeks. And we noticed.

It felt the same, exactly, despite its greater slowness. Normally, three weeks can seem like a long time. Not so in this case. I remember this immolation as instantaneous, and thus only have three images left in my memory of the three weeks that followed my birthday, all fragments. Tiny, twisted shards, each a highly polished mirror full of identical, surreal images.

I don't remember who broke the news to me, or where, or when, but shortly after that Thanksgiving birthday party—maybe even the next day—I learn that Tony and I must leave our foster homes immediately. The long-range plan is to send us to our uncle Amado, up in Illinois, but for now, while our uncle is getting his bearings up north, we're being moved to another foster home in Miami, run by a childless Cuban couple. It's a way station, I'm told, a temporary arrangement.

I bury the information deep inside, right away, and deny that this can really be happening. I don't want to leave home. Not again.

But the next thing I know—despite my superhuman powers of denial—Tony and I are being driven down Coral Way by a social worker, eastward, toward central Miami. We're in Coral Gables, the only part of Miami that reminds me of Havana. I'm staring at the giant trees on the median strip of this wide boulevard. Their branches reach over the roadway, making a natural canopy so thick that the sun is denied entrance. Their trunks are a tangled sinewy mass, a jumble of hundreds of smaller trunks all woven together, each shouting out its age, boasting of superior longevity, laughing at me and every other human being. Each and every one of those trees is a mirror image of those ancient ones in the park that was four blocks from my house in Havana, the park where I nearly blew off my hand with a firecracker. I think of my mother holding me close, pressing me to her chest as I clench my fist harder than I ever thought it was possible to clench a fist, telling me everything will be all right. I remember the pain. I don't hear her voice, but I sense again how it felt to hear it.

The social worker is droning on and on about something I'd rather not hear, giving us details about the foster home he is taking us to visit.

Before we know it we're in a shabby neighborhood that Lou Chait had once described to me as "very, very bad." We're just a few blocks from the Orange Bowl, part of which I see for an instant as we turn a corner. We pull up to a tiny, shabby house on a treeless street. The sun beats down on us as it does only in bad neighborhoods, in a foul mood, looking for things to burn and injure, memories to singe. The sunlight screams bloody murder as it hits the faded pale green stucco walls of the house that's about to become our new home. We go in, through the banged-up front door. It's my worst nightmare come true. Pure squalor. It makes the Becquer shotgun shack look good. A cramped sun porch wrapped in jalousie windows, sparsely furnished. A small living room, very dark, and an equally small dining room, slightly less dark. The kitchen is one of the circles of hell: Everything in it is scuffed and stained, and the linoleum floor is faded, cracked, and pockmarked. It looks like an unfinished jigsaw puzzle that's been left out in the rain. The smell is overpowering, and easy to identify. Garbage. Old garbage. The bathroom looks at least a hundred years old: A claw-foot bathtub hovers over a linoleum floor that makes the one in the kitchen look good. I can see dirt under the tub. Lots of it. The toilet might be an ancient Roman relic: The water tank sits above it, and a long rusty pipe runs down the wall. A pull chain with a well-worn wooden handle dangles from the side of the water tank.

I still don't know what mold smells like, since I've never encountered so much of it all at once, but I hate what I smell, all the same.

I ignore all the kids who are staring at us, as we make our way through the house. I ignore the woman who's in charge of this house, even though she's blabbering about this and that. I do notice, though, that there are about ten kids and only two very small bedrooms for them.

The woman who runs the house and her husband—who is invisible—
have the largest bedroom all to themselves, a room that's not included
in the tour. I ignore the fact that they're all Cubans, the people in this
house. I ignore the fact that the social worker is Cuban too.

Tony and I stay close to each other as we tour the house. We say nothing. Nothing at all. And suddenly we're not there anymore.

Black out.

Tony and I are in my bedroom at the Chait house. The door is closed,
and we're both sitting on my bed.

I hear myself say, "I can't live there. I can't live in that house." I feel
myself resisting what's about to happen, trying to will it away. If I object
enough, within myself, then it can't happen.

"This can't be my life," I tell myself. "No way." *De ninguna manera.*

I hear Tony say, "Stop it. Be quiet. *Cállate.* That's where we're going to
live from now on, and that's that. We can't do anything about it, so you'd
better accept it."

I might have been crying, but I'm not sure. Can't remember much,
save for Tony saying again and again, "We'll be all right."

Black out. Pitch black.

We're on Coral Way again, in the same damn car with the same
accursed Cuban social worker. He's very young for a grown-up. I notice
that this time around. He's droning on and on about how nice our new
home is going to be, how we'll now be part of one big happy family.

"*Calor de familia,*" he keeps saying, again and again. We'll be surrounded by "family warmth," and that's the most important thing of all.

How I wish he'd shut up.

Those trees on Coral Way suddenly turn into angels. Huge, powerful, muscle-bound angels. Terminators. Demon-slayers of the highest
order. Guardian angels thrusting spears and swords into demons, strain-
ing with every fiber of their being, driving their weapons into the Enemy
with resolve, their muscles rippling, their limbs perfectly poised to harness the power within them and do the utmost damage, their wings as
taut and perfectly angled as those of any eagle when it dives in for the
kill: the very essence of balance, of equilibrium itself, harnessed for a
singular purpose, divine in origin.

"As long as these trees are here," I tell myself, "I'll be all right."

Many, many years later, on a gray and rainy day, I'll see some statues of gilded angels swarming high above a baroque altar in Prague, and they'll instantly remind me of those trees, and I'll whisper, "What are you guys doing here, so far from Miami?"

It's just a few days before Christmas, and Coral Gables is all decked out for the holiday, full of all the stuff that's been outlawed in Cuba, where celebrating Christmas is now a crime. I tell myself again and again that I should get into the spirit of the season, but I'm not listening. It's not sinking in. It can't. These garlands and lights and Christmas trees and nativity scenes are a hoax. It's not Christmas. It can't be. Nothing bad can happen on Christmas, or just before it.

It doesn't make sense.

Images of Christmases past try to invade my mind, but they bounce right off my ramparts, like cannonballs fired from defective artillery. They won't get in; they can't get in. Even last Christmas can't get in, that Christmas when we had to pretend that we weren't celebrating it, and when there was nothing at all that could pass as a present because all of the stores were empty. Any Christmas past, no matter how rotten, has the power to kill me right now. So my fortress walls are raised and thickened and widened, and the moats around them made deeper and longer, and filled with the purest, strongest acid of all.

Fade to black.

I simply accept what happened as inevitable, for years, and I'll never ask anyone why it happened. I don't care to know, because I prefer to accept it as inevitable and foreordained. It couldn't have been any different. It's a lot like a car wreck: If you replay the scene before the crash, it only makes your scars hurt more, both the ones on your body and those in your mind. The best I can do is to guess, and to do so with one eye closed, and my hands over my face.

And the guessing always leads me to the same conclusion: Our foster parents had taken us in thinking that we'd be spending only a few months with them, but the fallout from the Cuban Missile Crisis changed everything.

No one knew now when our mom would be able to leave Cuba.

A month? Not likely. Ten months? Probably not. Sixteen months? Wishful thinking. Sixteen years? Maybe.

Would I have put up with me indefinitely if I were my own foster parent? No way. I was damaged merchandise. Very damaged. Would I have put up with Tony? No way, ten times over. The guy was nothing but trouble. Allergies, constant sinus infections, migraines, absolute sloppiness, and a dogged resistance to learning English were only some of his faults. The total list would be way too long. In a small house with two other teenagers, one male and one female, the guy was a constant drag. That abyss he carried around inside of him all the time was like a black hole that sucked in whatever light dared to enter the house. To top it off, he took showers that were about an hour long, and he ate way too many eggs.

To whom did we really belong? To whom did any of the ten thousand of us who were stranded belong? We were stuck here without our parents, and there was no going back. That was out of the question. Our parents had gambled and lost, but most of them never regretted the wager. Better that their children be alone in the United States than with them in that tropical hell, or somewhere behind the Iron Curtain. That's the way our parents saw it, and the way most of us kids saw it too. Vaulting over the Iron Curtain and returning to hell was not an option, even if that was where our parents were stuck. We were here for good, we of the silent unseen airlift that hardly anyone noticed.

I, for one, would have rather killed myself than gone back. I'd even have jumped into a sea full of sharks in a feeding frenzy before I'd set foot again in Cuba. It would have made as much sense for me to choose the Void willingly as to return to Cuba. And I have yet to meet another airlift kid who didn't feel the same way.

Tony and I were luckier than most: At least we had one uncle in the United States. So what if he was sixty-two years old, underemployed, living in a weird little town in the Midwest, and blessed with one child who needed extra care? He was our father's brother, our closest kin. Our foster parents were not really responsible for us, and all that they'd done for us was already way beyond any definition of compassion and selflessness. It was a mitzvah brighter than a billion suns, a good deed way beyond measure. The time had come for us to be picked up by Uncle Amado.

So the Chaits and Rubins tried to send us to Amado, through the same agencies that had brought us to their houses in the first place. Whoever they were. But something went awry, somewhere along the way. Something big.

Instead of being sent to our uncle, who was living in a hell of his own—trying to settle in godforsaken Bloomington, Illinois, knocking on every church door he could find, begging for used furniture and winter clothing, wondering how in the world he was going to pay heating bills that added up to about half of his income, or how he was supposed to get around in a town that had no public transportation—we were shelved, warehoused, tucked out of sight, call it what you will, in a holding tank.

We weren't supposed to stay there too long, in that house full of troubled, battle-scarred boys, gang members who'd already been in trouble with the law. Technically, it wasn't called a home for juvenile delinquents or an orphanage, but it sure qualified as both.

But what's supposed to happen is not always what happens, simply because there's a much larger and intricately complex plan that's way beyond our ken, an eternal plan. Parts of it occasionally surface in our dreams and are hard to recognize for what they are, and they are even harder to interpret correctly.

Tony and I were predestined to end up in that house, and to live in it for a specific number of days, a large number I've never bothered to count, simply because it wouldn't make any difference. What happened had to happen.

Meddling with the inevitable can only lead to trouble, even if the meddling takes place only in your mind. And the same goes for trying to forget about it, or to erase all memories of it.

Flash forward, twenty-nine years.

It's Christmas morning in Charlottesville, Virginia. The presents under the tree are all perfectly wrapped, perfectly laid out. The tree is nearly perfect too, as symmetrical as one could ever hope for, and it's loaded with lights and ornaments, none of which are heirlooms. My lovely wife Jane and I have spent hours assembling toys and wrapping packages. It's taken us nearly all night to do this, and we've barely slept.

This is all for the kids. Not for us. Before they came along, Jane and I never did this.

The cookies and carrots on the plate near the tree are full of bite marks, and the milk glass is nearly empty. Santa and his reindeer have sampled the snacks left out for them on Christmas Eve, and the evidence is there for the kids to examine.

We even have a fireplace, damn it, and stockings crammed with goodies hang from the mantel. It's a Christmas card, for God's sake. All that's missing is snow. It's Virginia, after all, where it rarely snows, but at least there's frost on the grass.

Our two kids come down the stairs, dressed in pajamas designed by descendants of the Vikings, purchased from a Hanna Andersson catalog. They're so little, so perfectly little: three years old and sixteen months old, a boy and a girl. So beautiful, both of them.

So perfect, they make the Swedish pajamas look better than they did in the catalog.

I'm ready for them, more than ready. The video camera is rolling. It's brand-new, just purchased with the money from a teaching prize. It's 1991, and video cameras still cost a lot. Way too much. Oh, but I don't care. I've blown all the prize money on this camera even though I have three monstrous credit card bills to pay off, all at killer interest rates, and I still have nine more years to go before I'm done paying my student loans.

I'm not going to let the moment slip away. No way. I've been waiting my entire life for this. And someday, these two cherubs will be so happy to see what it was like on this Christmas morning.

I hate Christmas. Loathe it. It's the darkest day of the year, something I'd run away from if it were possible. But I can't deny its pleasures to others, especially my own children. Maybe they'll have better luck with it than I did. Good God in heaven, I hope they do. It's my duty to make sure that their story turns out different from mine, that they never lose the magic, and if I try really hard, maybe it will all turn out all right.

The camera's rolling, and there's plenty of blank tape, just itching to be filled with images.

Jane guides the kids to the sea of presents under the tree. John-Carlos knows what this is all about. He's seen all this before, twice, but he inspects the scene with suspicion anyway. That's how he has viewed everything since he first opened his eyes. Grace has seen this bizarre set-up only once before in her brief lifetime, but she can't remember it, of course. She looks totally stunned.

They open a couple of presents, and react less than perfectly. To be honest, they both look a bit peculiar. They're acting sluggish, disinterested. They also have a strange look in their eyes, a look I don't quite recognize. I don't know if it's the early morning light, or the colored lights from the Christmas tree, but I could swear they both look a little green around the gills.

Sure enough, they do.

Then, in unison, both of them erupt like little volcanoes. Mount St. Helens and Krakatoa, twice over. Projectile vomit, the likes of which I've never seen before. I thought I'd seen it all by now, including that one time in church when my kid's mouth turned into a fire hose, spraying at the poor suckers seated behind us. But this is the biggest blowout ever.

They throw up all morning long, or so it seems. I didn't know they had that much in them to expel.

We'd had Christmas Eve dinner at a friend's house the night before, and two of his kids were sick. I knew we ran a slight risk of catching whatever was ailing that household, but I never expected this. This must be the fastest-acting bug in recorded history.

Perfect. Yeah. Sure.

As the kids recover and the now-well-cleaned presents sit under the Christmas tree, awaiting their perfect little hands, I rewind the tape and erase everything I've shot.

This didn't happen. No way. It couldn't. We'll start over.

Yeah. This works for me. They're better. The eruptions have ceased. And look at them go at those presents. Yeah—this is more like it. Now, this is Christmas!

Later that night, after the kids fall asleep, Jane and I plop down on the couch, exhausted, and prepare to watch the video footage from earlier in the day.

I rewind all the way to the beginning of the tape and press the play button.

"What the hell is this?" my lovely wife asks. "Where's the vomit?"

"I erased it."

"You what?"

"I wiped it out."

"Why?"

Silence on my part.

"Why?"

More silence.

"What's wrong with you?"

"Uh . . . I dunno . . . it didn't seem right to keep it."

Silence on Jane's part, for then. The worst kind of silence, the kind that you know is keeping the lid on a nuclear explosion.

Then for every Christmas after that and many occasions in between, again and again, up until this very moment, as I'm writing this, nothing but constant, detailed reminders of how truly stupid I was for erasing all of the vomiting.

Ah, but back then in 1991, on our television screen, the kids are giddily opening their presents, and there's no vomit anywhere in sight.

Perfect. Yeah. Sure. As perfect as any lie ever told. As perfect as my Vault of Oblivion. And as perfect as any perfect crime. Yeah. As perfect as anything one can regret for the rest of one's life, especially every time Christmas rolls around.

As perfect as dying for the second time in one's life, at the age of twelve.

Yeah, just perfect.

As perfect as finding a huge feather on my deck when I step out the back door, on the morning after I write about the trees on Coral Way. A feather large enough to belong to a heavily muscled angel, a feather that my lovely wife has left there untouched for me to find even though she has no clue about what I've just written. A feather that vanishes within the next hour, and is then nowhere to be found.

Nowhere.

Eleven

The mousetraps are snapping away at a fast clip. Just as soon as one goes off, we don't have to wait very long for the next one.

Snap. Snap. Snap.

It's damn cold in this living room as we huddle around the small electric space heater, which is nestled in the fake fireplace.

Snap.

"*Otro más!*" Another one.

The mice are dying like the troops at Verdun. We don't even bother to get up to see what we've caught. We took one look at the first one, and that was enough.

The metal bar had smashed the brains out of the mouse.

And he was a big sucker, all right.

Welcome to the house near the Orange Bowl, the house brimming over with *calor de familia*. The house of family warmth.

But damn, it's cold in here. And what's this wondrous cloud, issuing from my mouth as I speak? I've never, ever before seen anything like this. Why does it seem as if I'm smoking? And why is everyone else smoking too?

The filaments on the tiny space heater are bright, bright orange and they hum, but they don't seem to be giving off much heat. You have to get real close to it to feel any heat, but if you do that, the other guys start yelling at you.

"Egoista! Cabrón! Hijo de puta!" Selfish bastard, son of a whore! Bad words are not only all right in this house, but practically the only words spoken.

The light from the black-and-white television in the corner of the room competes with the orange glow from the heater. Some Western program is on the tube, and these guys have a comment for everything that takes place on-screen, something that always includes some swear word. A real one, not the fake ones I taught all of the American kids at Everglades Elementary School.

I keep hoping it will snow. It seems cold enough for snow. Damn it, if I'm going to shiver like this, there should be snow falling.

It's a few days before Christmas, and a record-breaking cold wave has hit Florida. After the Western show is over, the local news is full of reports about the orange crop. For some strange reason, the oranges are being sprayed with water, which freezes and creates icicles on them. I just don't get it. Why are they freezing the oranges in order to save them?

I don't know what's more interesting, or wondrous: the oranges covered in icicles, the smoke billowing from my mouth and nostrils, or the sound of the mousetraps.

Snap! Snap! Snap!

"Coño, carajo, como hay ratones en esta casa. Me cago en la puta ratona que los parió." Blankety-blank, there sure are a lot of mice in this house. Blankety-blank.

I still think that uttering words such as the ones I'm hearing will land a soul in hell for eternity.

Sometimes during the news show, the older guys get up and empty out all of the mousetraps and set them up again, with nice fat chunks of cheese. Not just any cheese, but that very special kind that is in plentiful supply in this house: government-surplus processed cheese that comes in large bricks, and never spoils, and tastes like rubber.

"Coño, estos cabrones son grandísimos." They're huge, those bastards.

The older guys report on their catch. And as soon as they're back in their seats, the traps begin to go off again.

Snap! Snap! Snap!

There seems to be no bedtime at this house. We're up way past eleven already, and no one is getting ready for bed. Tony and I have been assigned to bunk beds in the front room, which is crammed with three other beds.

Our roommates are aged seventeen, thirteen, and eight. The oldest one is counting the days until he turns eighteen and can leave this rat-trap. The thirteen-year-old seems to be a fairly normal guy, and very nice. The eight-year-old seems slow-witted. Or maybe he's just up way too late for his age.

There's one boy who sleeps on a couch on the enclosed porch, one who sleeps in the living room, also on a couch, and three others in the back room, off the kitchen. These guys in the back room are in their mid-teens, and they're all thugs. No one has to tell me. Any idiot could have figured that out immediately.

Bad news, those guys in the back room. Their eyes say it all, and so do their bodies. They're a lot like the caged tigers at the circus, which I'd seen back in Havana, before the end of the world. They're also poets. They can put bad words to use in ways I never dreamed possible. Not even the portrait of Empress Maria Theresa in my Havana living room—which used to swear most inventively in my dreams—could top these guys.

They also throw in their versions of English swear words, which are sometimes hard to identify. *Asjól. Shí. Fó yú. Modefoco.*

The seventeen-year-old guy digs his fingers into his nose and pulls out long stringy green boogers. "Hey, look at the bears I found hibernating in my cave!" He smears this treasure on the underside of his chair, and laughs.

Snap! Snap! Snap!

We all go to bed after the evening news, falling asleep to the sound of the mousetraps snapping away, one by one. And the sound of the guys in the back room shouting, *"Coño, otro más! Modefoco!"*

I have no idea what *modefoco* could be. But I know it can't be good.

Tony tells me he wants the bottom bunk. "You climb up; I'm getting the easy one." We cover ourselves up with our thin blankets and soon enough shiver ourselves to sleep.

In the morning, the body count is tallied. Twenty-two mice. Twenty-two in just one night. The guys in the back room are ecstatic. *"Veintidos, veintidos ratones. Coño, y quedan tantos más."* Twenty-two mice, and so many more left to go.

"Too bad we can't kill all the cockroaches the same way," says some other kid.

I'm impressed, and even take a look at the small pile of corpses in the kitchen garbage can. Not a pretty sight, but a cool one nonetheless. I've never seen so many dead mice, and neither has Tony, the great hunter of all creatures great and small.

I've never been so cold either. It's incredible. We're all wearing several layers, including our jackets. And we're all on fire inside, apparently, belching out smoke from our mouths and nostrils.

Breakfast consists of toast smeared with margarine and *café con leche.* It's not real coffee with milk, but instant coffee dissolved in water with powdered milk.

Tony and I march off to our new schools, accompanied by some of the other kids. Our schools are just around the corner, right across the street from each other: Citrus Grove Elementary and Citrus Grove Junior High.

As soon as we step outside, I notice something odd. The cars and the grass are all covered with something vaguely white.

Snow? Could it be? No, it just doesn't match the images on Christmas cards. But it sure does look white. I run to a car and scrape off the white stuff with my fingers. It's just like the stuff inside the freezer. The same stuff I used to scrape off the inside of my freezer back in Havana.

Back there, in that other world, I used to empty out the freezer, pile all the frozen food in the kitchen sink, and stick my head inside. I'd stare at that miraculous stuff, scrape it, dab it on my tongue with much more reverence than I'd ever shown for a consecrated host, and let it melt. I'd turn my head in there as much as I could to look at all sides of that small freezer and marvel at the fuzzy stuff that was totally unlike anything else on earth, and so imprisoned in there, so caged up.

I'd do this until the inside of the freezer started to drip or my mom or our maid would yell at me and chase me away. And whenever I could, I'd take one of the ice cube trays with me as I made my escape, so I could meditate on those miracles too, and pop them into my mouth, one by one, as they rapidly died in the tropical heat, giving up their souls and leaving nothing but water behind.

Heaven, I was sure, must be full of this stuff. Heaven must be piled high with this; it must be made of this, and this only. It was the stuff God sent to the Jews in the desert, which kept them alive for forty years. And it must be the stuff that the Christian Brothers used to talk to us about all the time, this stuff called grace, which came down from heaven and mingled with your free will and made you a better person. I ached to live where water could freeze outdoors, with frost and snow all around me.

And now I was scraping the stuff off a car. And it was all around me, on every car and on the grass.

Ecstasy.

I've made it. I may be living in a hellhole, but I've been blessed with some kind of ice and the kind of cold that makes people better. I'm out of the tropics for sure, out of that part of the world where the absence of cold and ice makes people inferior.

On the way to school, as I round a corner, I nearly bump into a burly garbage man hefting a large trash can. Two perfect columns of steam shoot out from his nostrils. Absolutely perfect. I stare at him, and he stares right back.

"Crazy kid," he mutters.

Citrus Grove Elementary School looks a lot like the school I'd just left behind, on the outskirts of Miami. It's not really a single building, but a collection of buildings, linked by covered walkways. There are no interior hallways of any sort. To get from room to room, you have to go outdoors.

On a frosty morning like this one, there's no escaping the cold.

Citrus Grove Junior High School, across the street, reminds me of my fourth-grade school in Havana. It's an older building, in Spanish colonial style, with an inner courtyard in the middle.

I say good-bye to Tony on the street that separates our two schools. He enters his old building and I go into my much newer nonbuilding. I walk into my school with the eight-year-old boy; Tony walks into his with most of the other kids from the house.

After a brief meeting with the principal and his assistant, I'm sent to a classroom.

"Boys and girls," says Miss Esterman, "we have a new student in our class. Let's welcome him, please. His name is Carlos."

Miss Esterman has no way of knowing that she just killed and buried Charles.

Everyone in that classroom looks at me. I don't know what to make of them, for they don't look very much like the American kids I'd just left behind at Everglades Elementary. For one thing, they are all a lot shabbier, and less American looking, save for two or three of them.

One guy is huge.

I know what will follow. I'm used to it by now. The Pledge of Allegiance. A Bible reading over the loudspeaker. Announcements.

Yes, we read the Bible every morning in Florida public schools. It's 1962, and the God of Abraham, Isaac, and Jacob has yet to be killed by a court ruling.

Nothing remarkable happens in school that first day, except that I immediately take to Miss Esterman. She's so much nicer than the teacher I've just left behind, so much friendlier, so much more motherly, even though she's just a "Miss" and therefore not a mother. And everyone in class seems to like her too.

I can also detect an undercurrent of tension in the classroom, unlike any I've felt before. Some of the kids in this class seem uneasy, restless, on edge, despite their obvious esteem for Miss Esterman.

Oddly enough, there are hardly any Cuban kids in my class. Because I am living in a house full of Cubans, I expected to see many more of us in school, but, as it turns out, there are only two other Cubans in my class, and both of them have been in the United States for so long that they speak Spanish with an American accent. Both of them came to Miami long before Fidel took over Cuba and turned it into Castrolandia.

Lunch is a new experience, for I had made it myself, following the instructions of my new foster mother. It was so easy to make, and it takes no time to eat it. It barely passes for a sandwich: two pieces of tasteless American bread smeared with Hellmann's Sandwich Spread. I'd had the stuff before, but with some meat and cheese thrown in for good measure. This so-called sandwich spread is nothing more than mayonnaise with some bits of pickle mixed in. It tastes good. So good, it leaves me craving a few more sandwiches.

This new foster mother is not at all like Norma, or Miss Esterman. There's nothing motherly about her. She seems more like a burned-out, rule-obsessed teacher, which is what she had been back in Cuba. She and her invisible husband had run their own small school, somewhere in Havana, a school I'd never heard of, which they'd named after themselves. Common sense and common decency dictate that I refrain from giving you their real names, for one or both of them might still be alive as I write this, and they've probably been hoping and praying for all of these years that none of us who were placed under their care at that house near the Orange Bowl would ever let the world know what that house was like. Who knows? Maybe they've repented and are now redeemed.

So let's call them Lucy and Ricky Ricardo.

Lucy was a short and wiry woman, about five foot two, maybe shorter. She was an old lady to me—probably in her late forties or early fifties—with jet-black hair, poorly dyed. She radiated apathy, laced with bursts of anger and resentment. Her sole job was to manage our foster home and to cook one meal a day. We kids did all the cleaning and our own laundry. And none of us could figure out how she spent most of her time, for whenever she wasn't scolding us or giving us instructions on what to clean, she was locked up in the air-conditioned room she shared with Ricky, the Invisible Man. Every now and then she'd come out to watch a television program with us, but her English was so poor she would end up asking a lot of questions and ruining the show for us.

Ricky was older by a few years. He had a debauched and menacing air that reminded me of Jack Palance, the Hollywood actor who always played villains. Years later, when I'd first see the 1962 version of *Cape Fear*, I'd instantly recognize this onetime foster father of mine in the sleazeball character played by Robert Mitchum. *There he is!* Ricky insisted that we always call him Señor Ricardo, and on those rare occasions when he was around, he always reminded us that he'd been the principal of his own school back in Havana, El Colegio Ricardo. He worked the night shift at *The Miami Herald*, doing some job that was never disclosed to us, and for this reason he was invisible most of the time. When we woke up in the morning, he was on his way home from work. Then he slept all day, while we were at school. And by the time we came home he was gone, off to work again. He worked a long shift, apparently. Or simply didn't like to come home. He also barely had any days off at all, and he wasn't around much on weekends.

This was all right, as far as all of us were concerned, for whenever he showed his ugly mug there was always some sort of unpleasantness.

The world-weary thugs in the back room and the seventeen-year-old guy in my room all say the same thing about him: *"Le está pegando los tarros a su mujer."* He cheats on his wife. Since these guys do nothing but talk about sex constantly, day and night, I figure that they must know something. They're self-proclaimed experts who've already had all sorts of sex, or at least think they have.

From the very start, Lucy and Ricky make it clear to Tony and me that they don't like us. Both of them tell us, to our faces, that we are *demasiado finos*—too refined—and too spoiled, and that we need to be brought down a few notches. In many ways, Lucy and Ricky remind me of Fidel, for they find it impossible to hide their contempt for anyone who at any time might have had a life even slightly better or happier than theirs. It doesn't matter much to Ricky and Lucy that Tony and I no longer have any privileges to boast of, or even any clothing from our former life. Our chief unforgivable sin is our past, and what they'll seek to beat out of us is anything that reminds them of that past: our softer tone of voice, our mannerisms, our politeness, our cluelessness, and our refusal to use bad words.

After that first day of school, as soon as we get home, Lucy Ricardo outlines the rules of the house for us, some of which we've already learned from the other kids in our brief time there.

We're to make our own beds, breakfasts, and lunches. Breakfast will consist of nothing other than toast, margarine, and *café con leche*. And with ten guys fighting over a two-slot toaster, breakfast is always guaranteed to be slow, and highly amusing. Lunch will be nothing other than two slices of bread with Hellmann's Sandwich Spread. The school will provide us with one small carton of milk, free.

Dinner will be served at five in the afternoon. Afterward, we'll all take turns washing the dishes and cleaning the entire kitchen. We're all assigned specific days, in teams of three, in rotation.

Snacks are your problem.

Saturday is holy house-cleaning day. No one is to go anywhere on Saturday morning, under any circumstances. All of us are expected to clean the entire house, from top to bottom, and we'll rotate our jobs according to a schedule kept by Lucy. After cleaning there will be an inspection, and anyone who hasn't done a good enough job will be grounded for the rest of the weekend.

Washing Ricky and Lucy's Ford Falcon and cleaning their room are two of the duties assigned to us.

Sunday is laundry day. We all have to walk to a Laundromat, where we'll wash, dry, and fold our own clothes and linens. Lucy will give us the quarters for the machines, and laundry soap. We're each assigned one drawer in some dresser for all of our clothes, and we are expected to put them all away neatly. The drawers are to be inspected randomly, so you can always be caught off guard. Messy drawers are punished by grounding, or other disciplinary measures, at the discretion of Lucy and Ricky.

Clothing is your problem. If you wear it out, damage it, or outgrow anything, tough luck. In dire cases, Lucy might take you to the social worker, who might come up with some funds for an item or two. Mending clothes is not part of Lucy's job, and pestering social workers is a great inconvenience, which she greatly resents.

We're to receive an allowance of seventy-five cents a week, every Friday.

If you don't want to use your allowance to pay for haircuts, you can go to the Miami barber college downtown, where some apprentice will cut it for free. Getting downtown, about thirty-five city blocks away, is your problem.

If you want to go to church and there's room in the car, Lucy might take you, if she feels like going. Or you can walk to church, if you feel like it.

School is your problem, if you care to consider it a problem at all. Getting help with homework is your problem too, if you think that something like that matters.

Staying in touch with your parents or anyone else is your problem.

Your health is your problem too, and so are your teeth and eyes. Doctors of any kind, or dentists, are for other people, not for you. Illnesses, cavities, and injuries are all frowned upon, and discouraged. Broken teeth or eyeglasses can't be mended, much less replaced.

If you have any disputes or difficulties of any kind with any other boy at the house, that's your problem too. Men are supposed to settle their differences like men, not by running to mommy or daddy or anyone else who might be taking their place.

Managing your feelings, if you have any, is definitely your problem, not anyone else's. And you'd better never cry or complain about anything, anytime. Real men never cry or complain. Nor do they ever say that they miss anyone.

Making friends is not only your problem, it is actually a problem. There are already way too many kids in the house, so you'd better not invite anyone over. If by some chance you make some friends at school or out on the street, you'd better hang out with them somewhere else. Anywhere else.

English is not to be spoken at home. That's for school and for the street. Only the television is allowed to speak English. Given the fact that there are no Spanish television programs, this has to be allowed, regrettably.

On the plus side, some major things don't fall under the rules at all.

We can go anywhere we want on our free time. Anywhere. And we have no curfew. We can come home anytime we want to, as long as we're there for breakfast and school.

Ah, but there's always a minus side too.

The thugs in the house have rules of their own, which Ricky and Lucy tolerate. And their first commandment is "Thou shalt not have anything I don't have."

So, by the end of our second day there, neither Tony nor I have bicycles any longer. The thugs in the back room take them, sell them, and pocket the money. Tony and I make the mistake of complaining to Lucy, and she admonishes us for thinking that this is a problem. After all, none of the other boys came to this house with bicycles, so why should we feel entitled to have anything that the other boys didn't have?

Selfish louts, she calls us. Spoiled brats. *Malcriados.*

We'd also brought a few other possessions with us: baseball gloves, the football that had made me cry, some comic books, my transistor radio. These, too, vanish immediately. And we know better than to complain.

"Now you're just like us," say the thugs after they've stripped us clean.

"No," says Tony. "You've got our stuff."

Their second commandment is "Thou shalt not fight back, ever."

And the third is "Thou shalt fear reprisals for not submitting to our will."

The worst one in the bunch is named Miguel. He's already done jail time, and he has a quick temper. He has a father somewhere in Miami, who is also in trouble with the law, on and off, and never calls or visits him. His real family is the Burger King gang in Little Havana, on Calle Ocho. The other two guys in the back room are less unpredictable than Miguel, but possessed by angrier spirits. Their names are Roberto and Mariano, and they'd come to the United States together on a fishing boat owned by Roberto's father. Sometime soon after their arrival, Roberto's father decided he couldn't take care of them all by himself, so he abandoned them. He never calls or visits, and their real family, like Miguel's, is the Burger King gang on Calle Ocho.

The Burger King gang is the sworn enemy of the McDonald's gang. *Madónal contra Bergekín.* The turf under contention is the heart of Little Havana, on South West Eighth Street, known to us as Calle Ocho. Our wonderful home is about thirteen blocks from there, so all of their street fighting is hidden from our view, most of the time.

Every now and then, they'll come home bruised up, and the rest of us won't ask any questions.

Mariano is a gifted artist. He can draw the most amazing pictures, or copy any image from any comic book and make it look better than the original. He also loves to carve old broom handles into clubs, with nothing but his switchblade and sandpaper stolen from hardware stores.

His clubs are amazingly intricate masterpieces; the angrier he is, the more intricate the carving will become.

"This will be perfect for smashing someone's brains out," I'll hear him say as he lavishes attention on one of his clubs, rubbing the grooves on its handle with fine-grained sandpaper, caressing it, almost.

An appropriate thing to say in our house, given our affinity for mousetraps. During the first few weeks in that house, a lot of brains will get smashed. Night after night, the mice fall for the traps we laid out for them, again and again, and after a while we no longer keep a body count. Then, almost suddenly, the snapping stops and the mice disappear.

We got them all, or maybe they wised up and moved to a worse neighborhood.

I wish I could follow the surviving mice to wherever it is that they go, but I'm stuck there, and so is Tony, and all the other kids too, including the Three Thugs in the back room, who deserve to have their name capitalized, like the Three Stooges. We're all in a trap of our own, one dubbed "family warmth" by the adults who dumped us there.

Snap. Gotcha, *modefoco.*

"A lavar mi carro, muchachos." Time to wash my car, boys.

Twelve

Christmas. Christ, no.

Please, no. *Por favor.*

It's Christmas Eve. *Nochebuena.* The most sacred time of the year. Whether you want it to arrive or not, whether you like it or not, it rolls around and crushes you under its weight.

Sacred time is supposed to be a foretaste of eternity, an irruption of heavenly life in the here and now. Redemption from the here and now, in fact.

In Cuba, even under the worst of circumstances, Christmas had never failed to tear asunder the veil between heaven and the here and now. Ripped it to shreds, every single time, even when it had nothing to rip it with: no food, no presents, no decorations, no trees, no lights, no Nativity scenes, no time off.

Here, in the house of family warmth, Christmas seems to be a heavy smothering thing, a choking column of smoke, a freakishly cruel joke.

We have no Christmas tree. Not even a tiny artificial one tucked into a corner of the living room. No sign whatsoever that Christmas is here.

Back home in Havana, my parents have to pretend Christmas doesn't exist. The ornaments and lights that once hung on our imported pine trees are all boxed up, tucked away somewhere in that cluttered house, along with the miniature Bethlehem that my father Louis XVI had gradually re-created piece by blessed piece, year by year.

God only knows what Louis XVI and Marie Antoinette are doing or thinking on this Christmas Eve. And God can keep that knowledge all to His Highest Self, as far as I'm concerned. I don't want to know what they're up to, or what any other loved one is up to either.

Images from Christmases past assault me all day long, pummeling my senses, piercing me mercilessly. Inverse transverberations, the very opposite of ecstatic raptures, but every bit as intense. I hear the sounds from Christmases past; I smell the Christmas trees; I see the lights strung out all over Havana; I taste the *turrones,* and the filberts and walnuts; I feel the warm night air blowing softly on my grandmother's porch, so thick with the sea's imprint as to be tasted, not just felt.

I'm far from alone, here in the house of family warmth, but the Void circles and circles all the same, like a hungry shark. I eye it, warily, suspecting a sneak attack unlike any other, in a house full of people.

"'Tis the season to be jolly . . ." "Don we now our gay apparel . . ."

I've been forced to learn some fiendish lyrics at school. Miss Esterman loves music, and the past few days have been a constant songfest. I'm thrilled to finally learn the English words that go with the Christmas songs I've been hearing all of my life. But it's just my curiosity that's pleased with this turn of events. I'm like a novice being introduced to the deepest gnostic secrets of an ancient cult. And I'm just as flummoxed as any of them. The mysteries ain't at all what they seemed to be, from far away. What once sounded like sacred hocus-pocus is now unmasked as the most banal nonsense.

"Oh, what fun it is to ride in a one-horse open sleigh . . ."

"And I've brought some corn for popping . . ."

"Tiny tots with their eyes all aglow . . ."

No me jodas. You've got to be joking.

Or the words prove to be the cruelest messages, carefully designed to enlarge whatever hole you might be sensing in your heart, or whatever happens to be missing from your life.

"May your days be merry and bright, and may all your Christmases be white . . ."

"I'll be home for Christmas . . . Christmas Eve will find me where the lovelight gleams . . ."

"Let nothing you dismay . . . O tidings of comfort and joy . . ."

Yeah, sure, go Yuletide yourself, and cram some tidings and popcorn up your nose while you're at it. What have I got to be jolly about? Or gay, or merry, or bright? Chew on your crappy mistletoe and choke on it. Not even that frost I saw and touched and tasted makes one bit of difference. None at all.

I won't be home for Christmas, ever again. In fact, I won't ever have a place to call home ever again. And Christmas has died. It's as dead and putrid as any Christ on a crucifix.

We have a lousy Christmas Eve dinner at the ever-inflexible time of five in the afternoon. It's just all of us orphans, and Lucy and Ricky. It's the first time that Tony and I lay eyes on Señor Ricardo, who, while apparently not invisible after all, does seem to be a man of few words, and even less capable of exuding family warmth than his frozen cod of a spouse. The food is awful: some greasy pork and the usual overcooked rice and black beans. No *turrones*, filberts, or walnuts. No special treats of any kind. We can't all fit at the table, so we scatter all over the house and eat wherever we find some comfortable spot in which to consume our feast. Then three unlucky guys get to clean up the mess.

Fade to black.

It's dark out, and we're in a car, with some social worker. Several of us are packed tightly into the backseat, so tightly that we have no room to move. Another car is following right behind, ferrying the rest of the residents of the Ricardo foster home somewhere, for a Christmas surprise.

We're on Coral Way again, apparently the only street ever traversed by social workers.

Those huge trees in the median strip cheer me up, much more than any of the Christmas decorations we can see around us everywhere. Much more than the gayest and merriest of Christmas trees. In the dark of night these huge trees look even more imposing, and reassuring. They puzzle me and gladden me all at once. I have no clue why they seem like the only good thing out there, in godforsaken Miami, on this Christmas Eve. But they do.

They're a promise, each and every one of them. And there are so many. Legions of them, lined up, perfectly arranged, messengers from forever, watchers, sentinels, guardians, ever eager to follow good orders, and only good ones.

We pull up to a building and park, right there on Coral Way, some-where. The building is plain and modern, with large windows. We pour out of the car and fill up the sidewalk, quickly. Above our heads the limbs from one of my giant friends hover graciously, shielding us from the stars above and the void in which they float. The specimen directly across from us in the median strip, the one under whose branches we're standing, is not much different from all of the others. It's simply doing its job, magnificently. The social worker opens a door and we follow him up a flight of stairs into a large room full of children and teenagers, both male and female, and a handful of adults.

A large and well lit Christmas tree fills up one corner of the room, and right next to it, a huge stack of presents calls attention to itself. The presents are all nicely wrapped.

Large rectangular windows directly behind the Christmas tree reveal a tangle of limbs outdoors, thickly covered with leaves, each of which is playing with light and shadow in its own way, waving in the slight breeze ever so subtly, whispering something to the street lamps.

Christmas music is playing from a phonograph, somewhere in the room. But since we're all Cubans in that room, our voices drown out the carols. Never underestimate the noise that a mere four Cubans can make while talking to one another. It's noisy and hot in there, and for a while it seems that there's no plan other than to have us stand around waiting for something to happen. The Three Thugs make a beeline for some teenage girls and start talking to them. The girls smile and laugh. Go figure. Tony and I stay close to each other and to the one guy in our new home who seems most normal, and most out of place, like us, a skinny thirteen-year-old boy named José.

The Christmas tree calls to me. My idol, my god from Christmases past. "Bow down and worship," it thunders. "Love me, honor me, return me to the inner sanctum of your soul." But, like Frederick the Great of Prussia—who once beat one of his subjects half to death with a cane while shouting, "You must love me!"—the tree fails to win my affection. It remains just a tree, despite its desperate efforts. For the first time in my life, I see the idol for what it really is: something I've been fooled by, something as deficient as I am, every bit as flawed and fickle.

I revel in my newfound wisdom and recoil from it, all at once. I don't know yet that I'm experiencing one of the worst feelings in the world, and one of the most valuable, full force. Disenchantment. My Spanish ancestors cornered the market on it, four centuries ago, as their global empire began to slip from their greedy hands. *Desengaño.* It's a rude awakening, a necessary step on the way to enlightenment. A blessing, really, and close to a sacrament.

There are plenty of refreshments and Christmas treats laid out for us, but I'll forget what they were soon after that night. What I'm focused on is the hollowness of this forced attempt at Christmas cheer, and on those presents piled up near the Christmas tree.

I'm just curious, not really eager to receive any presents. What could they possibly give us? What could I possibly enjoy finding inside whichever box is handed to me by a total stranger?

Soon enough I find out. Some clown dressed up as Santa Claus shows up and starts handing out presents. *"Jo, jo, jo, feliz Navidad,"* he says, in Spanish. *"Merri Kri'ma,"* he adds, in his own Cuban version of English. Some of the younger kids in the room—and there are many of them— seem to fall for his act, and get all excited. They get their presents first, and all of us older boys and girls hang back. Eventually, everyone gets their turn, and everyone discovers what they've been allotted.

Most of us boys get plastic model kits to assemble: one airplane and one battleship. They're nice Revell kits, the very same kind I used to put together in Cuba, before it joined Atlantis at the bottom of the ocean. Once upon a time, I used to love these plastic models. My room back in Havana was full of them: my medieval knights in armor, my gladiators, my Viking ship, my airplanes and battleships. Louis XVI promised he'd take very good care of them, as if they were part of his precious art collection.

"They're more valuable than anything else in this house," he said just before I left.

I'd spent a lot of time with those models. I loved every part of the assembly process: breaking off the parts from the thin plastic frames on which they hung, like fruit on tree branches; following the diagrams step by step; gluing the parts together, little by little; applying the decals; painting the finished product; finding a great place in which to display it. But what I loved most was the glue. Nothing in the world could compare to the smell of that adhesive, save for the DDT from the pesticide jeep that used to spray our neighborhood. I inhaled deeply, as deeply as possible, every time I squeezed out a dollop and applied it to those pieces of plastic. And I was amply rewarded. It wasn't just the model I was working on that seemed to assume a whole new depth of meaning, but everything else, even the dust motes that constantly hovered in my room, swirling like galaxies.

Everything made so much more sense, everything seemed so much more beautiful and enthralling. So utterly real, and worthy of affection.

Once, while working on a huge aircraft carrier, the room began to spin. At first the spinning was slow and hypnotic, but as I pressed on with my assembling and inhaling, the room began to spin faster and faster. And before I knew it I was flat on my back on the dining room floor, transverberated in the best way possible.

I get the two kits, and so does Tony: a battleship and some fighter jet. And we thank the perfect stranger who hands them to us.

Fade to black, again.

We're back in the Ricardo house of family warmth, on the enclosed sun porch, assembling our plastic models on Christmas Day. Tony and I don't have to spend much time on our identical kits. They're small and simple. But we put our all into it, from start to finish. José, the other normal guy, also assembles his two kits. Three identical battleships and fighter jets are now part of our household, and there's no place to display them.

No problem. The Three Thugs make their way to the sun porch, take the models, and smash them all to pieces as they laugh their heads off.

"*Comemierdas,*" they say to us. Shit-eaters. Idiots. Chumps.

I have to restrain Tony, who wants to lunge at them.

"You can't win," I say.

"*No me importa,*" he barks. I don't care.

I don't know how, but I manage to hold him back. I won't be able to do that again after this day. Never. And he'll never win either. But he'll never lose his dignity, even when bruised from head to foot.

"I kept you safe from those guys," he'll say to me many years later, on the phone, as he labors to breathe. And I'll thank him, from a thousand miles away.

Flash forward, sixteen years later, a thousand miles north of that sun porch in Miami. It's Christmas Eve again, and I'm in a loft in New York, on the top floor of an old warehouse in Tribeca, in lower Manhattan, on Duane Street. Some friends have lent the place to me because they've gone back home to Chicago for the holidays. They're great friends, and this is a great loft. I'd helped them move in four years earlier, and at that time no one else lived here in these buildings. My friends were among the first to claim some living space in these old abandoned buildings. Urban pioneers. Carrying all of their furniture up five flights of stairs had been a lot of fun, especially at the fourth floor, where the stairway suddenly narrowed into a ridiculously tight funnel. But the fun stopped when their couch got stuck on the narrow stairwell. It just sat there, suspended above the stairs, like some work of found art, only one landing away from the door to their loft. We'd tried to push it up, but all we'd managed to do was to wedge it even tighter. Getting it unstuck and hauling it back down to street level was quite a challenge, but we did it. Admitting that we couldn't bring it up again was an even greater challenge.

Rain is pouring down in sheets this Christmas Eve. I can hear it pounding on the skylight directly above me. The raindrops are drumming madly, the way they do in a storm, without a steady beat. But they're falling in patterns all the same, like waves. It's much too warm for snow. No white Christmas this year. No way. It's about twenty degrees Fahrenheit above freezing. And tomorrow promises more of the same treasonous disillusioning weather.

The Twin Towers of the World Trade Center fill all three of the front window frames. They eclipse everything else, they're so huge, and so near. They're just a few blocks away, and even though no one is working in there, they're all lit up, like two colossal Christmas trees. Years later, my friends' daughter will see people jumping from them to their death, close up, just before the Towers come tumbling down and fill that loft with the ashes of the dead and all of their hopes and dreams.

But tonight, on this Christmas Eve, that horror can't be foreseen. All that's certain is the lousy weather and my own dismal personal failure.

Crap like this is not supposed to happen. Where's the goddamned snow? Where's the comfort and joy? Where's the cheer?

I'm in this apartment with my soon-to-be-ex-wife, from whom I've been separated for the past two months. She's the first girl I dated, and the only one, ever, but I'm certain that I can no longer live with her, ever, under any circumstances. That's a hard thing to admit, and even harder to blurt out. Harder even than admitting that you have to leave a perfectly good couch on the street because it won't fit through the stairwell. This so-called holiday get-together is a last-ditch effort to live up to a vow I can no longer fulfill. Tonight, I've tried to be honest with myself and with her, and that's only made things worse.

If I were still able to think in Spanish, I'd say *"Coño, que mierda."*

This is as bad as it gets, short of some terminal illness, or war. Give me exile any day, or abandonment by your parents and foster parents. It's much easier than this. I don't want to be here with her. Not now. Not ever again. But it's not supposed to be that way.

The rain pounds on the skylight, right above my head. I'm looking at it, from the goddamned narrow couch that replaced the one we couldn't get through the door a few years ago, my arms folded under my head. I listen to the falling rain, searching for a rhythm. I study the fishnet pattern of the steel mesh embedded in the skylight's glass panes, lit from above by the glare from the gargantuan Twin Towers down the street. My soon-to-be-ex-wife is fast asleep. How she can do that, under these circumstances, I don't know. But, then again, I don't understand her at all and never have, and I don't know how I got myself into this mess in the first place.

I don't know anything.

I don't even know if I've wasted the last five years in graduate school, earning a doctorate, even though it sure seems like it. Two years of searching for a teaching post, and I still don't have one. I'm working at the Yale library for something close to minimum wage, at a job that requires a reading knowledge of five languages, but is every bit as tedious as any factory job I've ever held. My task is to make sure that none of the books being ordered for the library is already owned by it. I spend every workday pawing through card catalogs in one of the largest libraries on earth. I thought I could move "up" to a job as a salesman at a wine shop, but they've just rejected me for being overqualified. So much for the money I had to borrow to buy a pair of slacks for that interview. Of what use will those goddamned pants be to me now, save to wear to divorce court?

I don't know anything, except for two facts: First, nothing was supposed to turn out like this. Second, this Christmas is the worst ever.

As I try to force myself to sleep, an image creeps up on me, from an unexpected corner of my memory, probably from the antechamber to the Vault of Oblivion. I see trees. Lots of them. Big trees that have always existed, trees older than the earth. They're all lined up like soldiers ready for battle. Their enormous branches blot out the sun and filter all rainstorms. Each and every one of them is good, the very definition of goodness. Their will is one with the Creator's. They know things I don't, and that no one else on earth knows either.

Suddenly, the knot in my chest begins to loosen, and the fire raging in my mind is extinguished. I'm at peace, for the first time in months.

Sleep, sweet blessed sleep, begins to hover between me and the skylight, and it descends on me like grace, which is always the opposite of what we deserve. The trees reveal their true identity. Like Christmas trees, they're not what they seem to be; unlike Christmas trees, which are as hollow as any idol, they're much more, so much more than they seem to be. Suddenly I'm seeing angels, legions of them, lined up in perfect order, their weapons held high, bright shining as the sun. Big, serious weapons, all aflame. Their wings are huge, and they stretch across the entire span of Coral Way, like Gothic archways. These aren't wimpy angels with harps. They're terminators, as well muscled as an Olympic weightlifter, and just as incapable of plucking notes out of a harp.

They sing in unison, their voices in perfect harmony.

Hosanna in the highest.
Glory to God in the highest; glory to the lowest on earth.
Glory to the lowest of the low; glory to God in the lowest.
Glory to the stinking manger in stinking Bethlehem.
Peace on earth to those who fail most miserably.
Peace on earth to those who are stripped clean of their illusions and
*   of their love for them. This day is for you.*

Fade to the blackest of blacks. Then, suddenly, flash forward to today, the fleeting here and now, the day when I'm writing this chapter, on a perfectly hot July day, as far from Christmas as any day can be.

A certain feather reappears on my back deck, in the teeth of a tough old cat who's dying of cancer.

The veil rips open, and makes a roaring sound.

Thirteen

She's sprawled on the staircase, upside down, her head only about three or four steps up from a doorway on Flagler Street. Sleazy Flagler. Her sky-blue eyes are wide open, and they stare blankly at the three of us. Her handbag is lying on its side at the bottom of the stairs, within my reach, almost on the sidewalk. A thin man in a light-colored jacket stands above her, straddling three of the steps on the staircase. He's not moving at all; he's just staring at her face. The fluorescent lights in the stairwell seem as bright as any at the Orange Bowl, and they're reflected in her pupils, like sideways equal signs. Two bright vertical parallel lines in each eye. She's a blonde, probably bleached. Too old to be a babe, but not old enough to be a hag; too shapely to be called skinny, but not plump enough to be called fat.

One of her black high-heeled shoes is perched sideways on the edge of a step, about half a yard above her bare right foot. Her skirt is all crumpled about midway up her thighs. And she's wearing fishnet stockings.

I've seen eyes like hers only in the newspaper, back in my native land, Plato's cave, where the journalists loved to publish photographs of all the revolutionaries who'd been shot dead the night before.

"Keep moving," says Tony.

"But . . . take a look; I think she's dead."

"Keep moving, let's get out of here. It's none of our business."

José chimes in: "*Sí, vámonos.*" Yes, let's go.

"But what if she's dead?"

"Never mind; we'll miss the parade."

Happy New Year. *Feliz Año Nuevo.*

There are only a few hours left in the year 1962, and we've walked all the way downtown from our warm and fuzzy house to watch the Orange Bowl Parade.

We've just crossed the bridge on Flagler Street that spans the Miami River—a bridge that will disappear some years later when the wide concrete snarl of Interstate 95 is rudely shoehorned into this seedy corner of downtown Miami. The building and staircase we've just passed will disappear too, along with lots of other stuff.

Our three-mile walk had been uneventful up until then. There's not much to look at on this stretch of Flagler: nothing but rinky-dink shops, liquor stores, run-down apartment buildings, gas stations, vacant lots, used-car dealerships, and a sad-looking church or two. The clientele in this neighborhood—our neighborhood—is always a bit short on cash and liquid assets. They're not much into buying stuff or dining out. And shabbiness doesn't seem to trouble them much. The only remotely interesting thing we've seen on the way down here is a handwritten *Se habla Español* cardboard sign on the door of a barbershop. I hadn't seen one of those ever before.

We've been told that the parade is quite a sight, but that it can't hold a candle to any *Carnaval* back in Cuba, in the old days, back when having fun was still legal, back before the entire island was turned into a giant slave plantation.

I don't care how good or how lousy the parade is; I just want to be somewhere other than that stinkhole of a house. Tony and José feel the same way. José is quickly becoming our friend. So we're out on the town, the three of us, on the first of what will be countless excursions down ugly-ass Flagler Street, into downtown Miami, where—as we've just discovered—almost anything can happen.

The blonde sprawled upside down on the staircase lends an aura of mystery to our journey. I want to gawk at her and the man who towers above her, but Tony pulls me away and steps up the pace. I'm sure that I've just seen my first corpse, but I don't get the chance to find out for sure.

Rats; I'll never know.

So we leave her there, upside down, and walk a few more blocks eastward, toward Biscayne Bay. We find a good spot on a curb and watch the parade. Lots of marching bands and floats, but most of the music isn't that great. Neither are the uniforms on the marching bands. Where are the girls in skimpy outfits, shaking their assets to the beat of conga drums? What's the deal with these uptight girls and their baton-twirling, anyway? What genius came up with something so utterly vapid, so painfully far from a real *Carnaval*?

We endure the whole damn parade, even though it's as exciting as watching an old lady fall asleep while knitting. It's free entertainment, outdoors, and far from our foster home. If we could, we'd stay out forever and never go back, but we know we can't do that. So, as soon as the parade is over we head back to the house of family warmth.

We pass that same doorway again on Flagler, but there's no upside-down blonde on the staircase anymore. The glass door that opens out onto the sidewalk is closed, but I can see inside, and this time around the fluorescent lights have no dead-looking eyes to use as a mirror.

We get home a little before midnight, just in time to watch some of Guy Lombardo's New Year's Eve show on television with the whole gang, including the Three Thugs, who have a wisecrack for everything that flashes on the screen. If they weren't such jerks, I'd be laughing at their jokes, all of which are dirty, and some of which are very funny.

We all refuse to show any enthusiasm as the clock strikes midnight, and we go to bed shortly afterward. So what if it's 1963? We're all stuck here, and the date on the calendar changes nothing.

Having to go back to school in a few days seems a blessing, and it's just about the only thing that cheers me up. But before we all return to school, Tony and I are handed an unexpected present from an unlikely source. Juan Becquer shows up one morning and tells us that he's found us jobs. He says that we need to start saving money for the day when our mom finally arrives, and that we might as well begin right now.

Juan has begun to keep a close eye on us, now that the Rubins and Chaits have let go of us. He's been hovering as much as he can since we left those foster homes, calling on the phone, reassuring us that everything will be all right. So, we're not too surprised to see him show up.

We ask no questions, get into his car, and it's off to work we go. Before we know it we are standing inside a huge warehouse, somewhere in an industrial section of the city. It's Sid Rubin's warehouse, the place where Juan works as a janitor.

I've never been in a room like this before. It's enormous, about the size of half a city block, and it's all open space, save for the columns that hold up the roof, about twelve or fifteen feet above our heads. The walls are practically nothing but huge windows, with frosted glass, and most of them are open. It may be January, but this is Miami, and it's pretty hot inside. Boxes are stacked here and there, neatly, in piles.

The echo in this place reminds me of the *glorieta*, the huge gazebo in the park with the huge trees, near my house in Havana, the one where the firecracker ripped up my hand.

"It's high time that you boys learn some useful skills," Juan says, as he hands us big push brooms.

"Sweep the whole place, from one end to the other. Tony, you take this half; Carlos, you take the other. Start sweeping at that wall over there and work your way to that other one, then turn around and sweep in the other direction, and so on, until you've covered your half of the place. Here, this is how to get the most out of every sweep: press down hard on the broom handle with both hands as you push forward, and . . ."

He shows us how to be the most efficient sweepers on earth, and how to handle our dustpans like professionals.

It takes us about two hours to sweep the whole place, and we can tell that Juan is getting impatient. He keeps coming up to us, again and again, and asks why we can't move any faster. He also shows us all the dirt we've missed, and he keeps shaking his head.

"You know, you guys are lucky to have this job. I know grown men who would sell their soul for the chance to do what you're doing. Both of you are underage and can't get legitimate jobs; it's a good thing that you know me, and that Sid Rubin was willing to hire you."

He fails to expand on the fact that it's illegal for us to be working at our age and that our wages—thirty-five cents an hour—fall far short of the minimum required by the federal government of the United States.

Coño, que mierda.

I've never worked harder in all of my life. Not even that time when I had to clean up our street back home after we smeared it up from end to end with ripe breadfruit during a monster breadfruit fight. *Ay*. If this is what work is like, I'm not going to like work very much, I tell myself.

Sweeping is only our first task. Once we're done, and once we've gone back over all of our mistakes and all of the dirt we missed, Tony and I are assigned all sorts of other tasks, including moving boxes from one place to another and arranging them in a certain order.

By the end of the workday, Tony and I are both exhausted and stunned. We've worked about an eight-hour shift, and we can't fully take in what we've just been through. I can't tell what's worn me out the most: the sheer monotony of the tasks we performed, or the sustained physical effort. I'm not used to either of these things, and neither is Tony. Nor are we fully prepared to admit that we've now officially sunk to the rank of mere laborers. Quite a comedown for two boys formerly listed in the Social Register, and who were raised to believe that certain tasks were to be performed only by others, never by us.

We're both so sweaty and dirty we could pass for coal miners.

"You guys can come to work with me every Saturday from now on, starting next weekend. I'll pick you up and drive you back home."

I don't know what Tony is thinking, but as far as I'm concerned, this sounds like very good news to me. A whole day away from the warm and fuzzy house, the Palace Ricardo. Money in my pocket. Lots of money, more than I've handled since going into exile. For God's sake, I've just made three whole dollars. Juan was nice enough to give us a bonus for our efforts: an extra twenty cents. This rounds out our earnings to three dollars. Between the two of us, we now have six dollars.

"This will sure come in handy when our mom gets here," I say to myself. "And who's going to notice if I take out a little every week for myself?" Our weekly allowance at the Palace Ricardo is seventy-five cents per week. And that is supposed to cover all of our snacks and incidental expenses, like movies or a comic book now and then. Since most snacks cost about fifteen cents apiece and drinks about five cents, I'll have to be more frugal than Scrooge McDuck, or even my mom's parents, the greatest skinflints in the world. This extra cash can sure help *me* right now. Yeah. A lot.

Tony knows for certain that he's pocketing the whole sum for himself. I don't even have to ask him. I know how he thinks. His heroes all along have been Scrooge McDuck, Lex Luthor, and Ming the Merciless.

"Now, you be sure to put that away," says Juan. "You've got to start saving for your mom's arrival. Maybe next week or the week after that we can find some time to open a bank account for you." This is Juan's way of reassuring us that all is not lost, that our mom is still on her way, despite all evidence to the contrary.

On the way back to Palace Ricardo, I'm feeling pretty good about what I've just done. I'm wiped out, physically and mentally, and I'm hot and grimy, so drenched in sweat that even my pants are wet, but deep down I feel a very special and very new sort of thrill. Later on I'll learn to recognize it as satisfaction, but on that first day, all I know is that I feel good despite the fact that working was a pain.

I feel as if I'm almost a grown-up, and I am almost giddy at the thought of that. I'm not sure Tony feels the same way. His face shows no trace of joy, much less of giddiness over what we've just done and what awaits us every single weekend from now on.

I should have known better than to relish that moment. Disenchantment pounces on us the minute we walk through the front door of the Palace. *Desengaño*, of the worst sort.

"So, you boys had a good day at the factory today?" asks Mrs. Ricardo. I detect nothing peculiar in her voice.

"It's not a factory; it's a warehouse," I say. "And yes, we had a great day. We made three dollars apiece."

Ay. Whoa. Fireworks. I didn't know that icy Lucy could be so full of fire, or venom. She rips into us the way a great white shark goes after big fat seals. I have trouble following everything she says because it's all so tightly wound together and delivered at such a fast clip, and so loudly.

She shouts at the top of her reedy voice.

"Who the hell do you two *maricones* think you are? What gives you the right to think that you're better than everyone else? Well, the time has come for you to realize that you're just like everyone else, maybe even lower because of your selfishness, your unmanliness, and your attitude. *Niños bitongos, hijos de puta. Malcriados.* Spoiled brats, sons of a whore. You're used to having everything handed to you on a silver platter, to having people pull strings for you, or give you all sorts of special gifts and special deals, like those bunk beds you sleep in. *Cabrones.* Bastards. Why should you have bunk beds, when none of the other boys do? Is it because you went to such a fine school back in Cuba? Because you lived in Miramar? Because you have Jew friends? Who the hell does Mr. Rubin think he is, sending bunk beds to this house for you, and hiring men to assemble them? Why should you both sleep on soft, new mattresses? And why should you both come here with bicycles, and radios, and all that other stuff that none of the other boys have, and clothes from Burdines and Sears? And why do you two high-and-mighty princes think that you can now have jobs, when none of the other boys do? *Que coño . . .* What the hell entitles you to make more money than anyone else? And when the hell do you think that you're going to be able to go to work? On Saturdays? Well, forget that. No way. Saturday is cleaning day around here, and you have to do your chores. And forget Sunday too. You can't have jobs. That's that. No exceptions for anyone. Nobody can be special here. *Nadie, nadie, comprenden?* Nobody, do you understand? *Maricones, puñeteros hijos de un juez.* Fags, lousy sons of a judge. *Bueno, aquí, como lo ven, no hay juez.* Well, as you can see, there's no judge here. No judge to pull strings for you. No goddamned lawyer-janitor to get you jobs and stuff your pockets full of money. No favor-maker gets through my gate here, and no one here can be anybody's favorite. *Aquí me tienen que besar las chancletas.* Here, you have to kiss my flip-flop sandals. *Cabrones.* You bastards . . ."

Something like that, more or less. She went on and on in that vein until her voice gave out. Smiling from ear to ear, the Three Thugs savor every word, every syllable. Everyone else disappears more quickly than the cockroaches do in the kitchen when you turn on the light. Whoosh.

Ay. So much for our jobs. But at least I found out where the bunk beds came from. I thought it was weird that Tony and I were the only ones with new beds.

Fade to black.

Flagler Street becomes our best friend, quickly, our emergency exit, our link with sanity. Downtown Miami is full of movie theaters and a few of them charge only thirty-five cents admission for school kids on weekends. Every Friday night we run out the front door as soon as we can, after kitchen duty, and Tony and I walk all the way downtown, about three miles away. We'll see just about any movie, save for anything with Doris Day in it. We're not picky. Every now and then we luck out and the film turns out to be a great older one, like *Spartacus,* or great new ones like *The Nutty Professor* or *Jason and the Argonauts.* We can't even dream about getting into the nicer theaters, to see something like *Lawrence of Arabia* or *Dr. No.* That would cost way too much, maybe even a whole dollar. But we don't care. We even dare to see *Flipper.*

We'd love to go on Saturdays too, but our allowance can't stretch that far. On Saturdays we just go out and walk around at night, sometimes down on Calle Ocho, in the neighborhood that some of the English-speaking natives call Little Havana. We steer clear of the Burger King and the McDonald's, where the gangs hang out. There's nothing we can afford there, anyway. There's nothing we can afford anywhere, save for a Cuban guava pastry every now and then: a *pastelito de guayaba.* Tropical fruit milk shakes are out of our reach. Way out.

Being out, wandering around aimlessly—this becomes our obsession. We're not looking for anything or anyone, we're simply escaping, wearing out our shoes. Four months later, I'll be wrapping mine up in black electrical tape stolen by Miguel, just to hold them together. I'll be using about a yard per shoe, per day, because the uppers and the soles don't want to stay together. The holes in the soles will prove much harder to deal with.

Then we hit pay dirt, by accident. Tony discovers a public library. He's so desperate to find any escape hatch that he actually listens to what one of his teachers has to say about this tiny branch of the Miami Public Library on Seventh Street Northwest, and the next thing you know we're in there just about every single evening during the week, right after we're done with our kitchen chores. It's quiet. It's air-conditioned. We can read books in there, or check them out. Our library cards become our new passports, and replace our useless Cuban ones. Mine actually works as a passport to the past and the future, and eventually it gains me admittance to my chosen profession. Tony chooses not to use his that way, but rather to dive deeper into the abyss within him.

The world that opens up to me in that library has no boundaries whatsoever. It's infinite and eternal. And that boundless expanse calls to me, louder and louder with every passing day. Every time I set foot in that library I say "Whoa," like someone who gets to the top of Mount Everest or ingests a hallucinogenic drug for the first time. And my *whoas* keep getting louder and louder with every visit to that ragged, cramped little library that no one probably ever thought would make a difference to any of the slugs in that neighborhood.

And no quadrant of that limitless universe calls to me louder than the past. Before I know it I'm obsessed with time, and above all with the way in which all that we can really own is the past, what once was, but no longer is. The very thought that the present constantly turns into the past drives me wild with excitement, and the thought that there is so much to discover in the past pushes me further into fits of ecstasy.

I kid you not.

When I stumble onto the insight that the past is all there is, and that it is every bit as real as the present, or even more real than it, since there is so much *then* and so little *now*, I freak out at first, for my mind lags behind my soul, and, in the gap created by that lagging, it realizes for the first time that what it's been calling *real* all along is only a misperception of what is really *real*, and an infinitesimally small glimpse of it, on top of that. I don't realize it, of course, but at that moment, in the throes of that most peculiar transport, I've turned into a historian. A historian with taped-up shoes and no clue as to where he's headed, but a historian all the same.

The shoes have a lot to do with this life-altering insight, for they make the present look so bleak. And my own recent brushes with what people call *history* have a lot to do with it too.

I'm part of one of the largest exoduses of kids since the Children's Crusade, and no one seems to know about it or to care. I'm a pawn in something people call the Cold War, and no one seems to give a damn about that either. I've just seen President John F. Kennedy in person, on December 29, 1962, and also his wife, Queen Jacqueline, and the two of them have promised to the tens of thousands of us Cubans assembled at the Orange Bowl—including the returning veterans of the failed Bay of Pigs Invasion—that Cuba will once again be free. I've had a certain future promised to me by the most powerful man and the most charming woman in the world, but all I can grasp up here, at my high perch near the top row of the Orange Bowl, is the past that has brought me and everyone else to that spot. We're all there because the man who is promising us a bright future betrayed the Bay of Pigs veterans by sending them to certain defeat and also betrayed all of us Cubans by promising to Nikita Khrushchev that he wouldn't allow us to fight against the totalitarian regime that hijacked our native land. President Mr. Future, JFK, King of Camelot, has screwed up the past badly, as far as my fortunes are concerned, and also the present. To add insult to injury, I'm also saddled with a father who not only lives in the past, but also claims to remember all of his incarnations in great detail—a father whose memory spans millennia, but who is not here with me, at this modern Colosseum, or at that Palace just a few blocks from it, and who is also doing nothing at all, nothing whatsoever, to correct *that* injustice, or to fix my shoes *now*.

Never mind the hunger I feel, which could have something to do with my ecstasies. The Palace Ricardo Diet is beginning to take its toll on me. All of us at that house are getting only one real meal a day, and a poor one at that. Monks don't fast for nothing. Stop eating for a while, and you'll have ecstasies too. Hell, even if you're a goddamned atheist, you might get to see God, if you're hungry enough.

Ay. And José, poor José. The only real friend we have in that house. He's a year older than me and two years younger than Tony. He's our mirror image, although he's an only son and therefore in a darker realm of loneliness. He'd gone to a good school in Havana and had a nice childhood, full of love, the kind of love you can never, ever find in America, no matter what. All of his grandparents were from Galicia, like ours. His father owned a hardware store in Havana, but like every other shopkeeper, he had it stolen from him by the Revolution. It stayed open for a while and he was forced to work there as an employee of the state, but when there was no longer any hardware to stock the shelves with, the store ceased to exist. José has no clue what his father does now, or his mother. Like us, he was damn close to being reunited with his parents in Miami, but the reunion has been postponed indefinitely, thanks to the fallout from the missile crisis.

Cold War, my ass. All of us at the Palace have third-degree burns.

José is very thin. Too thin. He's been living on the Palace Ricardo Diet for several months already, and it shows. Tony and I briefly consider calling him *el esqueleto*, the skeleton, but we drop the idea once we find out what a nice guy he is. We have no inkling that soon enough, we'll look just like him.

José Cao will help to keep us sane. And when we finally get to leave that house, he'll be left behind. Tony and I will never check up on him, or return the two neckties lent to us by him, ties that have little labels with his name sewn into them, labels sewn with all the love that he lost. I'll have no good excuse for losing track of José and neither will Tony, save for one: All of us at the Palace Ricardo were desperate to forget our time there, to erase it and bury it in the deepest darkest Vault of Oblivion. He never wrote to us either, even though he had our new address.

Wherever you are, José, whoever you are now, you and Tony and I are still linked by a common timeless bond. That past is as real as today, perhaps more *real*, for it tested us and shaped us in ways we still can't discern. I hate to say it, I do. But that hellhole is in us, and we carry it around all the time, just like that upside-down blonde on Flagler Street carried the reflection of the fluorescent lights in her dead-looking eyes while she lay there, sprawled on the stairs, her hair and skirt a total mess, her shoe orphaned.

And, by the way, that brief moment when we saw her and did nothing but walk away, that moment will be with us eternally, along with every other one. And in the world to come we'll know once and for all, and forever, whether or not she was really dead when we saw her, or whether or not it was right for us not to linger and gawk, or for the lovely Mr. and Mrs. Ricardo to punish us for our past and theirs, and that of our parents.

Whoa.

Que hambre tengo.

My stomach is roaring. I need a snack.

Fourteen

There they go again, those roaches.

The instant you turn on the kitchen light, they all vanish. *Whoosh.* Motion is all that you can detect around you in that fleeting instant between darkness and light. *Whoosh.* Spots moving, running for cover, in unison. If only some artist could capture this and put it on display. Kinetic art of the highest order by Mother Nature herself. In its own twisted way, it's beautiful. Sublime.

We'd taken care of the mice, but the roaches were unbeatable. They're the real owners of this crappy old house. *El Palacio de las Cucarachas.*

We spray the kitchen from top to bottom with Black Flag insecticide, and a few others, to no avail. We even spray all of our dinnerware and the pots and pans, and ingest the stuff ourselves, every time we eat. You'd think that something that smells so foul could kill cockroaches, but they seem to thrive on it. They get fatter and fatter, and they multiply according to some exponential progression for which there is no equation. How I wish we could get our hands on some DDT. Now, there's some nice stuff. It not only smells like heaven, but it actually kills everything smaller than you that has an exoskeleton, three pairs of jointed legs, compound eyes, and two antennae.

Whoosh.

Damn roaches. We must have at least a thousand of them, mostly in the kitchen. They're everywhere and they get into everything. Sometimes they crawl over us at night and wake us up. If you've never had a dream interrupted by the feeling of a roach's six legs creeping over your lips or its twin antennae feeling up your nostrils, then you haven't lived, my friend.

One fine afternoon I reach in the cabinet above the sink for my cup—the red one—fill it with tap water and begin to drink. Wait, what's this? My upper lip is being tickled, ferociously. I pull the cup away from my mouth, look in it, and see a big fat roach swimming in there, treading water, waving its antennae around, struggling to climb out.

I spit the water out of my mouth, dump the contents of the cup into the sink, and watch the roach run in circles around the drain. I take off my taped-up shoe and crush it, gleefully. Yeah, I love it. Die, bitch. If you haven't ever heard the sound a fat roach makes when it's flattened, or seen its yellow insides spurting out, then you have something to look forward to, my friend.

We also have scorpions. The crawl space under the house is full of them. Inside the house, they're outnumbered by the roaches, but they're there all right, and they know how to hide even better than the roaches. We have to check our shoes carefully before we put them on, and we have to shake out all of our clothing when we take it out of our drawers. We also need to check our beds thoroughly before we get into them.

I've been on the lookout for scorpions all my life, already. My father, Louis XVI, was stung by a scorpion when he was a little kid, back in Havana, and he never tired of telling us that story. He was being dressed by his aunt Uma, sometime around 1912 or so, when ankle-high shoes were in style for little boys—a style that made it hard to check inside for vermin. Uma slipped on one of his shoes and he started wailing, and the more he cried, the harder she tried to get that shoe on him. She thought he was only being a spoiled brat. Poor Dad. That scorpion in the shoe stung him hard, and then he got very sick afterward.

Spiders, yes, we have them too. But they really know how to hide, better than any other critter. Every now and then we see a really big one and kill it. Yeah. Smashing one of them is way cooler than smashing any roach.

It's us or them.

Snakes, no, thank God. Every now and then we see a small one outside, slithering through the blades of grass on our patchy lawn. We leave
them alone. Why, I don't know. If Tony doesn't kill them, then there
must be something special about them. We have a few land crabs too,
and they aren't as lucky as the snakes. They make such a wonderful
crunching sound when you smash them with a rock.

Yes, it's us or them.

Lizards are in short supply. This surprises me, for the Chaits' backyard
was full of them. Maybe it's because we have so little greenery around
us, so few places for them to hang out and do lizard things. I'm happy
about it, but Tony is sorely disappointed. If he only had lizards to tor-
ment here, this house might seem more bearable.

No frogs either, probably because the whole neighborhood is so arid.
Back at my other foster home, every house had sprinklers, and you can
bet they were turned on at least once a day. The lawns were lush, and
the shrubbery dense. I once saw a frog near the front steps of the Chait
house that was about the size of a football, and no amount of pelting
with stones would make him budge from his spot. Here, no one ever
waters their lawn or their yard, and the frogs stay away. Tony is disappointed by that too.

And, speaking of the grass outside: We have no lawn mower. We do
have a nifty pair of hand clippers, though, and they do a fine job of cutting that thick Florida grass, which grows just fine without watering. So
what if it takes about five hours to do the entire so-called lawn on your
knees, *clip, clip, clip*? It's good, character-building exercise. One of the
Three Thugs claims that it's increased the size of his forearm muscles
considerably. He loves to show everyone how his right forearm muscles
ripple. He also does sit-ups and push-ups all the time. Mariano is obsessed
with his muscles, and sex.

All of the older guys are obsessed with sex. It's all that the Three
Thugs ever talk about, and also Armando, the oldest guy, who can't wait
to turn eighteen, and a few other older guys who pass through our house
for only a month or two and then disappear as soon as they turn eighteen
are all obsessed with sex. It's all they can ever talk about.

Mostly, they talk about their own frustration and how they'd love to
get their hands on some dirty magazines.

One fine afternoon, one of them comes home all excited, ready to burst at the seams. He's stolen a nudist magazine, which back then was somewhere between dirty and kind-of-dirty, and somewhat easier to find than a really dirty magazine, like *Playboy*. He runs around the house, showing everyone his treasure, flipping through the pages, saying, "Take a look, take a look! Oh man, take a look at this. Have you ever seen anything nicer than this?"

I remain unconvinced that these nudist women have the finest bodies on earth, or that they should be proud of displaying them. In fact, the few glimpses I catch of that magazine, the more I think that if anyone on earth should be wearing clothes, these are the most fitting candidates.

Even though it's a sin, I take a look. I can't help it. This guy practically shoves the magazine in my face. But all of the women I see in that magazine are so unattractive. I think that maybe this counts as a venial sin, rather than a mortal one. Or maybe it doesn't count as a sin at all. If someone is so ugly that you wish they'd cover up, can gawking at their nakedness be a sin at all?

I'd already seen better-looking naked women in some old *National Geographic* magazines that I'd found in a recently abandoned house in my neighborhood, back in Havana. Everything else in the house had been seized and taken away by the government, save for those magazines with the yellow border on their covers. A deceptively demure cover that denied the fact that naked women were hidden within.

The oldest guy in the house, Armando, is the most obsessed with sex. He sleeps in the same room as Tony and me, and he often says the rosary before going to sleep. He's tried several times to get us all to join in, but he's given up because the rest of us fall asleep one by one and he ends up reciting the Hail Marys all by himself. Apparently, he's had a very different sort of religious instruction from the one that Tony and I were cursed with, for he doesn't think of sex as a sin at all. According to him, you could say the rosary while taking part in an orgy, and then go straight to church and take communion. No sex act of any kind is ever a sin, he tells us, under any circumstances.

Sometimes he regales us with tales of whorehouses, and what he'd done in them. As was customary in some Cuban families, he'd been taken to a brothel for the first time by an uncle, at the age of fourteen, and he'd gone back many times on his own. Or so he says. He loves dwelling on the details of every visit he ever paid to these *bayús*, as they were called in Cuba. Unlike the rosary sessions, these late-night stories keep us all wide awake. I don't know about the others in the room—especially eight-year-old Paquito—but I'm overwhelmed. Later, when I get to driver's education in high school and see films of real auto accidents, full of mangled corpses, I'll get a feeling akin to that which Armando's tales of debauchery evoked.

One of our transient older guys, whose name I barely get to learn, much less remember, has tales even more lurid than Armando's. He's also full of advice.

"You've got to butter people up. Everyone will be much nicer to you if you kiss their behinds and pretend to like them a lot."

You have to hand it to the guy: He practices what he preaches. He's always telling Lucy Ricardo how nice she looks, and how kind she is, and what a great cook she is, and how he wishes that his own mother had been half as nice as she is. And so on. Lucy eats it all up and cuts him all sorts of breaks. More than once, we find the two of them having a pleasant tête-à-tête at the dining room table or in the kitchen, as Chef Lucy burns the rice.

"You guys are dumb," he tells us one morning at breakfast, while neither Lucy nor Señor Ricardo are at home. "You react too much to the crap these two scumbags dish out. You need to kiss their butts, the way I do. That's the only way to get through life: Pretend to love those who can do you favors, and soon enough they'll think you really do love them, and then you can get whatever you want from them."

None of us dares to call him a hypocrite.

"Do you really think I want to cozy up to this hag and her pimp of a husband? No. But do you see me being pushed around? No. And why is that? Because I've fooled her completely. When you're nice to people, even if you hate their guts, you can always get your way."

Some lesson. We all have to admit that his dishonesty has carried him very far indeed.

"This guy is no genius," says Miguel the Thug. "Yeah, Lucy may be cutting him a lot of breaks, but having to go to bed with her constantly day and night is more punishment than any of us gets. Hell, it's worse than anything I had to put up with in jail. I'd even take the electric chair over that."

I'm learning a few things at school too, but they all seem less practical, even when they're very interesting. Except for one unlikely subject.

Miss Esterman loves to introduce us to Broadway musical shows. I'd heard a lot of opera back home. It blasted out of Louis XVI's study constantly. I'd even memorized some of the lyrics to "Vesti la Giubba," not because I wanted to, but simply because my dad played that song so often, again and again. The words just stuck in my brain, and I couldn't ever find a way of dislodging them.

Ridi, Pagliaccio, sul tuo amore infranto! Ridi del duol, che t'avvelena il cor! Laugh, clown, at your shattered love! Laugh at the pain that poisons your heart!

Now I have other lyrics in there, lodged in the same spot, but these have been written more recently, in English, and are much less depressing.

There were copper bottom tympani in horse platoons, thundering, thundering all along the way. Double bell euphoniums and big bassoons, each bassoon having its big, fat say!

And many others like that one. Way too many.

I learn these lyrics because I want to, because they bring me closer to the roots of the new language I've fallen in love with. These words set to music make me feel American. Nothing else has the same hypnotic power, the same ability to fool me into thinking that I could shed my former self completely and leave it behind, flapping, like a lizard's tail when it's pulled off. Lizard tails eventually stop their spastic dance and rot away. That's what I want to happen to Carlos.

Living in the *Palacio de las Cucarachas*, being surrounded by Cubans at home, and being called Carlos at school only makes me wish more fervently for a total immolation of my former self. If I were able to strangle Carlos in his sleep, I'd do it. What a thrill that would be. Forget about strangling Lucy and Ricky Ricardo or the Three Thugs. The one death I hanker for most intensely is my own.

Why couldn't *The Music Man* belong to me, or I to it? Why couldn't I have been born in River City, Iowa, or Gary, Indiana; Gary, Indiana; Gary, Indiana? Why couldn't I be named Harold Hill or Meredith Willson? Why couldn't I just simply erase my past and start all over again, or just give myself a new name and birthplace? Who'd be able to tell? Do I look any different from any other white American? No. Have I ever been branded on the forehead like a slave? No. But I'm branded on the tongue.

I still speak with an accent. And Miss Esterman writes in my report card that I should work harder on getting rid of it. This comment makes me furious. Not at her, but at myself. She's only telling the truth, and I know it. And I also know that she only means to encourage me to try harder because she believes that I'm capable of killing Carlos. But there it is for everyone to see, on my permanent record: Carlos is still alive, embarrassing me, saying *easssy* instead of *eazy*, tripping all over *trough*.

At least I can write well in English. No accent there, on paper; I own those words completely. Words on paper are a lot like dollar bills or an American passport. Legitimate ones, I mean, not counterfeit. They get me to where I want to go, without anyone asking dumb questions or giving me funny looks. Words on paper make me totally unidentifiable. With them I can kill Carlos for good, make him disappear. A perfect crime, for there will be no body to dispose of, no body to see in the first place.

So, while I work hard on bending Carlos's tongue in strange new ways, I work just as hard on amassing an arsenal of words in English, which, if spelled correctly, will allow me to kill the Cuban in me. It's easy to love English: Some words are poems in and of themselves. You could write them on a page—just one per page—and pass each of them off as a poem. Or you could also pick some at random, like lottery numbers, string them together in alphabetical order, and have a Dadaist poem, which, if conceived in 1919, might have been worthy of publication in one of the Dada journals, maybe *Jedermann sein eigner Fussball* (*Everyman His Own Football*).

Ankle. Awkward.
Bark. Beef.
Clod.
Dam. Dribble. Drizzle. Drool.
Eel.
Fool.

Gaffe. Geek. Gawk.
Lawn mower. Love.
Neck. Nipple.
Oaf.
Pitch.
Shoehorn. Snowflake. Spill. Spool.
Warm. Whorl. Wrist.
Yardarm.

Spelling is no problem at all, even though the language is totally insane when it comes to that. In Spanish every letter is always pronounced exactly the same way. So whenever I learn a new English word, I also instantly memorize its spelling in Spanish. This makes all of the silent vowels visible, and each consonant too. *Omelette* is pronounced *umlet* in English but spelled *ome-let-té* in Spanish. *Treasure* is pronounced *trezur*, but spelled *tre-a-súr-é*. And so on.

This is why so many foreign kids tend to win the National Spelling Bee in the United States. It's easier for us aliens, especially when we're trying to kill the foreigner in us.

So, when my class is given a certain assignment in history one day, I decide to knock the socks off Miss Esterman with my writing. Our assignment is to compare ancient Greece and ancient Rome. I don't have to give it much thought. What would an American say? I ask myself. And how would he say it? Commercials, of course. What's more American than commercials? Having just lived with a family that had two babies, the next piece of the puzzle falls into place all by itself. A commercial about baby products, of course. I've seen enough of those already, and I understand the pitch used in most of them.

"It's here, the new Roman diaper. We've stolen the idea from Greece, but improved on it, as we've done with everything else that we've stolen from them. Those old Greek diapers are made from leather. They're great, yes, but they're so hard to pin tightly or keep clean. And you have to kill a lot of cows and goats, and that makes them very expensive, especially because after only one week, there's no way to make them smell good, no matter how many times you beat them with a rock in the stream. And they take forever to dry. The new Roman diapers are made of cloth. They're cheap. They're durable. They can be washed again and again and every time you wash them, they smell brand new. They dry fast and pin tightly and easily too, and there's no need to kill your cows and goats, at least not for this. Happy babies! Happy parents! Happy livestock! What else could you ask for? So, get with it, buy Roman now. We know how to improve on everything Greek."

Same sort of pitch for nipples and pacifiers. The Greek ones are made of tree bark. They wear out fast and the splinters are one huge drawback, especially if you want the baby to be quiet. Roman ones are made of leather. They're soft, they last awhile, and they're splinter-free. The Greeks were geniuses for inventing pacifiers, baby bottles, and nipples in the first place, yes, but they had trouble picking the right materials for things. Leather makes for awful diapers, but it's wonderful for nipples and pacifiers.

And so on. I pitch three other products in the same vein: rattles, high chairs, cribs.

Two days pass. Miss Esterman is at her desk, as usual. But this time she's speechless. Literally. She's holding my essay in her right hand and trying to get some words out, but none seem willing to leap from her mouth.

"Carlos . . . (silence) . . . where . . . how . . . (silence) . . . why . . . did you come up with this?"

Uh-oh. I'm not sure this is going to be good.

"This . . . this . . . is . . . like nothing I've ever seen before."

Uh-oh. Not good.

"This is . . . so . . . so . . . wonderful. How . . . did you come up with this?"

"I don't know. Is there any other way to do it?" I reply.

For a few minutes I savor the blood, exult over the sudden death of Carlos. I killed him, wiped him out. Give me a pen and a piece of paper and I'll kill him, bury him a little deeper, every time.

Damn Carlos. He should have said "I dunno," not "I don't know." But that's all right, I drove a stake through his heart. Next time, it will be a silver bullet. Let's see how long he can take this kind of abuse. Especially if I keep watching television and mimicking the accents I hear. Those favorite shows of mine should do the trick, especially *The*

Andy Griffith Show and *The Beverly Hillbillies.* Somehow, the actors on those two shows have accents that are so much easier to copy. They must be the most American, the finest actors, trained at the best enunciation academies.

So I teach myself to speak Southern, without knowing it.

Everything changes for me after that essay. I know for sure that I can be an American, that not only can I pass for one, but be one, for real. I don't have to be a refugee or an exile who happens to speak without an accent. I can own the accent and the language, and let it own me. I can sell my soul to it.

Quick, English, get me a contract, and I'll sign it in blood.

This is such an enjoyable death. Or should I call it murder? Or is it all right to call it both a death and a murder? What English word do you use when you kill yourself and become a new *you*? *Selficide*? No, wait, this is one of those annoying cases where Latin surfaces. *Sui.* Damn. That stands for *self* in Latin. The right word is *suicide,* and that word's no good. When you commit suicide there is no version of *you* left here on earth. None, save your rotting corpse. It means something else altogether, and it's way too close to the Spanish *suicidio*. All of those English words derived from Latin are so easy to learn, but they're not really English. They're words to avoid, at all costs. So, what do I call what I just did, in "gen-you-aynne" English, as Andy Griffith would say?

Cubanicide? Carloscide? No, damn, that won't work either. The *-cide* part isn't real English. That's Latin too: from *caedere,* "to cut, kill, hack, strike." Damn. The *-cide* in *insecticide* is the same as the *-cidio* in *insecticidio.* One of my favorite radio shows back in Havana made a running joke out of this Latin suffix, which also lives on in Spanish. In *La Tremenda Corte,* the permanently guilty character of Tres Patines was always brought to trial on charges of some kind of *-cidio* or *-cide. Lechonicidio* (porkicide), *retraticidio* (picturecide), *espejicidio* (mirrorcide), and so on.

So, sweet Jesus, what am I supposed to call this sweet death in English?

Self-squashing?

Why not? *Squash* is one of those sublime English words, a poem unto itself, whether used as a noun or a verb. It matters little that the noun and verb point to very different things. The word itself has been plucked from heaven, from the tongue in which our mother Eve wrote her poems, the one cursed by God at Babel. In the case of the noun, the vegetable in question is often odd enough in shape and color to deserve an odd and seemingly mismatched word. And the beauty of the noun is increased by the fact that *squash* is often associated with the fall season and the most beautifully named holiday in the English language, Halloween, and the second most beautiful, Thanksgiving. Or there's also that game reserved for the very privileged few, *squash*, played in suffocating enclosed spaces with skinny little rackets and a ball that can squash your eye and knock it out of its socket if you're not careful. In the case of the verb, *to squash*, the word conveys the sound made by a violent action. Squash a cockroach and you'll hear *skwash*. Smash a land crab or a scorpion and you'll hear the same lovely sound, only louder.

Yes, Carlos got self-squashed by that essay, all right. Squashed flat, like a cockroach in the kitchen sink. He couldn't move fast enough, like a real roach—*whoosh*—and his exoskeleton wasn't tough enough to take the blow dealt to him by those words on paper.

Skwash, you're history, Carlitos.

I'm through being nice to you. Being nice doesn't get you anywhere, no matter what that transient housemate at the Palace Ricardo says. Hypocrisy is never a good policy, especially with someone whose culture encourages uncles to take their fourteen-year-old nephews to whorehouses, or to say the rosary and talk about orgies simultaneously.

Any country with whorehouses deserves to be abandoned and forgotten. That's the lowest of the low, that cultural trait, more shameful than an ugly old nudist on display or any mispronounced word. More disgusting than a cockroach on your lips, or an accent on your tongue.

Time for Charles to take your place, *Car-lee-toes*. High time.

Fifteen

We're out in the Everglades, somewhere, and it's broiling hot. I've felt fired-up kilns and ovens cooler than this. And we're watching a bunch of men in camouflage gear prepare for the next invasion of Cuba.

These guys are serious. And those are real bullets they're firing. I miss the sound of gunfire so much. My nightly lullaby back in Havana. It's great to hear it again.

All day long they drill, and sit for lessons on tactics and hand-to-hand combat, and crawl through ditches and under barbed wire while someone fires live ammo over their heads. The guys in charge all behave like professional soldiers, or at least give the impression that they know what they're doing. Those doing the drilling and crawling are giving it their all.

Tony and I just watch. We want to take part, but are told we're way too young. It's thrilling, all right, but also extremely frustrating. I want to feel bullets flying over my head. And I wouldn't mind landing in Cuba with these guys a few months from now, or next year, or the year after that. Sometime. Anytime.

I'd like to do my share, even though deep inside I know it'll be a futile gesture.

At the end of the day, the top man in charge gives a rousing speech in which he thanks the men for their dedication and courage and assures them that their efforts will not go to waste this time. No mention is made of the Bay of Pigs. Bringing up that subject is as unnecessary as pointing out where the sun is, or how much we're all sweating.

We're all here because that invasion failed. And it failed because President John F. Kennedy and his brother Robert and their advisors decided to dump the exile invasion force in the worst possible spot—a swamp—and then to abandon them totally, after having promised military support. These men here in the Everglades have taken it upon themselves to try again, with no help from anyone. What they're doing out here in the bush is illegal, but they don't care. So what if John Kennedy promised Nikita Khrushchev that he'd keep the Cuban exiles on a short leash? Who cares? It's our island to reclaim, not his, or Nikita's. And Cubans have been invading their island from bases in Florida for a century and a half. It's such an essential part of Cuban history, an inescapable recurring pattern: A repressive regime on the island drives out those who dare to challenge the status quo; they go to the United States, gather funds, buy weapons, invade the island, and try to topple the oppressors; time and time again. Our greatest national hero, José Martí, spent a lot of time in exile in the United States in the late nineteenth century, mostly in New York, and also in Tampa. He landed with an invading force and was shot dead by the Spanish in a skirmish. Our first president, Tomás Estrada Palma, spent years fighting for independence from Spain, got tossed out, and then spent lots of time in upstate New York, teaching at a private school in a dinky little town. While stuck up there, in the middle of nowhere, he worked tirelessly to ensure the island would be invaded again. Most of our great heroes were exiles at one time or another, and all of them fought against oppression from bases in the United States.

This includes the current oppressor, Fidel Castro, who spent lots of time in New York and Miami, gathering funds and weapons with which to invade Cuba and topple Fulgencio Batista.

I'm only twelve and I know this. Every Cuban knows this, even the poorest illiterate peasant. You can't get rid of the oppressor from within; you need to invade from across the sea.

But John Fitzgerald Kennedy is a man of his word, and groups such as the one I'm with today are hunted down by all sorts of American authorities, including the FBI. If they get caught, all of their gear and weapons are confiscated, and they're prosecuted and sent to prison. The CIA has its own programs for dealing with Cuba, but they tend not to involve Cubans, and the few times they do, it always turns out poorly for the Cubans. We're shut out from their operations, for the most part, except when they need expendable foot soldiers who will fall on their own swords.

Flash forward, nine years: A handful of Cubans break into the headquarters of the Democratic Party at the Watergate Hotel in Washington, D.C., to look for documents that could link some Democrats to the Communist Party. In all of the news stories that follow, they are hardly ever mentioned by name. Even those for whom they're working fail to refer to them by their names as they are hauled before all sorts of tribunals. To them and to the press, they're simply "the Cubans." Everyone else involved who is not Cuban is always mentioned by name. All of the Cubans end up in prison.

Back to the Everglades, and 1963.

Tony and I are there with Juan Becquer, who has come to our rescue once again. Every two or three weeks he pick us up after we're done with our cleaning chores on Saturday and he brings us to his house. Almost every time we go to his house, there's some sort of surprise. This weekend it's men training for war. His role in all this is not clear to us. He's not giving orders or taking them. He's some sort of manager who seems to make things happen.

The Becquers are no longer living in the wooden shotgun shack. They've moved up to a small duplex apartment in a slightly less rundown neighborhood. I've never seen any building like theirs before. From the outside it looks like one house, but it has two front doors and two back doors, right next to each other. It's about a thousand square feet, at most, and it contains two apartments. We can hear everything that goes on in the other apartment, and they can most certainly hear us. But it's all right. The neighbors are Cuban too. Everyone in that redbrick duplex is used to loud voices.

Getting away from the Palace Ricardo is a blessing, anytime. Going away for a day and a half is an especially wonderful treat, even if there isn't much to do at the Becquer house. But they do try to keep us amused, along with their two young kids: a five-year-old girl and a two-year-old boy. Tony and I have trouble relating to kids that age, but it doesn't bother anyone. That house is a beehive, like every refugee household. It's a vortex of constant activity within minimal space, crammed full of bodies. When Tony and I come to visit that five-hundred-square-foot apartment, it houses four adults and four children.

And no one seems to care about personal space.

Tony and I depend on these getaways, for it's the only real *calor de familia* in our lives, the only semblance of normalcy. Juan and Marta Becquer are as nice to us as possible, and so are Marta's Spanish parents. Whatever they're doing includes us. We go shopping with them. We run errands of all sorts. We go to the beach. And we go to drive-in movies all the time. The oldsters stay at home, but the rest of us pile into a station wagon and usually take in a double feature. We have to pay only one entrance fee for the car, regardless of how many of us are inside. Refugees couldn't ask for a better deal.

I can't make up my mind whether I like drive-ins or not. There's definitely something magical about the outdoor setting. All those cars, parked beneath a giant screen, under the stars. The snack shack at the back; the constant foot traffic back and forth to that spot; the food itself, which tastes better than that in normal movie theaters. It's more like a carnival than a theater. And it reminds me of those outdoor film parties that our neighbors the Italian priests used to hold on our street in Havana. Like anything that's taken out of a familiar setting, the weirdness of it all makes it very special. But there's a downside too. The heat, for starters. There's no way to escape it. And in South Florida, you are always guaranteed heat at night. Then, those tiny speakers that you hang on your car's window are all as crappy as any speaker could possibly be. Listening to the sound track through them is hard work, especially with all of the ambient noise. Need I mention the bugs? This is Miami, after all, and the Everglades are never far away.

The Becquer kids bring pillows and blankets and usually fall asleep quickly in the back of the station wagon. Good thing, too. Some of the movies we see are not exactly kids' fare. Not because of sex scenes or foul language, which haven't yet made their way to the screen in 1963, but because of their themes. Above all, because they're so boring that you just want to scream. One double feature almost caused me to have a stroke: two insufferably turgid films with Paul Newman and Joanne Woodward: *From the Terrace* and *The Long Hot Summer.*

Returning to the Palace Ricardo on Sunday evenings is always hard, even after sitting through two lousy movies in a hot car. Anything is preferable to being in that house.

Of course, I give little thought to how the Becquer family is going beyond and above anything that they might be expected to do for two kids who aren't related to them. Instead, all I can think about is why they don't rescue us *every* weekend.

How I wish someone would.

I've stopped thinking about my real family back in Cuba. They may as well be dead, for, in essence, they are. Talking to them on the phone in three-minute increments every two months is a lot like talking to the dead through a Ouija board: You're never quite sure that those on the other end are anything but a figment of your imagination. Their letters are no better: They're always the same. Sometimes I get the feeling that there's only one letter, which I keep receiving again and again, with only one word or two changed. They're always fine, and our mom is always trying so hard to find a way out of Cuba. And then there's the same reassurance in letter after letter. It reminds me of the echo we used to play with at the Bosque de La Habana, on the cliffs above the Almendares River, which reverberated a few times before fading away. Our mom will be with us soon. Very soon, very soon, very soon . . . I read the same words every week, and with every reading they get fainter and fainter. Louis XVI and Marie Antoinette can't say that we'll be joining them there because all of the mail is opened and read by the Cuban authorities and if you say anything of that sort, which might imply that you think that Castrolandia will cease to exist, your letter gets destroyed and it never reaches its destination.

Deep down, I dismiss all hope of ever being reunited with my family. It's not despair that I feel, but sheer numbness, even indifference. I don't even have to make a conscious effort *not* to think about my parents, or anyone else. As I scheme ever more intensely to kill Carlos, time acquires a whole new feel for me. I have no past, and no future. All I have is the present, which is eternal. Even next week seems a long way off. Forget next year: That's way too far away, and not much different from a hundred years or a thousand.

The world has a past, which I'm beginning to discover as I grow ever fonder of history. But I have no past at all. This, too, makes history even more intriguing, for the world seems to have a dimension I lack.

At the Palace Ricardo no one is forced to write to their parents. We're forced to do all other sorts of stuff, but not that. I write anyway, and Lucy supplies me with an envelope and a stamp. Tony doesn't like to write. I encourage him, but Tony is not one for doing anything he doesn't really want to do. My letters are always the same too. We're fine. Can't wait to see you again. School is great. Miami is great. This house is so nice.

One of the few pieces of advice that Lucy Ricardo has for us is this: If you write to your parents, never, ever tell them that anything is wrong. Tell them that everything is all right and that you're very happy here. They can't do anything to help you, so it's best if you don't worry them too much about stuff they can't fix.

Good advice, especially when it comes to Tony. He's not doing well at all. Lucy and Ricky ride him hard, and the Thugs are always after him for something or other. He's always getting into fistfights with the guys in the back room. And more than once, Ricky Ricardo beats him up, badly. One time in particular was especially bad.

One of those odd afternoons when Ricky is home, he takes it upon himself to check all our drawers to make sure our clothes are neatly put away. When he gets to Tony's he blows a gasket.

"*Que coño es esto?* What the hell is this? Look at this mess! Who do you think you are; where do you think you are, *maricón?* Do you think you're still in your mansion back in Miramar where some maid or nanny will come and straighten out the mess for you?"

"No," says Tony. "I was expecting *you* to do it for me."

Ricky starts swinging away at Tony, and Tony tries to fight back. The kid lands a few punches, but Ricky is too big for him. He pins him to the wall and starts pounding away at him with his fists and feet, spewing venom from his mouth with every blow.

"*Cabrón, requetesinvergüenza, maricón,* who's going to help you now?

Where's your father? Where's the all-important judge? Huh? Let him come and help you now, you worthless privileged turd!"

And so on. Why elaborate? The insults and the foul language get viler and viler with every punch and kick, but one rhetorical question that Ricky keeps asking again and again sums it all up, and probably hurts Tony more than any bruising blow.

"Where's your father now?"

Good question, Ricky. Great question. I've been asking it myself.

And where am I? Why don't I do something to stop *you*? Why don't I run to the kitchen, get a knife, and stab you in your big fat gut? Or, better yet, why don't I come over there and slice you open, rip out your innards, and stuff Tony's clothes inside of you, all neatly folded? Why don't I cut off your tongue and cram your mouth full of dirty underwear?

I do nothing. I know better. I'm still a lot smaller than Tony. And this place is a lot like those Nazi concentration camps I've seen in movies. Every act of defiance is met with disproportionate cruelty.

The beating stops. Ricky takes the drawer out of the dresser and empties its contents over Tony's head.

"Now, clean up this mess," he growls.

This is followed, of course, by a few more inventive insults. Ricky was as much of a poet laureate when it came to swearing as the Three Thugs. And since he was older and more experienced in the ways of the world, one might say that he actually topped all three of them combined.

Fade to black.

Several beatings later, Tony is just as defiant. No one is going to make him fold his clothes neatly. No one can make him do anything. And no one can make him cry, either.

Unfortunately, his defiance extends to school, where he just shuts down. He drifts through Citrus Grove Junior High School like the opposite of a ghost. While a ghost is a spirit without a body, Tony is now a body without a spirit. A zombie. He goes to class and sits at his desk, and he's counted as present, but he's not really there at all. He's more absent than the kids whose desks are empty. God only knows where he is, and how far down he's managed to dive into the abyss he brought with him from Cuba. I feel him growing ever more distant from me too. I know he's there, with me, but I also know that he's not all there. I sense an impenetrable force field around him, which grows stronger and stronger with every passing day.

Fade to black again.

It's springtime, which really doesn't mean anything in Miami, except that it's now starting to get really hot. Report cards are handed out. We have to bring them home and get them signed by our "parent or guardian." Tony's report card could win a prize for consistency. Straight Fs. There's a certain beauty to it, physically. That one column filled with the same letter.

My own report card isn't anything to brag about. I'm finding it hard to focus on school. For the first time in my life, I get lots of Cs, and comments from Miss Esterman about how she knows I can do better than that, and how I should buckle down, put more effort into my schoolwork, and take it more seriously.

Ricky and Lucy Ricardo couldn't care less. They sign our report cards and say nothing. But Juan Becquer does care. He's been keeping an eye on our grades, even though he's not our legal guardian. When he sees Tony's Fs he loses his cool and does what no one should ever do with Tony. He tries to modify his behavior through punishment.

"No time with us this weekend," says Juan. "You've got to stay here. You can't be rewarded. You've got to learn responsibility, to realize that there's always a price to pay for every screwup. You stay here this weekend and think about what you've done, and how you can improve. We'll take Carlos."

I can't believe what I'm hearing. Even as a twelve-year-old I know that this is no way to deal with Tony. This is only going to push him in the opposite direction. And it's unfair. If he can't go, then I don't want to go either.

"I'm staying with Tony," I say.

"Oh no, you're not," says Juan. "You're coming with me. No arguments."

Several minutes of protesting and arguing get me nowhere, especially because Lucy steps in and orders me out of the house.

Tony says, "You'd better go; I'll be all right. Go before there's more trouble."

I know it's wrong, but I can't do anything about it. I get into the car with Juan and drive away, and that weekend proves to be the most miserable of all, ever. I feel dirty, literally, as if my body is covered with slime. And it's heavy, this dirt; it weighs me down. I've got something else inside that's even heavier. I can't locate it, physically, but I feel it inside, everywhere. Nothing has ever pressed down on me like this. Nothing has made it so impossible for me to feel good about anything, or so easy for me to hate everyone in the world, and myself most of all.

Judas must have felt like this, I think. "No wonder he hanged himself," I say out loud, as I wander aimlessly around the Becquers' yard. I study the blades of grass, so thick, so rough. I can't look up to the sky, the weight on me won't allow it. I bury every other memory from that lost weekend in my Vault of Oblivion, save for one: Juan Becquer lecturing me about responsibility, trying hard to convince himself that he's done the right thing.

Fade to black, once more.

Flash forward, a few months. The Becquers have moved again. Now they're in a larger and nicer place in Hialeah, an area that confuses me because it's in Miami, but not part of it. It's quickly filling up with Cuban refugees, and for the first time ever I see an *English Spoken Here* sign in Hialeah. The Becquers actually have a whole house to themselves, about twice the size of their duplex.

Hialeah is far away from the Palace Ricardo.

Tony tells me that the Becquers have invited us to their house for the weekend, but that Juan can't pick us up and we're supposed to get there by bus.

"Are you sure?" I ask. This sounds odd to me.

"Yeah. I took the phone call while you were outside."

It could be true. I'd been outside for a long time, catching grasshoppers. It was like a Biblical plague out there: thousands upon thousands of grasshoppers everywhere. Maybe they were locusts. They weren't green. No. They were black, with some yellow and red. And they were huge. I was filling jars with them, by the handful, just because they were there and seemed worth capturing.

Someone had to stop them. And Lucy Ricardo had a lot of empty jars saved up.

"Are you sure?" I ask again. "You're not making this up, are you?"

"I swear to God, I'm not lying. They want us to come over." *Lo juro; mal rayo me parta.* I swear; may I be cleft in two by a bad lightning bolt.

A transit map of Miami helps us figure out which bus lines to take. It's complicated, but we sort it all out and set off for Hialeah.

Somewhere along the route, on the second or third bus, we have an unpleasant experience with a bus driver who wants to send us to the back of the bus when he hears us speaking Spanish. And it's not just the bus driver who gives us a hard time, but some of the passengers too. I bury the details deeply in my favorite Vault, and make sure they can't ever be fully accessed. I decide I'll remember only the nature of the unpleasantness, but not the unpleasantness itself. I do remember the word *spic* being used several times, however, and Tony saying, "No way we're budging from these seats up front. Don't even think about it. Stay put."

We get to our final bus stop, which is still many blocks from the Becquers' house. We walk forever, it seems, under a merciless Florida sun. By now it's summer. And there's no shade here on the streets of Hialeah. I think of all of those cartoons I've seen with a man walking in the desert, a cow's skull at his feet, a buzzard circling overhead. This is worse than the Sahara, I tell myself. I'm parched, and the electrical tape that's holding my shoes together is reaching the limits of its endurance. The fact that I don't have any underwear on doesn't help either. My pants are scratchy.

I no longer have any underwear. Worn out.

We cross a vacant lot and I'm stunned by what I see. Cactus. The lot is full of little cactus plants, hundreds of them. So, this is a desert after all. If I didn't know better, I'd think this was a mirage. But I know what real mirages look like. Miami is full of them in the summer. Just look down any long street, and you'll see some shimmering off in the distance that looks like a glistening lake. The cactus plants are up close, however, and I can touch them. I try to pull one out of the ground, and its thorns fight back, successfully. I leave it alone and suck the blood from my fingertip.

We finally make it to the Becquers' house and ring the doorbell. Marta's mother comes to the door. The look on her face says it all. I don't need to ask any questions. She's not only surprised, but horrified to see us standing on the front steps. She also expresses her total surprise and annoyance in no uncertain terms.

"*Pero, qué hacen aquí?*" she asks. Why are you here? "*Qué se les metió en la cabeza?*" What got into your head? "*Y ahora, qué?*" And what now?

She's nice enough to let us in. And when Marta and Juan get home, they allow us to stay. But I can tell that they're not too happy about it. They've just moved in and they've got a lot to do. Tony says as little as possible, but looks totally comfortable with the discomfort he's causing our benefactors. He wanted to get out of the Palace Ricardo, and he did.

This lie, this trek, can't ever fit into the Vault of Oblivion. It's too big. And it feels too much like some sort of omen, or foreshadowing.

Flash forward, eighteen years. It's the Fourth of July, 1981, and I'm at Tony's house in Chicago. It's as small and as cramped as the Becquers' duplex. It's way out in the northwest corner of the city, a Polish neighborhood still unfamiliar to me. Too far from the lake. I'm spending that summer in Chicago after being away for many years, and I am trying to reconnect with my brother, whose force field has been impenetrable for a long time. I'm doing research at the Newberry Library and writing lectures for my fall semester courses. Come September, I'll have a new teaching job at the University of Virginia, and I've got to get my act together. Tony works at O'Hare airport, loading food onto planes.

"Time for fireworks," Tony says.

He goes into his bedroom and I follow. He opens his closet door. There are hardly any clothes in there. No room for them. This is an arsenal. All sorts of weapons: rifles, pistols, machine guns. Boxes and boxes of ammunition. Grenades. A grenade launcher. Not toys. The real thing.

"Side benefits. It pays to work for the CIA," he tells me. "The only drawback is getting shot at now and then, or getting screwed by the agency."

I identify an AK-47 Kalashnikov assault rifle in the arsenal.

"Here, take this," he says, handing me a very nice and heavy .45 caliber pistol.

He grabs an identical M1911 for himself, and a box of bullets.

"Let's go up on the roof," he says.

"How about the AK-47?" I ask.

He laughs.

We climb up on the roof, using a tall stepladder. It's a one-story ranch house, and it's easy enough to get up there. We sit on the gently sloping roof for a while and scan the pinkish sky for fireworks, over the rooftops. Fireworks are illegal in Chicago, but some of Tony's neighbors know how to get around the law. So it seems. We see a few rockets light up the sky. And we hear explosions all around us. It sounds like a war out there. A familiar sound, a comforting one, in an odd way. Up on that roof, I feel like Tony and I are back in our bedroom in Havana, joking around the way we used to at bedtime, listening to the bombs and the gunfire off in the distance.

"Party time," he says.

He fires first. *Pow.* I follow his lead. We unload our guns into the pink Chicago night sky. Reload and unload again. The noise we make is heavenly, and so is the smell of gunpowder that envelopes us. I know that what we're doing is wrong, but I don't care. I'm with Tony.

Surrender. Release. Absolute freedom. Peace.

I haven't felt this good in a long time, or as reckless, or as whole.

A very, very long time.

Sixteen

Miss Esterman isn't here today. Instead we have a substitute teacher: an old lady, very small and thin. She gives you the impression that her bones might break at any moment, for no apparent reason, and that not a single one of those bones is a mean one.

She looks like a grandmother.

That suppressed undercurrent of restlessness that had been flowing through our class for the past few months surges to the surface as soon as the Pledge of Allegiance and the Bible reading are over.

It begins with the roll call. She calls out a name and several kids say "Here" at once. And it happens with every name. One guy, Richard, says "Here" to every name but his own. Richard is one of those Cuban kids who've been in Miami so long that they have English first names and can't speak Spanish correctly. He's the tallest kid in the class, and he has blond hair and blue eyes. He looks like an English choir boy, but beneath the cherubic exterior, a volcano is waiting to erupt. He's full of hell, and so far it's surfaced only on the playground. Miss Esterman has him under some kind of spell in the classroom. The same one she uses on the rest of us.

No Miss Esterman, no spell.

Everyone who'd been restraining their worst impulses breaks free, and Richard leads the way. The roll call takes about a half hour, and God only knows what the substitute submits to the principal's office. There's no way she can figure out who is really there, or who is who.

Time for the first lesson of the day. The substitute asks a question, and Richard raises his hand. She calls on him.

Richard stands up and replies in his rusty Spanish: *"Tu eres la vieja más fea y más flaca y mocosa que he visto en toda mi vida."* You're the ugliest and skinniest sniveling old bag that I've ever seen.

"What? Could you please repeat that? I didn't get what you said."

A few giggles from the few kids who know Spanish. I'm too stunned to giggle. The rest of the class looks puzzled, but highly amused.

"Te dije que eres feísima, y más flaca que una vaca muerta de hambre, y que tienes la nariz llena de mocos." I said that you are very ugly and skinnier than a starving cow and that your nose is full of boogers.

Richard sits down.

"Oh, I'm sorry . . . I didn't get that again. Could you repeat it one more time?"

A girl in the class shouts: "He can't speak English. He just got here from Cuba."

"Oh . . . I see."

The legitimate question she asked is answered by some other kid, and the class moves along. Or so it seems for a few minutes. Then Richard begins to interrupt the substitute continually, blurting out more insults in Spanish.

All it takes is about ten minutes of this, and the class begins to disintegrate into chaos, rapidly. The substitute teacher, who seems unable to realize what's happening, keeps trying to move the class along whatever lesson plan Miss Esterman had left for her.

Within an hour, we're all talking to one another and carrying on as if the substitute were not there at all. After a while, she just gives up and sits at her desk, doing nothing.

"All right, kids, if this is how you want to behave, so be it," she says. "It's your problem if you don't want to learn what you're supposed to learn." Or something like that.

By lunchtime, we're all having a grand old time in there, talking, joking, doing whatever we want. Since Citrus Grove Elementary doesn't have a lunchroom—only a cafeteria with no seating space—we do lunch in the classroom, as always. I have nothing but my usual Sandwich Spread sandwich—*pain américain à la Hellmann's*—but most of the other kids buy real lunches and bring them back to their desks. This means that some of them have several items to play with. I eat my sandwich and drink the eight ounces of milk I get for free, but many of the other kids start playing with their food.

Food fight!

Much to my dismay, I see really good food being tossed around the room, stuff I'd love to eat. The brownies, especially, look very good. Even worse, as far as my dismay is concerned, I have nothing to throw, save for what gets thrown at me, most of which I eat.

At this point, the arrangement of the desks in the room comes into play. Miss Esterman is always changing our desks around. They're not fixed to the floor, so she's constantly coming up with new patterns for us, to keep us off guard. On this day, our desks are perfectly arranged for war: We're in four rows, perpendicular to the teacher's desk, with two rows at either end of the room and a wide aisle between them. This means that we are evenly divided, with two rows on one side of the room facing two rows on the other, with a trench and no-man's-land in between.

Fortunately, no one throws anything at the substitute teacher, who continues to sit at her desk through all of this, as if nothing unusual is taking place. Sparing her makes it possible for us to carry on.

The bell rings. Lunch is over. The kids who had trays and plates return them to the cafeteria and come back. There's been a lull in the fighting, a momentary truce. Just like the one that took place between the Germans and the Franco-British forces along the western front on Christmas 1914, which didn't last long.

With no food to throw, we dig into our desks and look for suitable projectiles. At first it's wads of paper and paper airplanes. But the mere act of having to dip into our flip-top desks for ammunition accidentally reveals to all of us a crude defense strategy. If you keep your desk top flipped up, you have a nice big shield to hide behind.

Hiding behind our shields, we reach for the one item that is crying out to be used, precisely because it's shaped like a bullet: our coloring crayons. We let them fly. And when I say "we," I mean all of us. Not one kid in that class is a conscientious objector or a pacifist. Each and every one of us is launching colored projectiles across the room.

The crayons smash into the desktops and break into smaller pieces. They smash into the walls too, for not everyone has good aim or a good throwing arm. As we run out of whole crayons to throw, we begin to pick up their remnants from the floor. Throwing crayons across the room and ducking behind the shield of your raised desktop is hard enough. Throwing them while you try to pick up pieces from the floor is even harder. So, this is when the casualties begin to mount. I get hit several times. Good thing I'm wearing glasses, for someone lands a shot right over my eye, and it's thrown hard. It leaves a purple blotch on my lens. I score a few hits myself, including one that lands squarely in someone else's eye. It's one of the nicest guys in the class, someone who is as close to a friend as I can hope for. He winces and puts his hand over his eye. My conscience bites hard, and I do some wincing of my own, inside. But that doesn't slow me down or stop me. It's kill-or-be-killed in there, everyone for himself and God against all.

Crayons give way to pencils and pens, and the chalk from the blackboard, and even to ink cartridges—those little plastic tubes full of ink that you could insert into fountain pens back then in the early 1960s. Some of the ink cartridges burst. On the desktops, on the walls, on the floor, on the warriors.

It seems to go on forever. Then the bell rings. School's out. I don't know about the others, but I don't even see the substitute as I file out the door. I go home a bit ruffled and stained up, just like everyone else. And we leave behind a classroom that looks as if it has been hit by a tornado.

I know we're all in trouble, and that there will be hell to pay. Big-time. But that's not going to happen today, I tell myself. That's tomorrow's problem. I live for the present, the eternal now moment. All I can think about is how much fun I had, and how I wish I hadn't hit that one guy in the eye.

The rest of that day is like every other one at the Palace Ricardo. A bad dinner at five o'clock, kitchen duty, a walk to the library, a walk back during which we look for empty soda-pop bottles that we can redeem for two cents apiece, an hour or two of television, and off to bed.

Morning breaks, and I get out of bed feeling shaky. Suddenly, *now* has turned into a day of reckoning. In the kitchen, it's the usual rush and the usual pecking order. Like the lowest monkeys in a monkey tribe, some of us have to wait until the alpha monkeys are done eating before we can even begin to think about our turn. Tony and I eat our margarine toast and drink our instant *café con leche*, and we head for school. As soon as I walk through the classroom door, I know that judgment day has arrived.

The principal is in our room, and he's just standing there, tight-lipped, up in front, next to Miss Esterman, who looks thoroughly mortified. He says nothing, and neither does she. There are also a couple of janitors in the room, cleaning up the mess we made. One of them is scraping crayons off the wall. The other is collecting debris from the floor. We go through the usual sacred morning ritual: Pledge of Allegiance, Bible reading via the school's sound system. The janitors stop their cleaning while this takes place. We students eye one another and make subtle facial gestures, all of which indicate apprehension of the highest order. I catch a glimpse of Richard. His gaze is fixed on my end of the room, like a needle on a compass pointing to true north. But I catch him glancing at Miss Esterman and the principal out of the corner of his eye, furtively.

Much to my relief, no one has shown up wearing an eye patch.

Miss Esterman is the first to break the silence.

"Class, you know why Principal So-and-So is here. He has something to say to you."

He rips into us, not by screaming and yelling, but by subtly needling our consciences with red-hot reminders of everything we've ever been taught by our parents and our teachers—the very same principles that all of us had been trying not to think of ever since yesterday. I can't speak for the others, but my conscience has been released from the cage into which I put it yesterday, and now it's like a wounded rampaging bear, in there, wherever it is that it dwells and does its work.

Ay. It hurts. I'm getting mauled. And the guilt is flowing like red-hot blood from gaping wounds. But I have to admit to myself, as my own conscience is ripping me to shreds, that what I'm looking at is kind of funny, maybe even hilarious.

As Principal So-and-So talks, the janitors are hard at work, scraping crayons off the walls and floor, wiping stains, sweeping, mopping. Somehow, something deep inside of me tells me that I should laugh at this, that it's one of the funniest things I've ever seen. It's a lot like the aftermath of a pie-throwing scene in a silent movie, except that in this rendering, we have a principal scolding us, the pie throwers. And I'm waiting for a pie to hit the principal squarely in the face.

I half expect the overture from Rossini's *The Thieving Magpie* to start playing over the loudspeaker that has just delivered the Word of God to all of us reprobates.

But this is no silent film. It's real life, and Principal So-and-So gives us a tough assignment. We're asked to write an essay in which we explain our behavior: "Why did I do what I did, even though I knew it was wrong?" This is a low blow. The lowest of the low. What does he expect us to say?

But wait, maybe it's not such a low blow. Is that it? Is this the extent of our punishment? No suspension? No detention? Nothing else?

Damn. Yes, there's something else. He's going to write a letter to all of our parents and guardians detailing the nature of our appalling behavior, and they'll have to sign it and return it to him. He's also going to turn our essays over to our elders, and they'll have to sign and return those to him too.

I breathe a huge sigh of relief and laugh, inside. In my case, this turn of the screw will be painless. Lucy and Ricky won't give a damn about this at all. They might not even read what I give them to sign. That's what they always do. "*Qué es esto?*" Lucy will ask. What's this? She's the only one who signs our stuff. She always asks about what's on the pieces of paper we give her to sign, and she never reads it herself, to check and see if we've told her the truth. When it comes to things of this sort, she trusts us completely because her English is so poor, and also because she couldn't care less about any of us.

I luck out. For once, being an orphan works in my favor.

Writing the essay is every bit as hard as I expected, even though we're given the rest of the day to do it. This is no homework assignment, but our sole activity for the day. I approach my conscience with caution, since it's on the rampage. It roars, and mauls me. I back off. If I rely on this beast, I'll have to write my essay in blood. Hell, no. No way. So I do the only thing I can: I turn to the other beast in me, the one that's always nice and sweet and wicked to the core, the one that thinks highly of me and all of my worst impulses.

Doctors Freud and Jung and all of your disciples—wayward or not— please feel free to laugh. No need to hide your feelings. This is the kind of stuff that keeps you gainfully employed.

"It wasn't my fault," I say in my essay. "I had to defend myself." Yeah. I didn't start this, I say, but once it got going and stuff started flying around the room, it became a question of honor and self-defense. What was I supposed to do? Let others pelt me with crayons and chalk and ink cartridges willy-nilly? Hide behind my desktop like some sissy girly-boy? Even the girls were throwing things. What kind of boy would that make me, if I were to just sit there, passively? And where was the substitute teacher during all of this? Why didn't she do anything? Why didn't she protect *me* from all of those projectiles? Yes, I know it's wrong to trash a classroom and to disrespect a teacher, but I got hit hard by some of those crayons. They hurt. And my clothes got all stained up, maybe permanently. I live in an orphanage, you know. I have to wash my own clothes, and I don't have much in the way of a wardrobe. If something is damaged, that's it: I don't get to replace it. So, where was this teacher? It was her job to keep the natives from getting out of control. I'm not one of *them*, the real troublemakers. I just had to defend myself from *them*, under the most pressing of circumstances. I'm really a good boy. A very good boy, living in hell. Yeah. I have a lot to put up with once I leave the classroom, so the least that the school could do for *me* is to provide me with a safe and nurturing environment.

Yeah. And I'm sorry too. So sorry. I wish the *others* hadn't turned me into a hoodlum.

Some essay. If this were a trial, with a judge and jury, I'd surely be acquitted. But there's still one dark shadow in there, in my conscience, which my essay fails to exorcise: the image of one of my crayons striking that one guy in the eye. The image won't leave me alone; it bothers me more than anything else that happened yesterday. That's how it is with me. It's always images that reveal the truth to me, silently, without words. Words can be used to deceive oneself and others. Somehow, images never lie.

The crayon struck his eye while it was wide open. He wasn't looking at me. He was peeking from behind his open desktop, in another direction. He held his hand over his eye for a long time, and he stopped throwing stuff. I saw the pain in his face, and then in the look he gave me with his one good eye. Not a pretty sight. That look said it all, and I knew it.

No way I could admit that in my essay. And that's the worst problem of all.

But, by the same token, why is it that I have no image at all of that teacher after the first couple hours of that day? Where the hell is she? Why isn't she there? Why aren't my mother and father there either, to read the principal's letter and my own wretched essay? Where? Images never lie, but it takes a lifetime to interpret them. And even by the time you get to the end of your life, to that final death that takes you out of your body, you won't have exhausted their meaning.

We're born liars, but the lies we tell ourselves are a lot like the promises we make and the vows we take. They're what we wish could be true.

Flash forward, twenty-eight years or so. My firstborn son is only about three years old, and he's taking amoxicillin, a liquid antibiotic, for some infection. Talk about looking cherubic, this little guy is straight from the highest heaven. He radiates light, literally. There's no guile in him, whatsoever, no hint of a shadow within, much less of any beast.

He has to take some of this pink antibiotic several times a day. I know he understands that. I also know that he's getting old enough now to figure some things out for himself, such as the need to take one's medicine when one is sick. So, I decide to let him take his own medicine. He's our first, so Jane and I are learning as we go along, trying to do our best as we fly by the seat of our pants. This seems like a logical step to me.

I fill a little thimble-like plastic cup with the right dosage. I place the cup on the coffee table. He's watching a videotape of his favorite television show, *Thomas and Friends*. Man, how I wish this show had existed when I was his age. Sometimes I think I enjoy it more than he does.

"Time for your pink stuff. Here it is," I say. "Drink it up."

I leave the room, patting myself on the back for being such an enlightened father and so unlike my own Louis XVI, who used to whip me with his belt. He wouldn't have even bothered with something so beneath him as to dispense medicine to his sons. That was woman's work. Plus, neither he nor my mom would have trusted me. My mom would have shoved that pink stuff up to my lips and tilted the cup with her hands until its contents were safely down my gullet. And she'd have watched for gulping, and maybe even asked me to open my mouth and stick out my tongue, to prove that I really had swallowed it.

Not me. I'm enlightened. This kid will live most of his life in the twenty-first century. High time to leave the sordid past behind, and to do things differently. I can trust my son to take his own medicine. He's such a good kid.

I busy myself with feeding our daughter Grace, who is only about a year old. Now, there's a kid who needs all sorts of help, simply because of her age. Her older brother is old enough now to do some things on his own.

About a half hour later I go into the downstairs bathroom to rinse something out in the sink, and what I see makes me reel.

There's a large pink puddle inside the sink.

Yeow. This one hurts. "Hey, John-Carlos, come here, please. I'm in the bathroom."

The cherub comes in from the living room. He stares at me with his big blue eyes.

"What's this?" I ask, pointing to the pink puddle in the sink.

He peers over the edge and takes a look. He hesitates for a while. "I dunno," he says, finally.

"Did you take your medicine?"

"Yes," he says, nodding. But his eyes tell a different story. He's shocked, bewildered, and frightened.

"What do you think this is in here?"

More silence.

"Is this your medicine?"

"No." Perfect shaking of the head. Perfect befuddlement in his eyes.

"But it looks just like your medicine, right?"

"Yeah." More nodding.

"Well, huh, this leaves us with a mystery. The medicine bottle is on a high shelf in the kitchen, and it has a childproof cap, which means that you can't reach it or open it. I didn't do this. Mom didn't do it. Grace can't do it. The only medicine that could be spilled was in that cup I gave you, out there in the living room. But you drank that. So where did this come from? How did this get here, if you drank your cup?"

"I dunno." Shrugging this time. And his sky blue eyes are now bottomless pools. I can see the vortex of a black hole forming inside of him. It's an amazing sight.

"Are you sure you don't know?"

Silence. Lots of it.

"No."

"Don't do this again. All right?"

End of conversation. His first lie. His first failure at lying. He knows it. I know it. There'll be other lies. Many more, each and every one of them a wish, and an echo of a beastly howling within.

Like father, like son.

Seventeen

Kirk Douglas is hanging on a cross, just like Jesus Christ. This doesn't seem right. I knew he couldn't beat the Roman army, but this is too much. Kirk and Christ are total opposites. Kirk is Einar, the Viking, not the Prince of Peace. Kirk doesn't look good up there, and neither do the hundreds of other extras who are hanging on other crosses along the Appian Way. You might as well put Santa Claus suits on all of them, it's that much of a mockery of Christ. Jean Simmons shouldn't be there either, showing Kirk their baby. Guys who hang on crosses don't have girlfriends, much less babies. What kind of sacrilege is this? And there's been damn little action in this movie too. Yeah, the gladiator fights were all right, and some of the battle scenes too, but this is nothing like *The Vikings*, even though Tony Curtis, another actor from that movie, is also in this one.

I've been waiting to see *Spartacus* for three years, about one quarter of my whole life. I'd followed the making of this movie back in Cuba, in 1959, in the same magazine that had previously covered Fidel's guerrilla theater in the mountains, a weekly rag called *Bohemia*. Every week we'd get an update on the making of *Spartacus* and on the progress of Fidel's so-called Revolution, now that he had switched roles from glamorous jungle revolutionary to maximum leader of the whole island. *Bohemia* was still partial to Fidel in late 1959, even though he was clamping down on the press, in a heavy-handed way that made Batista look about as repressive as a kindergarten teacher at a Quaker school. Censorship was the order of the day, and the censors were ultrasensitive. By the time *Spartacus* was released in 1960, Cuba had entered its Dark Ages, and the thought police wouldn't allow the film to be shown, even though it was about a revolution.

So, ironically, none of us got to see *Spartacus* in Cuba, thanks to the so-called Revolution. I guess that seeing a revolution fail on the big screen might be perceived by the authorities as some kind of threat to correct thinking. Kirk/Spartacus does end up getting crucified after all.

Imagine Fidel on a cross, with Che and Raúl on either side. If you were in charge of thought control for the so-called Revolution, you wouldn't want anyone to imagine that. No way.

But I'm no longer in the land of censorship and thought control. I'm free as a bird, right after Noah's flood has subsided. Not only am I in the United States, I'm living in a house where no one cares what I do as long as I tackle my chores. If I were somehow to get roaring drunk or high on heroin, no one would notice or give a damn. And now that I've developed a passion for ancient history, seeing this film or any other set in yesteryear has become an obsession. I need to see the distant past re-created on-screen. So, I'm delighted to learn that *Spartacus* is showing at one of the theaters on Flagler Street. I blurt out the news, thinking no one will care.

Apparently, I'm not the only one who's been waiting to see this movie. Everyone at the Palace Ricardo is just as interested in seeing it, and we end up having a rare mass excursion down Flagler Street. The Palace empties out and we amble down Flagler as a wolf pack. Even the Thugs come along.

I expect something to go wrong, at some point. This is much too weird.

But nothing goes awry, much to my surprise. No arguments, no fights, no unpleasantness of any kind. It's a long and slow-moving film, but we're all drawn into it. No one but Tony and I have a gold standard to measure it by—*The Vikings*—but even the two of us have to admit that for all of its languor, it's a mighty fine film. Everyone's deeply moved. All of us grieve for Spartacus at the end. The slaves should have won, no doubt about it; at the very least, Kirk should have slipped away in disguise, or let someone else die in his place. He should have thought of himself, rather than his noble cause.

But, then again, Kirk Douglas does have a habit of playing characters who do stupid things at the end, like being unselfish. As was the case in *The Vikings*, Kirk embraces total detachment at the end, and he ends up losing his life in the bargain.

Although I grieve with everyone else, I've known all along that Spartacus is going to fail because I've read up on his story at the library. I expect a sad ending, but no one else does. They all expect a happy Hollywood finale. And this leads to trouble, once we all get home.

Roberto, one of the Thugs, can't shut up about how unfair it was for Spartacus to be defeated. He goes on and on, repeating himself a thousand times, ignoring the fact that this was a historical epic, based on real events. Everyone nods in unison, except for me. The more that Roberto expresses his disgust with the movie script, the harder it becomes for me to bite my tongue and refrain from speaking.

Ay. But there comes a point when I can't take it anymore. Right after Roberto says for the thousandth time that the film had the wrong ending, I put in my two cents. Unfortunately.

"Spartacus couldn't win because Spartacus really lost, in real life."

"What do you mean?" asks Roberto.

"The real Spartacus lost. This movie is just telling that story."

"You mean to say that you weren't rooting for Spartacus to win?"

"I would have loved for him to win, but I knew he'd lose. He was fighting Julius Caesar, after all."

Yeow! That's it. Watch out! Roberto starts screaming at me, using every foul word in the book. I'll spare you those details. The gist of his outburst is this: I'm just as bad as the Romans who owned slaves and crushed Spartacus's slave uprising.

"There you go again, *maricón*, you bastard, defending class privilege!"

Punch. Kick. Punch, kick, punch. Kick. Punch some more . . . kick some more.

If you've ever thought that all Cuban exiles were rich or middle class, forget about it. The Cuban exodus was not driven by class tension, but by political repression, and all of the unresolved class issues went into exile too, along with all of us who left. We had as much class tension in the Palace Ricardo as in Cuba, Manhattan, Liverpool, or Hong Kong. Roberto's father had been a poor fisherman, and Roberto resented me as much as Fidel did, with only one huge difference: Roberto wasn't a revolutionary megalomaniac.

Poor Cubans could hate Fidel as much as rich Cubans, and often did. No one likes to be told what to think, or to be permanently gagged, or to be promised nothing but poverty and struggle forever. No one does, save for those who are out for revenge against perceived oppressors, or those who think they can switch roles with the so-called oppressors and take all of their stuff from them.

The same class tensions that drive Ricky and Lucy Ricardo to loathe me and Tony drive Roberto to explode when I observe in a matter-of-fact way that the real Spartacus had really failed and the movie could have had no other ending.

I say nothing in response to Roberto's outburst, or his kicks and punches. I know that anything I say won't make a bit of difference. Even though he and I are in the same tight spot, he's not ready to let go of his prejudices or his resentment of me. And I'm not ready to get clobbered again.

Tony and I get beaten up a lot. Tony fights back. But I'm much smaller than the Thugs, and I learn the hard way that any defiance on my part will only lead to more bruises at the end of the day. I've also learned that the Thugs love to make the rest of us miserable, no matter what. Anything can set them off.

A few weeks prior to the Spartacus outburst, Roberto and Mariano had both beaten me up for making a simple observation about a science-fiction movie we were watching on television about an expedition to outer space.

"Hey, look, here we go again: There's only one woman in this movie," I'm dumb enough to say. The responses are too predictable. I should have known better than to open my mouth.

"Yeah, so what? She's hot."

"Yeah, look at those boobs. *Coñooo.* I'd love to get my hands on them."

"Forget the boobs. Look at the rest of the equipment."

My stupidity knows no bounds. I speak up again. "These movies are all alike. Her role is to be dumber and weaker than the men and to fall into the monster's hands, and to give the men an opportunity to come to her rescue. And she has to have big boobs. It's part of the deal. That's why the monster or space alien abducts her in the first place. Hollywood monsters love big boobs as much as any earth man."

"*Maricón, hijo de puta . . .*" blah, blah, blah . . . I don't need to spell out the rest of the venom spewed at me. Even at their most inventive, these guys are hamstrung by a finite number of foul words at their disposal. And they're also handicapped by a machismo that borders on hysteria. Everyone who disagrees with them or questions their judgment is a fag.

They accuse me of not liking women as they pound me with their fists.

Idiots. If they only knew the full extent of my obsession with women, and how many mystical experiences I'd already had simply by contemplating the way some girl's hair flowed over her cheeks, or the shape of her calves, or the line of the bridge of her nose, or just the sound of her voice. *Comemierdas.* Their blows don't hurt me nearly as much as the sight of perfect lips or ankles, or breasts. You want to hurt me, you morons? Do you really want to injure me severely? Show me a pretty girl. Nothing hurts more than that.

Truth, beauty, and goodness. All of them hurt, way deep inside, any time they cross your path. But a beautiful woman hurts the most. *Ay.* Sometimes, it's almost enough to kill you, or to make you wish for death, right there and then.

Up on the screen, in the movie theaters, I see some beautiful women who slay me. Honor Blackman as the goddess Hera in *Jason and the Argonauts*; Stella Stevens in *The Nutty Professor*; Jean Simmons in *Spartacus*. Stella, especially, causes me exquisite pain and suggests to me subliminally that I should become a professor. On television I catch glimpses of Marilyn Monroe, who is now dead and rotting in her grave, much to my dismay. I'm especially thrilled when a news program shows footage of her singing "Happy Birthday, Mr. President" to John Kennedy. I'd missed this epiphany when it took place originally in May 1962, shortly after I'd moved in with the Chaits, and I'm transfixed by what I see. *Whoa* doesn't even begin to cover it. Too bad she was singing for such a knucklehead. Too bad they didn't allow her to stay onstage when Mr. President John F. Bay of Pigs Kennedy took the podium. She was so much more important than he, and so much nicer to look at. I hope they buried her in that dress. No other woman ever will ever be worthy of wearing it.

I haven't seen a beautiful girl in real life for a very, very long time, however. Citrus Grove Elementary School seems to sift them out, somehow. None of my female schoolmates causes me the right kind of pain. In a way this is good, for given my circumstances and my taped-up shoes, I'm in no position to cause any girl a commensurate measure of grief.

We have no full-length mirrors at the Palace Ricardo, so I have no clue as to how the house diet has changed my appearance. I'm not only alarmingly skinny, but also sort of deformed. My back, especially, is twisting and curving, and, as a result, my rib cage is bulging out. Since all I ever see of myself is my face, in our tiny bathroom mirror, I can't notice this. In my mind, there's nothing wrong with my looks, save for my clothes and footwear.

Flash forward briefly, just a few months. Tony and I climb out of an Ozark Air Lines plane in Bloomington, Illinois, and we're greeted by our uncle and aunt, and their daughters, along with some other nice people we've never met before.

Our aunt Alejandra holds her hand over her mouth when she first sees us. Then she hugs us and says: *"Ay, Dios mio, que flacos están!"* Oh my God, you're so thin! *"Y qué te pasa en la espalda, Carlos?"* And what's wrong with your back?

News to me. I don't know what to say, save "Glad to see you."

Fade to black. Return back to late spring 1963, which is really already summer in Miami, and hotter than a blast furnace.

Paquito, the eight-year-old, catches the chicken pox while visiting some of his relatives. Like Tony and me, he gets away every few weekends. He's covered in sores from head to foot, and he is quarantined on the sun porch.

Too late, too bad. It doesn't take long. Within a few days, nearly all of us at the Palace Ricardo are stricken too. Only two or three guys are spared because they've already had the pox. The Palace turns into an infirmary of sorts, in which there are no doctors or nurses, no medications of any kind. We all broil in the Miami heat, as we wrestle with our fevers and sores. Jesus H. Leper-curing Christ, this is really bad. I've never felt so sick, or so uncomfortable. Tony and I are both riddled with pox, even in our ears and inside our noses and mouths, and down yonder in the nether regions. Our friend José wins the prize for the highest number of sores. We pass the time counting them on one another, when the fever subsides, save for those on our private parts. The count for those is left to each individual, and is accepted unquestioningly, on our strictest honor code.

"*Lo juro. Mal rayo me parta.*" I swear, it's true. May an evil lightning bolt cleave me in two. I have five on my *cojones.*

During the worst of the worst, when our fevers are at their highest, Tony and I get one of those unexpected three-minute calls from Cuba. And we tell Louis XVI and Marie Antoinette that everything is hunky-dory. We've never had it better, and can't think of what more we could ask for. We're in a lovely home, we're loving school, and we've never felt better. Never, ever. Don't worry about a thing. And, yes, we'll see you soon, here, not there. Bye.

We miss nearly two weeks of school and go back to our classrooms as summer vacation is about to start. On the last day of school Miss Esterman turns into a psychic and predicts what each of us is going to do with our life. She tells me I'm going to work for the United Nations, and master several languages. Little does she know what effect the second half of that prediction will have on me.

Tony remains consistent: He fails every single subject and isn't allowed to proceed to tenth grade. This makes me happy in a perverse way, for it means that next year, when I'm in seventh grade, he and I will be attending the same junior high school. He's already earned a reputation as one of the scrappiest fighters in the school, and no one messes with him. At home, of course, it's different. The more defiant he becomes, the more Ricky Ricardo and the Three Thugs make life difficult for him.

But every now and then miracles happen and redemption sneaks up on you from the most unlikely quarter. As soon as school lets out, when we're all staring at the prospect of three months of unrelenting boredom and incarceration, the worst thug of all, Miguel, discovers a way of turning all our free time into gold, literally. A Cuban humor magazine, Zig-Zag, is looking for door-to-door salespeople, and they don't give a damn about your age. All they care about is selling as many copies as possible. The magazine sells for ten cents, and the salesperson gets to keep half of that for each copy sold, a whole five cents. You merely have to go down to the Zig-Zag office in Little Havana, ask for as many copies as you think you can carry, and walk away with an armload of potential profit. You don't even have to put any money down; they trust you to come back because they know that if you do manage to sell some, you'll want to come back again the next week and the week after that. Or maybe, if you're a really good salesperson, you'll come back several times a day, for another stack to sell.

Refugee ethics. A bit different from those of the world of the fully settled.

The best thing about selling Zig-Zag is the money, no doubt about it. But a great added bonus is the magazine itself, which is beloved by Cuban exiles. Zig-Zag had a long history back in Cuba: It was one of the most daring satirical publications, always dripping with political acid. I loved reading it. Zig-Zag respected no one in authority. And it was full of great cartoons, including those of Antonio Prohías, who, in exile, would sell his "Spy vs. Spy" strips to MAD magazine. Many of the Zig-Zag's covers I handle, week in and week out, are drawn by Prohías. As one might expect, Zig-Zag was one of the first publications to be squashed by the censors of Castrolandia. And, as one might also expect, when it was resurrected in exile, its acid content increased exponentially.

Each and every one of us boys at the Palace Ricardo, save for Paquito, turn into Zig-Zag salesmen. They would take Paquito too, even at eight years of age, but he just doesn't want to do it. We go down to Little Havana, pick up our big fat stacks, and fan out in different directions, having reached some sort of agreement beforehand about how to carve up the territory. Sort of. We're not precise, but we're all on the same page about not competing with one another. We all know there's maximum profit in spreading ourselves out as much as possible. God bless America. God bless free enterprise and freedom of expression. I want to change my name to Zig-Zag, I love it so much.

This is why I came here. This is why I'm in exile. This is why I have no parents, so I can sell this magazine. If I'd stayed in Cuba, what I'm doing would be not only impossible, but also illegal. Not just the anti-Castro humor I'm peddling, but the very simple act of selling something door-to-door and pocketing a fair share of the profits for myself.

I haven't been this happy since I first set foot in the Palace Ricardo. That fat stack of magazines under my arm weighs nothing. It buoys me up, in fact. It's an antigravity device, which helps me levitate from door-to-door, along with Tony. We walk miles and miles, knock on every single door with all the obsessive-compulsive thoroughness of Immanuel Kant, and sell most of our stash. Little Havana is the best territory, and it's large enough for all of us. When you knock on a door there, you know you're bound to have it opened by a Cuban. But after a couple of weeks, Tony and I decide to branch out to *terra incognita* because too many of those Cubans in Little Havana tell us that they've already bought one. We know there are Cubans scattered everywhere, so we decide to go north of Flagler Street, where no one has gone before.

We strike it rich. Sort of, as we see it. But it takes a lot more walking and door-knocking, for only about one in ten doors you knock on has Cubans behind it, and only one in eight of them buys a *Zig-Zag*. Many of them tell us that they would love to, but can't spare the ten cents. We have a lot of doors slammed in our faces by non-Cubans when we say we're selling a Cuban humor magazine, but we don't care. Every now and then, some English-speaking person will be nice enough to buy one anyway. I'm way beyond shame now, and I don't care if the line between begging and selling gets blurred every now and then. Every *Zig-Zag* Tony and I sell means five more cents in our pocket. This means we can buy food for ourselves, even get sandwiches, and Cuban pastries, and chewing gum, and Twinkies, and candy bars, and Cokes and 7•Ups to slake our thirst as we wear out our shoes some more, along with the tape that holds them together.

We learn a few things along the way. For starters, we become intimately acquainted with seediness and many of the down-and-out non-Cuban residents of Miami. We Cuban exiles had nothing, and we filled up these crummy neighborhoods because all we could afford was at the absolute bottom of the heap. But these neighborhoods hadn't been built with us in mind, and they had become slums long before we showed up, penniless. Before we came, these neighborhoods were full of American bottom-dwellers, men and women who had flocked down here to the absolute South from somewhere up north. God only knows what dreams they'd harbored when they fled here, seeking sunlight, fun, and fortune, only to end up in some ramshackle hellhole of a home, every bit as derelict as the Palace Ricardo, or worse, where they had to spend a good part of the day squashing cockroaches or hiding from bill collectors and boys who sold Cuban magazines.

Children were scarce in the area around the Orange Bowl. So were young adults. Almost every door we knocked on was opened by older American men and women, all of whom looked as if they'd had the stuffing knocked out of them day after day for the past forty years or so. Apartment buildings were the worst. Sun-scorched, half-ruined, the nadir in shabbiness, those stuccoed caverns were full of wrinkled oldsters who smelled awful and had bulging bags under their eyes and nicotine stains on their teeth and fingers. Many of them had no teeth, at least when they came to the door. Sometimes they'd say, "Wait a minute," and come back fully toothed.

The very act of going door to door and not skipping a single one is at once a thrill and a tremendous chore. But, since you never know where you'll find a buyer, the challenge of finding them keeps you going. *Knock, knock. Ring, ring.* You could tell right away whether you were staring at a Cuban or an American. Facial features and skin tone had nothing to do with it. The Cubans looked stunned and stressed, but healthy. Most of them were youngish, too, and some had children. The Americans all looked as if they'd already given up the ghost, or sorely wished they could.

To Cubans, we simply say, "*Zig-Zag?*" To Americans we say, "Oh, sorry, we're selling a Cuban magazine; sorry to disturb you."

Every now and then we run into something unsavory, maybe even dangerous. One day we run into José, our housemate, who's walking across the street from us, going in the opposite direction. A tall, portly man is walking beside him, talking up a storm. What we see looks peculiar, but Tony and I don't give it a second thought because José waves at us as if he doesn't have a care in the world.

Later, at home, he tells us that the guy was a total pervert who was trying to get him to go to his house and had spent more than an hour following him around, describing in detail how much fun they could have with each other's private parts.

Tony and I are invited into a few squalid apartments by old geezers and old bags, but we know better than to accept these invitations. It's the geezers who worry us the most.

We don't make tons of money, but we're deliriously happy with every nickel we pocket. Sometimes we make as much as one dollar apiece, after an entire day of selling. Returning unsold copies to the *Zig-Zag* office always hurts, but the people down there are so nice, and so much more like family than Ricky and Lucy Ricardo, that they always find something to say that makes us feel better.

"Hey, count how many you sold, not how many you've returned."

And they never stiff us, or scramble the numbers in their favor. They actually seem happy to give back to us half of what we turn in to them.

Had we stayed in Cuba, where everyone works for the government and everyone gets paid exactly the same salary regardless of what kind of work they do or how well or how poorly they do their job, Tony and I would be nothing more than glorified slaves. Both he and I know this, even though we're just kids. We also know that one dollar per day is more than any adult makes in Castrolandia, thanks to Marxism-Leninism.

I can't speak for Tony, but selling these magazines is the ultimate pay-off for me: the surest vindication of my life as an exile. I couldn't spark a slave revolt back home, like Spartacus, but I've rebelled nonetheless. I've slapped my masters in the face, and spit at them, merely by slipping out of their grasp and selling magazines that poke fun at them. Like Sparta-cus's son—the one held up at the foot of his cross by Jean Simmons—I can be free even though my parents are still in bondage. Like Spartacus, they're happy to know that their son has eluded a life of coerced ser-vitude and silence, even though, as he walks from door to ramshackle door in Miami, they both hang on their crosses, back in Cuba, along with millions of others who line the Carretera Central, the highway that runs from one end of the island to the other. Our version of the Appian Way.

Now, if I could only find a Jean Simmons of my own, to constantly slay me with her beauty, this slave revolt of mine would be a total victory.

Eighteen

C ottonmouth!"

"*Que carajo es eso?*" says José. What?

I've never heard the word before. But I don't have to ask what it means, for I see that snake right away. I've never seen such a big one, or any so aggressive.

It darts out from under a rock at the river's edge and lunges at the guy with the smallest fishing pole. He backs away and whacks it with his pole, but it just keeps coming at him, its white mouth agape, its fangs on full display.

The more he whacks it with his teensy-weensy fishing pole, the more aggressive the snake gets. It's full of hell, and it fears nothing or no one. All of us who are there at the river's edge back away several feet.

I pick up a rock and throw it at the snake. Others join in. With six or seven of us pelting the snake, it starts to back off. No one hits a bull's-eye, but the stoning gives the fisherman a chance to jump away safely, out of the low riverbank, up into the grassy field above it. As the stoning continues, the cottonmouth turns around, slithers into the water, and swims away.

The sight of that undulating V-shape in the water—something I've never seen before, not even in movies—evokes the same feeling in me as a shark fin breaking the water's surface.

We pelt it with rocks until it disappears down the river.

"Thanks for the rocks, boys. Thanks a lot."

"Nastiest water moccasin I ever saw," says another fisherman.

"Close call, bud," says the guy who first yelled "Cottonmouth."

None of us from the Palace Ricardo say much, other than "Wow" or other such one-syllable summary expressions of sheer amazement. In English, of course. All of these guys with fishing poles speak English. Two of them are black, and they've obviously come here from some other part of town, for this is 1963 and Miami is still segregated. As the local elites would say, there's nothing but spics and poor white trash in our neighborhood.

We don't care much about all of this civil rights stuff we keep hearing about in the news. It doesn't include us, even though hardly anyone considers us white, and often enough we're told to ride in the back of the bus.

Of course, unlike black Americans, we haven't had to put up with segregation for more than a few years. And that makes one hell of a difference.

We don't care much about anything that's happening in the wider world either. We've got troubles of our own. And we've discovered the Miami River, about ten blocks from the Palace Ricardo, near the intersection of Eleventh Street and Twenty-second Avenue Northwest. It's a wild place, still untouched by the city. To get to it we have to walk through a big open field with lots of tall grass, which we know could be full of snakes. It's not the main branch of the river, but a smaller one. There are small fish in there, and we take off our shoes, go into the water, and scoop them up with jars. Then we take them home and try to keep them alive, but nothing seems to work. We even use some of our Zig-Zag money to buy fish food, but they still die.

So, we've settled for watching guys with poles catch bigger fish. Every now and then they catch something edible. We hang out there for hours and hours, exploring the riverbank or just sitting there. Every now and then we see someone cruising down- or upriver on a boat. They always wave at us, and we never wave back.

"Why don't you ask us to join you, bastards?"

Years later, the Dolphin Expressway will go right through here. Much of that toll road will be laid right along this waterway, erasing what is here now, and no one will foresee its constant, monstrous traffic jams. But right now, in the summer of 1963, this is one of the last wild places left in this part of town. We hear stories from the fishermen about alligators and manatees. "I know of boats being overturned by gators and manatees, not far from here," says an old guy with a heavily creased face. "If you follow this river up, it gets wilder and wilder."

That's all he had to say to spark our interest in going upriver.

Exploring on foot, we go upstream as far as possible, and also downstream, to where this branch empties into the big one, where there are all sorts of docks and boats.

Tony gets an idea. Why not borrow a boat? A little one. No one will notice, especially if we do it at night. It sounds a bit crazy to me at first, but the more I think about it, the more I like it. A rowboat would be nice. No engine to start, no noise. Who would know?

Our first excursion is a great success. In the dark of night we "borrow" a rowboat and set out for the jungle upstream, the one the old guy told us about. It's a moonless night, and without any streetlights nearby, the river is a dark black ribbon surrounded by shadows and silence. Rowing against the current isn't as hard as we expected. The oars dip and dip. *Slish, slosh, slish, slosh.* It's all we hear. We don't say a word, so no one will hear us.

Upriver we go, quite a ways, looking for the jungle. But like those of our ancestors who wasted their lives looking for El Dorado or the Fountain of Youth, we find no jungle. We do find trees hanging over us in places, and nothing but pure stillness all around us, but we can sense the city just beyond either bank.

"What if a manatee or a gator is right under us?" whispers José.

"We've got oars we can hit them with," says Tony.

I immediately sense huge shapes under us, of course. I see nothing. It's too dark to see anything. But the mere mention of gators and manatees sets me to imagining their presence. I picture us being overturned, like the whaling skiffs in the movie *Moby Dick*, tossed into the water. Alligators, manatees, and cottonmouths gang up on us, and we're history.

"Shut up," I whisper. "We'll get caught."

The large shapes below don't go away. They just multiply in my mind. But this is too great an adventure, well worth the risk. Tony is right: At least we have oars with which to beat the crap out of the gators and man-eating manatees. But what can we do about the cottonmouths? Better not to think about it, to enjoy our adventure.

And how beautiful it is, the river at night. How dark and quiet. Above us, through the haze created by the city's lights, a few stars poke through. Shadows large and small lurk off to our right and left, and we can imagine whatever we want: virgin forests, ancient ruins, Amazon villages. We're so free, so totally on our own, the three of us: Tony, José, and me. We're so far from everything and everyone, we really could be in some far-off jungle, even on another planet. I don't know about the others, but the danger that lurks under us and around us and in my mind doesn't scare me that much. Neither does the prospect of getting caught with a "borrowed" rowboat. Just the opposite: It revs me up, steadies me, and makes me feel more alive.

This is the high life.

We'd row all the way to the end of this river, given the chance, up into the Everglades, the real jungle. If we rowed long enough, maybe we could be there by daybreak, and no one would be able to find us. But then what?

At one point we all agree that it's time to turn back. So we do. And we return the boat to its mooring, cross the big empty lot in total darkness, and head home.

While we're crossing the field, Tony starts talking about coral snakes, and how poisonous they are, and how many are probably ready to bite our ankles right now.

"Shut up," I say. He laughs.

We borrow that boat often, so often that I lose count. And we make it upstream a little farther each time. But still no jungle. None at all. No alligators, manatees, or cottonmouths either. But the fear never loses its edge for me, or its kick. Miami is full of alligators, and everyone knows that. Miami is also full of boat owners who wouldn't like to see theirs being "borrowed" late at night by three hoodlums.

Going up and down that river in total darkness calms me, despite all of the obvious perils. It soothes me like nothing else has lately. It's not at all like being held by my mother when I was very little—in fact, it's just the opposite—but it has the same effect on me. I don't have my ear pressed against her chest. I don't hear the air going in and out of her lungs, which has the same rhythm as the waves that crash against the Malecón. And I certainly don't hear the sound of that heartbeat, that eternal heartbeat, the sound above all others, the pulse of the entire universe echoing in her and in me. But I feel the very same calm, the same dissolving of boundaries between me and the pulsating source of life, the same exact sense of total well-being, the certainty that I was born for this moment, which, of course, is eternal.

If you can't see yourself or anything else around you, and all you hear is the sound of oars dipping in the river, where do you begin and end? Where are you, and where is the world? Isn't the world in you, and aren't you in the world, each in the other, completely?

The more that the boundaries of my body dissolve, the more that the danger soothes my soul. And the same goes for the dissolving of the normally thick boundary between right and wrong. I'm being bad right now, yes, but not totally bad. This is good for us, and the boat's owner will never know. We'll return the boat, undamaged. Being bad while also being good is the ultimate thrill ride.

No amusement park will ever top this. No way. None will even come close.

But nothing good can last for long, ever; especially in the Palace Ricardo, where the Three Thugs insist on knowing everything so they can lay a claim to whatever you might have found that isn't theirs yet.

"Where have you guys been?" It's easy to lie when asked that question.

"What's the deal with that mud on your shoes?" That's easy to evade too.

"Where'd you get those fish in the jars?" Impossible to evade.

So, they find out about the river, and they check it out for themselves. A couple of times they show up while we're there. They find the docks and the boats, which interest them a whole lot more than the jungle.

Miguel gets it into his head to steal a boat. Not "borrow," but steal. Not a rowboat, a motorboat. "I can hide it upriver, and I can steal gasoline from the other boats," he says.

Eventually, he figures out that this isn't such a great plan. So he decides to steal an outboard motor. It's portable. It can be brought on land. And someone might want to buy such a thing, especially from a sixteen-year-old kid who's selling it for far less than retail or wholesale.

Our resident criminal mastermind tries to recruit us as accomplices. But even the two other Thugs, Roberto and Mariano, refuse to do something so utterly stupid. They're more interested in fighting the other gang on Calle Ocho and stealing small stuff from stores.

As his frustration intensifies, Miguel gets increasingly violent and unpredictable. One morning he emerges naked from the back room, pees on all of our breakfast toast, and howls with delight. He threatens all of us nonviolent types constantly, promising swift retribution if we refuse to join in the heist of the century. One evening, as I'm throwing out the trash, he sneaks up on me from behind and bashes the back of my legs with a huge club, made from a palm frond. He howls with delight again, thinking that he's broken my legs. They're not broken, but it takes me a while to get up off the ground, and no bruise, ever, will match that one.

Then he disappears for long stretches. And whenever he does show up, he keeps to himself and talks to no one.

One afternoon, the police show up and arrest Miguel. A recently pilfered outboard motor, it turns out, is up on our flat roof, which has a ledge around it. Perfect hiding place. Less than perfect accomplice, however. As it turns out, Miguel is turned in by a snitch from one of the gangs on Calle Ocho who agreed to "help" him as a way of currying favor with the cops.

Good-bye, Miguel. Off to the hoosegow again. He doesn't howl with delight on his way out. Not at all. The other Thugs say nothing: Roberto and Mariano have one less roommate. More room for them.

And as Miguel exits, a new guy joins the household. A redhead with freckles who looks just like Archie, the comic book character. All he needs is a bow tie. Nice guy. Very nice. Normal. A great relief. Fortunately for him, he's given a couch on the sun porch rather than Miguel's empty bed in the back room. And as soon as I lay eyes on Archie, I realize that José is the spitting image of Jughead. I kid you not; all he needs is that stupid crown-like hat. This should be interesting, especially with no Veronica or Betty anywhere in sight.

Yes, we have redheads in Cuba.

In the meantime, Lucy Ricardo is making life hell for Tony, who gets phone calls from a friend he made in school. Tony always calls him *Gordo*, or "fat guy." Since we have strict instructions not to bring friends to the house, Gordo is confined to the phone. But that's a problem too, it seems. Lucy resents the fact that Tony spends a lot of time on the phone with Gordo, because it runs up the monthly charges. But there's also an undercurrent of ill-will embedded in her resentment. Soon enough, Lucy starts accusing Tony of being a *maricón*, and she threatens to write to our mother and tell her that her oldest son is a homosexual if he doesn't stop getting phone calls from Gordo. She openly mocks Tony's masculinity, and she pretends to be him on the phone, saying such things as "Gordo, oh Gordo, how much I love you," again and again.

Tony swears to me that he's going to kill both Lucy and Ricky.

One night, as all of this is going on, we go to bed as usual, late at night. Normally, Tony goes to the bathroom first and I follow, and he gets into his bunk while I take my turn. But this night, unlike other nights, I beat him to the loo. So flushed with pride about being first in line, I climb up to my perch on the top bunk and the whole thing collapses. It pancakes, the whole top, right onto the bottom bunk. *Crash, kaboom.*

I'm not hurt at all, just stunned. Tony rushes out of the bathroom and finds our roommates gathered around me and the collapsed bed. Had he been in his place, as usual, he would have been crushed. We have a good laugh about it and find a place for his mattress in the living room. How funny. We all chuckle our way into dreamland.

A close inspection the next day reveals that all four corners of the top bunk gave way simultaneously. The screws and brackets simply decided, all at once, not to hold anymore. They were tired, it seems. Or maybe someone made them feel awfully tired, on purpose.

I say nothing. Neither does Tony. But we know this is no accident.

Jesus H. All-seeing Christ. Are you watching from way up there, at the right hand of the Father?

Apparently, yes.

Soon after the bed collapses, Tony finds a prayer card in his pocket. It just shows up in there. He has no clue as to where it came from. It's just simply in his pocket, one day, as the downward spiral is pulling him deeper and deeper into his abyss. It's a holy card of St. Martin de Porres, recently canonized by Pope John XXIII in 1962. Pope John has just died, by sheer coincidence, shortly before the card mysteriously appears in Tony's pocket. We see the huge headlines on a newspaper stand on Seventh Street as we're returning from the library one night.

I look up St. Martin at the library. Martin de Porres lived in Peru in the late-sixteenth to early-seventeenth century. It took him a long time to be canonized not because he lacked miracles or local admiration, but because he was of African descent. St. Martin wanted to become a priest in the Dominican order, but couldn't because of his race. So instead, he became a lay brother, and swept, and cleaned, and cooked for all the white Dominicans in Lima. He also ran their infirmary and worked miraculous cures, and soon enough all of Lima was seeking him out. Martin could also communicate with animals—just like St. Francis of Assisi, St. Antony of the Desert, and Adam in the Garden of Eden before the Fall—for he was in perfect touch with nature. He even talked the mice into staying out of the kitchen, back in Lima.

So Tony prays to St. Martin for help. Get us out of here. The quicker the better. Please hurry. We can't take it much longer.

As for me: I'm not praying anymore.

One very hot afternoon, a social worker suddenly shows up out of the blue to handle some other business at the Palace Ricardo, probably something having to do with Archie or the recently departed Miguel.

She takes one look at Tony and me and gasps. "What are you boys doing here? You're supposed to be with your uncle."

She's horrified. I can tell. We're a big mistake. No doubt about it.

Next thing you know, we're shopping for new clothes with her at Sears in Coral Gables. She tells us how much we can spend and helps us pick out stuff, including new shoes. On the way there, of course, and on the way back to the Palace Ricardo, the giant trees on Coral Way stand guard, as always. I haven't seen them in a long time, these great friends about whom I think all the time, whose images flood my imagination way too often. In the dense shade provided by their powerful limbs and foliage—under the winged arch that stretches over the roadway—Tony and I make our way back to the warm and fuzzy home run by Ricky and Lucy Ricardo.

In the meantime, all sorts of things have been happening out of our field of vision. Our uncle Amado has been contacted, up in Bloomington, Illinois, even though it's hard to reach him since he has no phone. In order for him to take a phone call, arrangements have to be made for him to be at a pay phone or a neighbor's house at an appointed time. Letters take a long time. Telegrams can't say very much. But, somehow, all of the obstacles vanish, and solid plans are made to send us to him, as quickly as possible.

Elation is too weak a word to describe how Tony and I feel when we hear the news. So is *ecstasy.* Spanish is no better, and neither is any other language. There's no earthly tongue that contains any word capable of describing how we feel, save for the original one lost at Babel, the one used by Eve in all her poems. She had a word for this feeling because she could remember it, way back before she and Adam screwed up everything. It's how they felt all the time, way back then.

We race to the library and look up Bloomington in all of the encyclopedias. As it turns out there are a lot of Bloomingtons, one in nearly every state. But the one in Illinois seems like a great place. It has only around thirty-six thousand people, which makes it seem tiny to us. It's right next to another town with the howlingly funny name of Normal, which has only about fifteen thousand people. Imagine that. Normal! And these twin towns are right smack in the middle of something called the Corn Belt. Bloomington/Normal, as some encyclopedias call it, has some factories, large insurance firms, two universities, and a mysterioussounding Scottish Rite Temple where a Passion Play is performed every spring.

Oh no. Holy Week, up there too. Can't we ever escape it? Even if they dress everyone up in kilts at the Scottish Rite Temple, rather than period costumes, it'll still be a grim play.

They do make vacuum cleaners up there, though. That's a plus. They make stuff. We'll be living in the industrialized world, finally. And it snows. It snows! Good God in heaven, we're going to where it snows, finally.

Tony and I go to the barber college on Flagler in downtown Miami for one last free haircut. This time we hit the jackpot. Tony and I are both assigned to absolute novices. His head and mine will be their first ones, ever. My haircut comes out halfway all right, just as slightly bad as all the others: about a half dozen rough spots and one monster untamable cowlick. My barber-in-the-making shows promise. Tony is far less lucky, however. His novice barber struggles to keep his cool, but finally gives up. The master barber who runs the school comes over and takes a look.

He shakes his head and says, "Sorry, kid; this one can't be fixed." *Whirrr.* Taking the electric clippers from the apprentice, he attacks Tony's head with absolute resolve and shears off all that was left of his hair. He walks out looking as if he's just joined the Marines, with a total buzz cut.

A date is set for our departure to the land of snow: Sunday, the first of September. Nine months and two weeks since we were first thrown into the Palace Ricardo. We don't have much to pack, so there's not much to get ready. And we have no neckties. Sometime during our stay at this house, the ties we brought with us from Cuba have vanished. So José lends us his only two ties. This is 1963, and, if you're Cuban, especially, you can't get on an airplane unless you're wearing a coat and tie.

Lucy Ricardo gives us a weird gift to bring to our uncle: a chunk of the stinkiest cheese I've ever had the misfortune to smell. I ask no questions. Neither does Tony. And we're dumb enough and hungry enough to bring the cheese with us, which is in a paper bag. The cheese drips and leaks, and we have no choice but to carry it on board with us. No way we're going to put this in our luggage. The cheese bag will get increasingly stained and its powerful stink will be released more and more as the day wears on. All along the way, people will ask us what that awful smell is. We'll have to say, "It's cheese."

Now, this is a nice death. We say good-bye to José and promise to keep in touch. We say good-bye to everyone else too, and promise them nothing. As always, Ricky Ricardo is nowhere to be found. Just as well. The guy was getting increasingly creepy, on top of everything else, pinching us on the cheeks and assuming an effeminate voice.

It's a beautiful day, this first of September. The sky is heartbreakingly blue, and the cumulus clouds at their most boastful. This time around there's no fishbowl at the airport, no *pecera* where you are strip-searched and made to say farewell to your loved ones through a thick glass enclosure. And we don't have any loved ones to say farewell to, anyway. We've already said good-bye to the Becquers on the phone, and also to the Chaits and Rubins.

We board this Eastern Air Lines plane in much the same way as we boarded the one from KLM in Cuba, eighteen months ago. But we're not the same boys. Far from it. Tony and I have each died at least three times since then. And it's getting so much easier to go through it.

The burning silence strips us clean one more time, inside that cabin. It doesn't surprise us, and we welcome it. This is one life we're both glad to slough off.

It's going to be a long travel day. It's a prop job, our plane, not a jet, and it has to stop in Atlanta and Cincinnati before it gets to Chicago, where we'll change airlines at the busiest airport in the world, the one where Tony will end up working for many years.

What a beautiful death. And how utterly painless. The opposite of pain, in fact. This is a mystical transport. This is how saints who know they're going straight to heaven must feel when they die, or how souls feel when they're released from Purgatory.

A nice family is seated across the aisle from us: a man, his wife, and two teenage kids, a boy and a girl. The boy looks just like Jimmy Olsen, from the Superman comics. I've already met Archie in person, and I've been living with Jughead for a while. Who's next? I hope it's Lois Lane, or Wonder Woman. Or Betty and Veronica. Females, please.

These good people are headed for Cincinnati, where they live. Real Americans. Ohio has to be the most American of states, I think, if this is what people from Ohio look like.

We take off. I'm used to it now: It's a familiar tug as the burning silence envelopes me. *Fire! Fire! Fire!* Thank you, brother fire, *gracias*, sister death. I see the Orange Bowl from above for the first time, and the Miami River too. I see that there's no jungle anywhere near that river. I see the angels on Coral Way—they stand out like a long green ribbon. I see a turquoise sea below me, and the islands offshore, briefly. It's vaguely familiar, that sea, but that water isn't part of me. I hardly ever got to swim in it. Off to the east, the sun is low on the horizon, having just risen less than an hour ago. It has a long, long way to go before it gets to sink in the west, that incandescent yellow host, so similar and yet so different from the glowing orange one, the setting one that I left behind in Cuba.

The plane veers sharply, to the northwest. And the sea disappears.

North by Northwest. Off to the Corn Belt.

Jimmy Olsen's dad asks us, wincing, "Say, kids, what's that awful smell?"

I say it's cheese, but what I really want to say is "My former self."

Nineteen

I'm laughing my ass off. There's nothing in the world that can match this. No way. I'm laughing so hard I think I might pass out.

And I'm not drunk or high, or anything like that. Just a couple of beers. They're too expensive in here, and I'm a refugee. Once a refugee, always a refugee.

"What? You want how much for this beer? Sure, give me one that will last all night." Please imagine a thick Chicago accent, which is how I speak now: *Waaat? Ya waaant how much fer dis beeerrr?* And we say "sure" all the time here in Chicago. It's an all-purpose word, pronounced *shurr.*

It's summer, in the year 1973. I'm at Second City, in Chicago, and these people onstage, just a few feet from me, in this very cramped space, are redefining funniness minute by killer minute as they improvise, following our cues or totally ignoring them. They're probably all high, but it seems to help them rip open some veil that no one has ripped before.

The funniest guy, hands down, is some hefty Albanian named John Belushi, who transcends the tiny stage in this incredibly small space. This guy's a wayward angel, not quite fallen all the way. He has to be. There must be some of those, in between. He probably made God laugh too much and got sent to earth rather than to hell. He's on some celestial wavelength, poking fun at Creation itself, bringing us all in that room to an uncanny level of enlightenment, somewhere between blasphemy and beatitude.

I'm addicted to laughter. It obliterates all polarities and helps me see that opposites can, in fact, coincide. For a refugee, all of life is nothing but a welter of contradictions, and holding two contradictory thoughts as true, simultaneously, is essential for survival. So I can't ever get enough of this spasm caused by our highest brain functions, this uncontrolled winking of our third eye, this flare-up of the divine spark at the core of the soul.

Belushi knows all about the true nature of laughter, though he may not be able to explain it to you, especially tonight. Or maybe any other night, for that matter. Every time I've come here, he's been in an altered state. He *is* an altered state, come to think of it.

The others onstage are also wayward angels, probably. But they came from some rank just one smidgen below Belushi's. One of them, Bill Murray, is damn close; so is the fat guy, John Candy; and the tall guy, Joe Flaherty; and the ones from Toronto who show up sometimes: Dan Aykroyd, Eugene Levy, and Gilda Radner.

I come here as often as I can. Tonight I'm here with my bride of six months and a couple of good friends who will also get married and move away in less than a year. They're the ones who will end up with the loft in Tribeca. But this night we are all in Chicago, where we all live and where we went to high school together.

I have long hair and a moustache like Pancho Villa's, and I am about to grow a full beard. I think I need one in order to succeed in graduate school. I've just finished college, and in less than two months, I'll be heading east to Yale, to study religion and history. I don't know yet that I've managed to get into a PhD program rather than a master's program, because no one has spelled it out for me. I'm an ignoramus when it comes to these things. Once a refugee, always a refugee. I've simply assumed that if all I have is a BA, I have to prove myself at the master's level before I can move on to doctoral studies. In a couple of months, I'll be pleasantly surprised and terrified, simultaneously.

As soon as I get to New Haven, I'll discover that I'm a PhD student and that nearly everyone else in my seminars has some sort of master's degree, save for just two or three of us schlemiels who've had only four years of college. I'll also find out that although I have a fellowship that covers my tuition, this award prevents me from working and making any money with which to live. A tough catch-22. And a very serious problem for my bride, and therefore also for me. A marriage-killer, in fact.

I'll be right about one thing, though. When I get there, every other male in my program will have a full beard. And eyeglasses.

I'm sporting antique gold frames designed in 1911. No more plastic crap. The age of plastic is behind us, forever. No one, ever, will wear plastic frames again, especially black rectangular ones, or any with right angles, or especially those that look like the mask on Robin the Boy Wonder from Batman comics. Round is in forever. And the wet head is dead too. Men will never, ever again, put any goop of any kind on their hair, and they're never going to shave again either.

By the way, I'm not Cuban anymore. I stopped being Cuban when I got married and moved out of my mom's basement apartment. I'm a Chicagoan. Everyone in Chicago came from somewhere else, even our Native Americans. We have a neighborhood full of them, Uptown, which is only five blocks from my mom's apartment. But all of those Indians have come here from other states, mostly from out West. The native Pottawatomies are all gone. Long gone. All that remains of them are the names they gave places. And my bride and I live right across from Indian Boundary Park, which was once the line between the white settlers and the natives they itched to exterminate. The street we live on, North Rogers Avenue, was the boundary line itself. And we live on the settlers' side.

My bride's family is Jewish and they came from Eastern Europe.

Everybody here is from somewhere else, including John Belushi's parents. And everyone is a Chicagoan, and an American. Hell, you don't even have to be a citizen to be an American, or speak English to be an American citizen. My mom took her citizenship exam last year in Spanish, and she still doesn't speak English, and never will. But she's a citizen. And my high school principal had a map of the world in his office with colored pins all over it. Each pin marked a country represented by at least one student at our school. Every continent but Australia and Antarctica was full of pins. If he'd placed one pin on the map for every student, the entire island of Cuba would have been blotted out.

Hell, the overflow alone could have filled Australia and New Zealand. Many of us were airlift kids too. Way too many of us. So many that I started to think that no family had ever left Cuba intact. We never talked about it, those of us who had lived through the airlift and the foster homes, and the resettlement and all that. Unfortunately, too many of us were too busy putting up with bad teachers and rough classmates. Only a handful of us were allowed into the honors courses because the counselors had trouble conceiving of us as bright or sufficiently motivated. And, despite the pins we could have claimed on the principal's map, we were sort of invisible. The school was so huge that we simply disappeared, like some spice sprinkled on a stew. We were unnoticeable until the time came, once a year, to photograph the Spanish Club for the yearbook. This club was practically one hundred percent Cuban. We'd fill up the entire stage in our auditorium. I wasn't in the club, but I'd sneak into the picture, just to be with my fellow *Cubiches*. Many of them took Spanish in order to get an easy A, or to give our Spanish teachers a hard time. Payback for the grief experienced in other classes.

"Excuse me, Mrs. Throckmorton, that's not how *arrastrar* is pronounced. You need to roll your *r*'s like this, rrrrrrrrrrrrrrrrrrrrrrrrrrrrrrrrrrrrr."

I'm working two jobs, as I do every summer: one full-time and one part-time. About sixty hours a week. My full-time job is a farce. I'm working for the Social Security Administration, transferring information on disabled workers from the files of local agencies onto paper forms that are to be sent to Washington, D.C. A well-trained monkey could do my job—probably better than me—but it requires a college degree. There are more than a hundred of us involved in this farce, in one huge room in a building in downtown Chicago. It's supposed to take us two months to complete this process, but some genius in Washington didn't do the math right, or something. We hardly ever have any work to do, for as soon as the files come in, we dispatch them in less than two hours. Since these deliveries take place only about three times a week, we don't have much to do at all. But we get paid for a full week's work, anyway.

So we read a lot, all of us, and collect our paychecks. After a month or so we become more brazen and bring cards and board games to work, and while away the hours playing poker, or Risk, or Monopoly, or whatever. I read a lot of novels I never had time for in college, that I know I won't have time for in graduate school. I round out my education.

I finally get to read *Moby-Dick*. And the book is so much better than the movie.

It's the best job I've ever had. How I wish they'd all be like this.

My part-time job is the same one I've had since 1966. I'm a grocery clerk at a Jewel supermarket. This summer I'm a produce man. I get to unpack and stack fruits and vegetables, and weigh whatever the customers want to buy. It's a wonderful job, and I love it. This is my second Jewel. I had to leave the first one because a bigoted, racist manager chased me out. He went to great lengths to make me uncomfortable by constantly bringing up the subject of my ethnicity and complaining about how many spics worked at his store. He also tried to get rid of me by assigning tasks that I would fail and he could count against me, like assembling grocery carts with a stopwatch running.

"Even a dumb *amigo* should be able to put this together in five minutes, tops. An *amigo* in college should do it in three."

The unassembled carts came with no instructions, so it took me a lot longer than that.

"One more screwup and yer outta here, *amigo*."

So I found another store to work at before he could fire me.

The new Jewel store is just about three blocks from my apartment, and I can get there quickly by climbing over the Chicago and Northwestern railroad tracks, which run right behind the store. It's against the law to do that, of course, but this is Chicago, and I'm not the only one breaking laws.

We have our way of dealing with infractions here.

Waaat? But, officer, de light was yellow. Hey, officer, ya know, cut me a break . . . Oh . . . Jeezus . . . waat's dis? Hey, look, officer, sir, it looks like ya dropped a twenty . . . Look, dere at yer feet, sir.

I should be more careful, though, with my long hair and Pancho Villa moustache. It's much harder to deal with Chicago cops if you look a certain way. My customers call me the "hippie guy."

My bride and I think we're happy. And perhaps we're as happy now as we'll ever be. I'm great at overlooking anything unpleasant, avoiding arguments, denying the obvious, and burying anything that hurts. She's the opposite, and I refuse to acknowledge it. We were made for each other, I'm convinced.

Sure.

My mom and brother are out of the picture now. My bride wants me to cut ties with them, as much as possible. They're such a drag.

My mom is living with my father's sister, Lucía, who came over in 1971, at the age of seventy-six. Lucía went to live with her brother first, our uncle Amado, in Bloomington, but that didn't work out. So my mother took her in, and they now live in the basement apartment from which I've fled, the one with the pipes and radiators on the ceiling.

Tony is living with his new girlfriend, way out in the northwest corner of the city, not far from O'Hare airport. He's already been married once and divorced. His first wife was Cuban, and I'd rather say nothing about her, save that watching Tony exchange vows with her at St. Ita's Church was a lot like watching a train wreck in the making and not being able to stop it from happening. The marriage actually lasted longer than I expected, about eighteen months. His new girlfriend, whom he'll marry within a year or so, is part Polish, part German. She's divorced too, and has a daughter from her first marriage.

Tony and I hardly ever talk or get together. His force field is totally impenetrable now, and I'm living in a totally different world from his, the world of books. He gave up the printing trade, lied his way into Northwestern University's business school, dropped out of that, studied computers, and got himself a decent job as a computer technician. The place where he works is one giant computer. It takes up the whole building, practically, and there are wires running everywhere—under the floor, above the ceiling—all hidden behind removable panels. Reels and reels of tape too. And rooms full of reels. It's 1973, and microchips are about to change all of this radically. So, rather than keep up with the changes, he'll bail out of that too, and go to work as a dog catcher and debt collector before he ends up at O'Hare airport, loading food on planes.

The airport will be a wild nonstop party for him. And he'll fit right in, because, when he's on a roll and high as a kite, he can be very funny. Funnier than John Belushi, at times.

Pretty soon, he'll start to disappear for long stretches of time, and no one will know where he's gone, or even whether he's dead or alive. Our mom will go nearly insane with worry every time this happens, but no one will be able to do anything about it. And he'll reappear just as unexpectedly as he disappeared, and somehow, he'll keep his job at the airport and party on while he's there, nonstop.

Quite often, at the end of the workday, he and his coworkers will hop a flight to Las Vegas—for free, of course—party it up, and fly back for work in the morning. Again and again and again. And eventually the party will come crashing down.

Flash back, ten measly years. The first of September, 1963.

Tony and I have made it to Chicago, and it's late afternoon. Only one more flight left to go.

We've just flown over six states, in perfectly clear weather. Not one cloud to block our view from Miami to Chicago. Tony and I have shared the window seat, in half-hour intervals, and what we've seen defies description. This is no jet plane we've been on, so it flies low, and we can see a lot.

I'll never think of the earth the same way again. It's too small. Way too small. If we can fly this great distance in less than a day, and feel as if we're flying over a map, then we're all in trouble. A "world" should be bigger than a map. It should be nearly infinite.

But what we've seen from our perch in the sky, no matter how seemingly small, has left us speechless. The red earth in Georgia. The mountains in Tennessee. The lush green farms in Kentucky. The patchwork quilt landscape of Ohio, Indiana, and Illinois, all laid out in perfect grids. All those roads, going in all directions. So much land.

Lake Michigan. Good God in heaven. I've been waiting years to see this marvel. A freshwater lake so big that it could pass for a sea, joined to four others, all splayed out like a weird flower or an inkblot. An inland sea that freezes over. Who could ask for more? I'd spent hours and hours back in Plato's cave, poring over maps of the world, meditating on the places where I'd love to live—rather than in my own benighted land—

and the Great Lakes were always high on my list. Any of the three big lakes would do. Erie and Ontario would be all right, but not as good. I'd prefer all those lakes in Manitoba. And also Hudson's Bay, Nova Scotia, Newfoundland, Scandinavia, Scotland, Greenland, Iceland.

Chicago. Ha. What a joke. I've been laughing about this place for years. *Cago* means "I defecate" in Spanish. But this city we just flew over is nothing to laugh at. It's large. It has a whole forest of skyscrapers, not just some small thicket of them downtown. It's beautiful too, and it reminds me a lot of Havana. As we approach the lakeshore, I spy a road that looks a lot like the Malecón. And the lake is almost turquoise.

O'Hare airport is nothing but straight lines. Horizontal and vertical. No diagonals, no curves of any kind, save for one spot where a couple of terminals converge and they put in one circular atrium just for the hell of it. This is the very definition of modern. And, despite the fact that it's sheathed in glass, it feels more solid than any building I've ever been in.

It's also huge.

Tony and I have to walk a long way to get from one terminal to another, but we have no trouble finding our way.

We wait at O'Hare for about an hour, and then board our Ozark Air Lines flight to Bloomington. This is one hell of a beat-up plane. It looks like a relic left over from the Second World War. The two wooden boards fastened to the tail rudder worry us a little. And the interior of the plane doesn't inspire any more confidence than the fuselage. It's as worn out inside as outside. Could this help explain why there are so few passengers?

It's a smooth flight, though, and we get to see many more details below because we fly lower than we did in the Eastern Air Lines plane.

Illinois is made up of straight lines, just like O'Hare airport: squares and rectangles, in various shades of green. The slanting sunlight from the fast-setting sun lends an amber tint to the corn and soybean fields. We see a few trees, here and there. It's mostly wide-open farmland. So much of it, and so utterly flat. A house here and there, clumps of trees, some squirming streams that seem to annoy the straight lines, a town or two, a few lakes.

I'm on the lookout for pines, even though I'm no longer an idolater. This is where Christmas trees come from. I'm just curious: I want to see huge ones, a hundred feet tall. And every now and then I see some, near farmhouses. Or so I think.

In about forty-five minutes we begin our descent. In the waning sunlight, everything is bathed in gold. But where's Bloomington? Or Normal? It's all cornfields, and suddenly, *yeow*, an airstrip. Down we go, steeply. The descent is quick and the landing rough. Very rough. And the plane shimmies and spins all out of whack, because the third wheel is in the rear rather than the front.

Tony and I look at each other and laugh, nervously.

We look out the window and are surprised to see a lot of people milling about. It's a mob out there in the open, with tall corn as their backdrop. They and the corn are all awash in gold.

"Are they here for us?" asks Tony.

We climb down onto the tarmac and see our uncle, aunt, and cousins, leading the mob toward us. They look about the same as the last time we saw them. The girls are a little taller, but basically the same. It feels so good to see them. We approach, in what seems like slow motion. Our aunt covers her mouth and gives us an odd look. Our uncle smiles. Hugs for everyone. Our aunt observes we're way too thin, and asks me what's wrong with my back. We're introduced to everyone in the mob. They're the good people who've been helping our uncle and his family for the past year or so, without whom their life would be unbearable.

We meet Mr. and Mrs. Foster, who allow our uncle to use their phone. Mrs. Foster will end up being my math teacher in eighth grade. We meet Reverend Nordquist and his whole family. He's a Presbyterian pastor and is always doing favors for our new family. Most of their used furniture came from his flock, as did their winter clothes, and the clothes that are waiting for us at our new home. He's a civil rights activist, and he wears a little piece of burlap on his lapel all the time to let people know that he won't rest until the Civil Rights Act is passed. We meet Mrs. Junk and her teenage kids. She drives Uncle Amado and the family to the supermarket every week, so they can shop. She has a nifty Volkswagen bus, a brown one, and it's in that van that we're driven home from the airport. We can't all fit in there, since so many people came to greet us, so we end up with a small caravan.

But before I get into the minibus, I hand over the stinky cheese to my aunt Alejandra. Mission accomplished, and preserved for posterity. Someone snaps a photo of this slice of eternity, at once infinitesimally thin and infinitely vast. In it, Tony is giving some babe the eye, and I'm holding the stinky cheese bag under my left arm, looking delirious.

I have never, ever been so happy. No lie. On the way into town I see many huge Christmas trees, everywhere. Enormous pines. And other sorts of trees I've never seen before, some of which make the ones on Coral Way seem puny by comparison. All of the houses have sloping roofs, and most of them are wooden, with elaborate trim. I've never seen houses like this before, except on Christmas cards. Many of the streets are paved in red brick, and the cars make the most wonderful sound as we roll over them: one long constant low *whrrrrrrr*. We pass a very modern looking building, with a wing that looks a lot like a flying saucer.

"That's our high school," says Mrs. Junk.

I'm a little thrown off by her surname because at this point I'm not sure if it's really "Junk" or "Yunk" or "Yonk." I'll find out soon enough that she's a widow, and that her husband died a few years back when their furnace exploded.

She asks us questions about ourselves and points out landmarks. I'm so high I can barely answer her questions. Everything here is enthralling. Every little detail. It's so different, so totally unlike anything I have ever seen, even in movies. This is the real thing. This is the land of snow, and I'm higher than I ever was on airplane glue or Robert Mitchum on marijuana *and* cocaine, together.

We pull up to an old house with two huge Christmas trees in front. "Okay, here you are, your new home," says Mrs. Junk. It's a little run down, but still very attractive. Later, when I learn more about architecture, I'll be able to tell that it's an Arts and Crafts house, built in the early 1900s. It's a riot of triangles juxtaposed against one another, low-slung in front, with a glassed-in porch that's topped by a peaked roof line that runs east to west, and two gables sticking out of the steeply sloping roof that rises above the porch, sloping from north to south. The driveway is empty.

"Our very own Christmas trees," I say to Tony.

The house next door is enormous, and the largest Christmas tree I've ever seen is sprouting from the front yard. It's as tall as the house itself, and it reaches all the way to the top of the steeply sloping roof, three stories above the sidewalk. Unlike the two trees in front of our house—which are a bit ratty looking—this one is perfect.

"Look at that," I say to Tony.

"It's a blue spruce," says Mrs. Junk. My idolatrous instincts reawaken.

We go into the house. It's a bit like the exterior: somewhat scruffy, but beautiful. A long curved archway separates the living and dining rooms. The living room has one wall that's all windows. These windows open onto the front porch, which is itself totally wrapped in windows. If it weren't for the tall Christmas trees out in front, which cast a dense shade, a lot of light could stream in. The space is furnished with an old couch and armchair, both of which look slightly worn out, yet decent enough to let you know they have a lot left to offer, much like a pretty woman whose face is just starting to wrinkle. A very square television set fills one corner, directly beneath a framed print of a garden scene. The only other decoration on the walls is another framed print, a portrait of Jesus Christ. It's an image I've never seen before: a rendition of the face of Jesus that doesn't scare me to death. This Jesus isn't bleeding or suffering in any way, and his eyes aren't looking straight at you. He can't follow you with his gaze, either, for his head is turned sideways to the right, nearly into a full profile. You can still see both of his blue eyes, but they have a far-away look. This Jesus seems kind and slightly weary. Maybe worried too. Come to think of it, he looks as if he's waiting for a haircut at the barber college. I have no way of knowing that this is an American Protestant icon I'm staring at: Warner Sallman's *Head of Christ*, painted in 1940, in Chicago, and reproduced half a billion times by the time I lay eyes on it. This icon hangs right above the armchair, which—as I'll soon find out—is strictly reserved for my uncle. Jesus H. Midwestern Christ, what a contrast with every tormented, bloody, pain-inducing, terrifying Catholic image of Our Savior! No doubt about it: Even the Son of God looks better up here in the Corn Belt. One wall in the dining room is all windows, which open onto the empty driveway and the house next door, with the giant blue spruce. The kitchen is large and has a breakfast nook: two benches and a table tucked away, with a window that looks out onto the backyard. Tony and I get a large room downstairs. It has two big windows and a walk-in closet with built-in shelves and drawers. We have our own clean bathroom right next to our bedroom. The other two rooms downstairs are vacant, and it's a shame, for they're both beautiful. The front room, especially. Two of the walls are nothing but windows, and the ceiling light fixture is made of stained glass. It has dragonflies on it, blue and purple when the light shines through them, set in the midst of all sorts of greenery, with traces of yellow and orange. It's a work of art, far superior to any of the crystal chandeliers in my house back in that place that doesn't exist anymore. Uncle Amado says he has to keep these two rooms closed up and empty because he can't afford to heat them.

For the rest of my life I will ache for that unused and drafty study.

Uncle Amado, Aunt Alejandra, Marisol, and Alejandrita have rooms upstairs and their own bathroom. And, as a bonus, there's an attic crammed with stuff, including old family photo albums that belong to the owner of the house, a certain Mr. Guttman.

Then, another bonus: There's a cellar, or as they call them in Bloomington, a basement. It's the first one I've ever seen, other than in a movie. It's huge, like some medieval dungeon, only very clean and well-lit. It makes me think that we've moved up to a castle.

By now it's pitch black outside. We have a simple meal. Ham sandwiches with stinky cheese, which, as it turns out, tastes much better than it smells. The sandwiches are on white American bread, whole. No diagonal or vertical or horizontal cuts. I devour mine and don't take the time to thank God. The ham slices have been carefully prepared by Uncle Amado, who trims all the fat away, patiently, with ultimate concentration, much like a watchmaker working with tiny gears and springs. I'll see him do that every night at the breakfast nook table during the two years, two months, and two days that I'll spend in his house. It's a ritual for this architect who has lost everything and has to count every penny at the checkout counter at the A&P, literally. He needs to trim the fat from everything in the universe, to reduce everything to the bare essentials. And this includes the ham. I'll have many a great conversation with him as he performs this essential nightly ritual. Trim, trim, trim.

I will learn a great deal from this wise man.

We have nothing uniquely Cuban to eat, save for the stinky cheese, because there's no place to buy anything slightly tropical in Bloomington. No black beans. No plantains. No mangoes. No malanga. No yucca. No saffron with which to turn our rice yellow. No thinly cut steaks. No guava paste. No espresso coffee. It's even hard to find French bread, the closest thing to Cuban bread.

So what? Maybe these things are worth discarding in exchange for a life up north, where it snows and everything is nearly perfect.

We watch television after dinner. It's Sunday night, so it's *Candid Camera*. We missed *The Ed Sullivan Show*. I discover another minor drawback: We have only one channel to watch. Bloomington has no television stations. Our television set—an ancient model—receives only VHF signals, which means that it can't pick up signals from very far away. And all we get is the CBS network, broadcast from Champaign, about thirty miles southeast of us. Nothing else but snow on the other channels, the wrong kind of snow. The other networks broadcast in UHF, from *big* cities such as Peoria, and we're as unable to pick up their signals as those broadcast by alien beings in other galaxies.

We also don't have a telephone. Can't afford one.

But I don't care, not one bit. Tony and I have been redeemed from bondage, and from a tropical existence. From now on we'll be real people, not troglodytes chained by our necks to a cave wall, constantly duped by shadows. Miami was only the mouth of Plato's cave. This place, I know, is way beyond that. Here, the true light bathes everything, fully, all the time.

And it will be in this living room, where I'm watching *Candid Camera*, that I will see the true True Light for the first time. I don't know this yet, of course.

Flash forward, ten years again, to 1973.

We've been driving all day, and my bride has been crying nonstop, all the way from Chicago to Buffalo. It's August, and beastly hot. Our crap-brown Chevy Nova has no air-conditioning, and I've been driving about eighty to ninety miles an hour the whole way, with the windows wide open. The rushing cyclone that flows into the car keeps us sort of cool, and its unrelenting roar muffles her sobbing. Under the circumstances, we don't have much of a chance to talk.

In Buffalo, at a Holiday Inn, she soaks a pillow with her tears. It's like a giant soggy sponge now. I don't want to wring it out because, unlike the God of the Psalms, I don't want to keep track of the number of tears. I just want them to stop.

We're moving to New Haven, Connecticut, and my bride of eight months is most unhappy.

And I'm trying to relive the first of September, 1963, moment by glorious moment. I play it over in my mind, again and again and again. Every little detail. I've been doing it in the car all day, and I'm doing it now. Oh, but for some of that stinky cheese now.

Some deaths are so much sweeter than others.

Ay.

Twenty

"You can't have a name like *Carlos* around here," says the salesman at the sporting goods store on Main Street where we're being outfitted for gym class. "That's not American. Is there an English version of that?"

"*Charles*," I say.

"Oh . . . great. But you don't want that either. Nobody's going to call you that. You'll be either *Charlie* or *Chuck*."

This guy seems to know a lot. And he's asking about my name because when he sells me these Converse high-top sneakers I've just tried on, he's supposed to write my name on them with an indelible marker.

"If you want to know, *Chuck* is better than *Charlie*. It has more weight to it; you'll be a lot happier with *Chuck* than with *Charlie*."

"Oh," I say, weighing my options. I need to think fast. Whatever he writes on that shoe is going to be my name at school, maybe forever. *Chuck* certainly sounds tough. I've never heard that name before, but it has a ring to it like Buck or Flash, the two space heroes played by Buster Crabbe. Come to think of it, *Chuck* is also like Buster. Man, this is a killer name.

I hesitate. This is hard. Can I change my name so completely without having thought about it first? You bet. "Thanks, make it Chuck."

So he writes *Chuck Nieto* on my sneakers, smiling as he does it. A very fast-germinating seed has been planted in me that will soon choke out both Carlos and Charles and turn me into *Chuck Neat-o*. It's a lethal combination, this pairing of name and surname—Chuck and Nieto— because no one in Bloomington will be able to pronounce *Nieto* correctly.

"What? Say that again? *Neat-o?*"

"No, it's *Knee-a-toe*."

"Oh, okay, *Neat-toe*."

Aaaaaargh.

Having been stripped in Miami of *Eire*, my other surname, I've given up on reclaiming it. It's as dead and buried as my Cuban self.

All of my life, up until the day I set foot in Everglades Elementary School, I'd had two last names, each equally significant: one from my father, Nieto, and one from my mother, Eire. But everything changed in an instant at that school in Miami. "Only one surname per customer," the assistant principal said. "You can't have two. Pick one."

Sophie's choice, in reverse: Is it better to reject your father or your mother?

I briefly ponder what might happen if Chuck were to reclaim *Eire* tomorrow, during the first day of school. Given the enormous trouble that Americans seem to have pronouncing anything in another language, it might be risky. *Eire* is tougher on American tongues than *Nieto*. *Chuck Eerie. Chuck Ire. Or Chuck Air.* Man, those are no good at all. Or how about the full combination: *Chuck Neat-o Eerie, Chuck Neat-o Ire,* or *Chuck Neat-o Air.* Holy smokes, forget about it.

I like this new name, *Chuck.* It suits me, the new me, here up north, in the realm of light—and snow. Hell, I could be like Buck Rogers now, if I go with that name, or Flash Gordon. Then I could be super-American.

Comemierda, says Carlos. He doesn't like being shoved aside again like this. And he swears revenge against both Charles and Chuck, and threatens Charlie just in case that moron decides to stake a claim.

School starts tomorrow. We got here just in time. Monday was a holiday called Labor Day, when everything was closed. Today we're getting ready for school, buying all sorts of stuff with money that we were given by the social worker in Miami. My uncle could never pay for this stuff. We've gone up and down Main Street and found everything we needed.

Downtown Bloomington is close to home; we can walk there, easily. Uncle Amado walks to Lundeen and Hillfinger, the architectural firm where he works as a mere draftsman, which is near the domed courthouse that squats right in the middle of downtown. This courthouse looks like a small version of the Capitol in Havana, which, in turn, is a small version of the Capitol in Washington, D.C. I'll soon discover that fat old men like to sit on the courthouse steps all the time. They're almost like sculptures, permanently affixed.

Every building on Main Street is made of red brick. None of them is very tall, and none of the stores is very large. The largest building is the twelve-story headquarters of the State Farm Insurance Company. It dwarfs everything else. The largest store is one block west of Main, and it's one I'd first learned about in Miss Esterman's class, while listening to *The Music Man*: "Montgomery Ward sent me a bathtub and a crosscut saw."

Uncle Amado tells us everything at Ward's is way, way too expensive. Once we've used up this money, he says, there are only two stores in town that we can go to: Goodwill and Salvation Army. He says that the used clothing they sell is practically new, and that you can get great bargains. Fortunately, they're both close to our house, in one of the shabbier corners of downtown, which surprises me when we walk past it. What? Squalor, here, up north?

The public library is downtown too, much closer to our new house than the library was in Miami. I make plans to check it out as soon as possible.

Our neighborhood is a bit run down, but you can tell that it was once the best in town. The streets are all lined with old giant trees, taller than most of the houses. Many of the streets are still paved in red brick rather than asphalt, and some of the houses still have hitching posts for horses. There are palatial houses everywhere. Many of them have turrets, and lots of gables. I'll find out soon enough that most of them are called Victorian houses. I'll also discover that many of them have been turned into apartment houses, and that the few that haven't are usually occupied by lonely old ladies.

Our house looks a little more run-down in the full light of day than at twilight, especially when viewed from the backyard. The Christmas trees out front could use some trimming, and the siding and windows could use some paint. And the backyard could use a lot of work. You can tell it was once beautiful. There's a scruffy old trellis out there, and also a cement fishpond, about the size of a large bathtub, crammed with rocks and debris. This rubble looks as if it was deliberately dumped in there, and it's all under three inches of stagnant water. The edge of the fishpond is inlaid with river pebbles of different colors, and it looks a lot like a tarnished jeweled necklace. As soon as we lay eyes on it, Tony and I decide we will restore this treasure to its former glory. We'd like to freeze stuff in there, once it gets cold, and see it suspended inside the ice. I try to imagine what it'll look like as a block of ice, with toy soldiers sticking out of it at all angles.

The fence along the edge of the backyard has seen much better days. So has the garage at the far end of the yard, which faces the alley.

What a concept! An alley. A street that runs behind the houses, and is used as a service road. Your trash goes out there, not on the street. How utterly civilized, how perfect. Every block in Bloomington has an alley. We also have a huge steel barrel out there, where all of the paper trash gets burned. More than perfect. Fire! Yes!

As soon as we find out what the barrel is for, Tony and I both volunteer to burn the paper trash every day. We'll spend a lot of time out there and become creative incinerators, and scientists too. We'll not only toss all sorts of nonpaper items in there to see how they fare under scorching temperatures, but also test each and every aerosol can our family discards, to see whether or not it will really explode when tossed into the fire, as the dire warnings printed on such cans predict. We'll also keep track of time as we wait for them to explode—or not explode—and determine which ones detonate faster than others. After two years of testing we'll fail to find a single aerosol can that won't explode immediately.

None of our groundbreaking research will ever be published, however, until now.

The garage is full of interesting stuff, which we can see through the window that faces the backyard, but it's locked and we wouldn't dare break in. Everything in there belongs to Mr. Guttman, our landlord, and we don't want to mess with him.

Oh, but what we'd give to go in there and poke around. It astounds me that anyone could have so much stuff that they never use and never even come to look at or paw through. The Guttmans are the opposites of refugees. Tony is not as amazed by this as I am. He'll simply observe that the Guttmans are no different from our father, Louis XVI, and that he and I had more stuff than that, and more valuable, back in Plato's cave.

I'll realize then, when he says this, how deeply I've buried my past self. And then I'll forget this insight, almost instantly, and go back to being Chuck Neat-o.

On Wednesday, a mere three days after our arrival, we start school. Bloomington Junior High School is only a block and a half from our house, and it serves the entire town. It's housed in what was formerly the high school, a large brick building from the 1930s, slightly art deco, three stories tall, with a cafeteria in the basement. It has a huge gym and an Olympic-size swimming pool. It's set back from the street and has a lawn in front, with maple trees that are taller than the building itself. Inside, the hallways are lined with lockers. All of this blows me away, for I've never seen a school like this before. What amazes me the most is the fact that not a single square inch of this school is open to the outdoors. Everything is so contained, so protected from the outside world. So untropical. So real in its acknowledgment of the harshness of cold weather, which I can't wait to experience fully, sometime soon.

I'm both excited and terrified as I set foot inside this building. I'm not only in a new school, in a new town, but also moving up from the safe and protected environment of elementary school to the bewilderingly new world of junior high school, where you don't have the same teacher all day long and need to change classrooms all the time. I know I'll also have to wear a uniform in gym class—something totally weird—and, on top of that, take a shower afterward, even if I'm not sweaty.

This is the freakiest thing of all, and the most troubling. What? Don't they trust me to take one at home? And they expect me to get naked in front of all these other guys every day? What? Are they crazy? Sadistic? But I'm painfully aware that this would have happened in Miami too, where the rules were the same. It seems to be a very peculiar and extremely perverse American fixation. So, at least I'm partially relieved to know that I'll be getting naked in the world of light as opposed to the entrance to Plato's cave, which was full of all sorts of thugs and potential perverts.

I see some thugs milling around outside the school, and it surprises me. Thugs, in the real world? Wait, this is the realm of light. How is this possible? But there's no use in denying the obvious. They're here too. Thugs are easily identifiable, anywhere, regardless of geography or culture. But there seem to be far fewer here than I saw at Citrus Grove Junior High, which is where I'd be right now if St. Martin de Porres and God had not intervened.

I'm immediately set at ease by my homeroom teacher, a tall blond guy with a flat-top haircut and black plastic eyeglasses. He calls the roll and when he gets to my name, he actually gives me a choice: "Charles, Charlie, or Chuck?" I hesitate again, for an instant, and then say "Chuck" as if that's been my name all along. He explains what our first day will be like in great detail, and sets us loose.

I almost miss some of his instructions because I'm transfixed by the maple tree outside our homeroom windows. It's right up against the glass, this tree, and it blocks whatever is beyond it. All you can see are leaves and branches. The dappled sunlight is in constant motion as the leaves wave in the breeze, and the room itself is bathed in a greenish glow. The only other window I've seen that comes close to this is the one in Coral Gables, in that room where we had a Christmas party. It pains me to admit it, but this one tops the one in Florida. These leaves play with the light and share it with you. And the leaves themselves have a beautiful shape. The trees on Coral Way made me feel protected, but these trees make me feel as if I need no protection at all, from anything or anyone.

I go from class to class and meet one nice teacher after another. Man, this world up north is so much better. Then I get to gym class and meet Mr. Henker. He's different, all right, but I can't put my finger on it. Icy. This guy radiates the opposite of warmth. He has a flat-top haircut, just like my homeroom teacher, but he also has a tattoo on his forearm: a bulldog's head with the initials U.S.M.C. He tells us that he's going to whip us into shape and turn us into real men, and that we'd better put one hundred percent or more of our effort into this class.

I turn to the guy sitting to my left and say something appropriately skeptical and sarcastic. He responds in kind. I don't know it yet, but I've just met my new best friend, one of the best ever. His name is Gary, and he, too, is new in town. His family has just moved here from farther downstate. Of all the guys I could have sat next to, it had to be him.

Mr. Henker tells us that tomorrow we'd all better have the right gear for gym class, assigns us lockers, explains how it's possible to shower and get dressed in less than five minutes, and lets us go.

The rest of that first day is as wonderful as one might expect in the realm of light. By lunchtime, I notice that we have a lot of black kids in this school. This is something new—I thought all American schools were racially segregated. Wow—what a great change. That march on Washington and Martin Luther King's speech from just a few days ago are already making a difference. I also notice that no one is asking why I have a funny accent, or where I come from. No one: not the teachers, not my fellow students. I also can't help but notice that this school has more beautiful girls than I've ever seen thus far in my entire life. It's not just the blondes, though there are so many of them and they catch my attention first. In this school, here in the realm of light, hair color makes no difference. Perfection abounds. I'm overwhelmed, and by sixth period the pain in my soul is getting in the way. Too many perfect features on too many girls. I find it hard to focus on anything else. Name a feature, I can count at least two dozen girls I've seen with perfect ones. And it's not just a case of girls with one single perfect feature. No. I've seen some with multiple ones, and a few who seem to be totally perfect. Wholly and mindblowingly perfect.

Legs are by far the most common perfect feature. Calves such as I've never, ever seen before, on any girl, anywhere. Perfectly symmetrical curves tapering down to a perfectly taut, inward-curving ankle. So, so many of them. The pain they cause is exquisite.

By the end of the day, I'm practically levitating. In spiritual distress, yes, but euphoric. I'm overwhelmed by all of this beauty, and even more elated than I was when I landed at the airport. To say I'm high doesn't even begin to cover it.

I go to more classes, and get higher and higher. Industrial arts. What a concept: a class where you get to play with wood and metal and learn to use power tools. This isn't school, this is a playground. I don't know it yet, but this class will eventually lead me to many blissful moments with sawdust, metal filings, drills, chainsaws, and backhoes. And that teacher for my last period, Mr. Noden, put me over the edge. He was on fire. Social studies, of all things. I thought this was going to be a boring class, but hey, in this world surprises, along with perfect legs on girls, abound. This guy loves what he teaches. You can tell. All he did was lay out what we'd cover this year, but he made it seem like an adventure. I don't know it yet, but Mr. Noden will know exactly what to do with my raw passion for history, and he'll also teach me how to teach, even though doing any such thing has never yet crossed my mind.

And I love my hallway locker, and the combination lock, and the combination. 17–8–23. Perfect. The gym locker I can do without.

After school, I come home to real family warmth. These are my kin. I've known them forever, going back even to the lowest depths of Plato's cave.

Uncle Amado has always been the only sensible and pragmatic member of my father's family, and, as one might expect, this has caused him some measure of grief, given how utterly dysfunctional everyone else is. I've always liked him, though, no matter how much the others carp about him. He can seem cold at times, but he's never harsh, or mean-spirited. I've never seen him angry either. Tony and I will find it odd and irrational that he should harbor hopes of returning to Cuba and reclaiming his business and his property. As Tony and I see it, that's all gone, vaporized, irretrievable. Of course, Tony and I are two punks who don't have a clue and can't even begin to imagine what it must be like to abandon absolutely everything that you've worked for your entire life at the age of sixty-two, or how it must feel to go from the top of your profession to the absolute bottom. He'll write letters to American newspapers tirelessly, correcting their abysmally poor reporting on Cuba or praising the wonders of America, which Americans fail to appreciate. He'll ask me to help with the English, and going over those letters with Uncle Amado will become one of my favorite moments of the day. He'll write about two or three letters per week, during the two years, two months, and two days I'll live with him. Tony and I will think he's wasting his time, of course. But I'll enjoy helping him with this quixotic obsession, while I puzzle over the fact that this man who knows so much more than I do about everything needs to ask a kid to help him with English.

His wife, our aunt Alejandra, is much younger than him. She's always been very nice to us. She has a great way of turning any awkward moment around and finding the right thing to say. She suffers from frequent migraines, though, and sometimes has to disappear for a while. She doesn't speak a word of English, and after two years, she has made no effort to learn the language. In a town like Bloomington, where no one else speaks Spanish, this isolates her completely. It's understandable. Like many refugees her age, she doesn't see her present situation as permanent. As she sees it, this is a blip on the screen. She'll be going back to Cuba any day now. Maybe next week. What amazes me the most about Alejandra is the way in which Amado loves her, and tries constantly to please her. Whatever she wants is what he wants. This was certainly not the case with my long-dead parents, Louis XVI and Marie Antoinette.

Marisol, their older daughter, is sweet, but a bit slow, physically and mentally. She's slightly older than Tony, and during the first three or four years of their childhood, the difference in their development was so disturbingly stark that Amado and Alejandra asked our parents to stop visiting. Seeing what Tony could do broke their heart. Marisol is in junior high school, but in special classes. Two years after her arrival in the United States, she still has some trouble with English, as she does with every subject. Her balance is poor, and she has to wear orthopedic shoes. You can guess how all the other students treat her.

I don't know it yet, but a day will come when I'll hear someone call her "Moose," and I will lose control completely. I'll punch the guy out before I can realize what I've just done. Chuck Neat-o will be shocked, unable to figure out where this violent response came from. Carlos will try to shout to him that it's what he was supposed to do, to defend the family honor, but Chuck will pretend he doesn't understand him.

Alejandrita, their younger daughter, is just a few months younger than me. We've always gotten along well. She's smart, funny, and talented. She's everything Marisol can't be. She does suffer from one handicap, however: She has to put up with the nearly paranoid protectiveness of her father, who, like all members of the Nieto family, thinks that the world is too dangerous and that the only way to survive is to stay indoors as much as possible. Amado doesn't let her walk to school alone, even though she's in sixth grade and her school is only three blocks from home. As soon as Tony and I arrive, it becomes our job to walk her to and from school every day. Tony will shirk this responsibility, but I'll enjoy it, in part because I like Alejandrita very much and also because, finally, I get to be an older brother.

During these first few days I ask my new family a million and a half questions about the climate up here. What's fall like? Winter? Spring? I'm especially interested in knowing when it'll start turning cold and when the leaves will change colors. Right now, in September, the weather here is no different from what I'm used to. It gets warm during the day, and it doesn't cool off a lot at night. We sleep with the windows open and hear the most amazing symphony of insect noises outside, very different from any that we've heard before. The yard is full of large grasshoppers—green ones—and I imagine they're the ones serenading us to sleep.

It's a comforting sound. So much better than gunfire and bombs.

I see my first cardinal. My first blue jay. Rabbits. Squirrels. And no lizards—none at all. Free at last! Around here, the squirrels seem to have taken the place of lizards. They're everywhere. Uncle Amado has built a shelter for them on the cherry tree outside the kitchen window. He's built them a little architect-designed shed, about six feet up the tree trunk, in which he places ears of corn. Given how careful Amado is with his money, this expense shows how deeply he cares about these exotic creatures. We watch the squirrels more than we watch television. My aunt Alejandra is especially taken with the way in which they hold the corn cobs, and how methodically they chew them up.

"Look, they eat the same way we do!"

Alejandra is at her best when she contemplates the simplest things. She has a way of making the most mundane things seem marvelous, even miraculous. She won't know she's doing it, but she'll be teaching me a most useful skill, which is also, at the same time, a great way to get high, naturally.

I sleep as never before and have trouble telling the difference between my dreams and my waking life. They seem equally unreal, equally enjoyable. No nightmares. No fears as I drift to sleep. There's nothing to dread, no roaches or scorpions to worry about. Nothing is scary. Not even the portrait of Jesus above my uncle's chair, which is always the first thing my eyes fix on when I walk through the front door. Jesus H. Comforting Christ, how nice. The Void has been off my radar screen for nine months or so, and I've almost forgotten about it. No reason to worry about that now. This house is not only full of people, but they never go anywhere. Without a car, they can't.

Fade to black.

Havana, at exactly the same time. The sunlight is screaming, as always, and slamming into everything. The tree outside my house has grown a lot since I left. A whole lot. The house has filled up with more art and antiques, surreptitiously acquired from collectors who left the country before the door was slammed shut. Ernesto now sleeps in the room that once belonged to Tony and me. Next door, the Committee for the Defense of the Revolution keeps a sharp eye on my house, and my parents. They don't like the fact that Tony and I got away.

My parents get the news about our move to Bloomington, and they are relieved. I'll find out years later that they had no clue how bad the Palace Ricardo was, but that they suspected it was awful. What they didn't know was a blessing of sorts, given the fact that they could do nothing for us.

Louis XVI goes around with a huge hole in his heart, and the bigger and more painful this hole gets, the more he immerses himself in his art collection and the more out of touch he becomes with the reality his absent sons face, day to day. It pains him that Amado, a brother he never liked too much, should now be raising his children. His cluelessness keeps him sane. In the meantime, his real heart—as opposed to the figurative one with the hole in it—gets worse and worse. None of this will be reported to Tony and me, of course.

Lying is sometimes the kindest sin, perhaps even a virtuous deed.

My mom, Marie Antoinette, has been trying to find a way out of Cuba, with no luck. Finding out that she couldn't leave in November, 1962, was a devastating blow, almost more than she could bear. The door out of the island has been shut tightly. But if you persist and find connections in the right places, you can luck out. She wears herself out, tries everything, pesters everyone. And she gets nowhere. The relatives in Spain can't do anything for her. Uncle Filo's diplomatic connections prove useless. All of the doors are shut tight. She cries a lot. A whole lot, too often.

Fade to black. Back to Bloomington.

I never think about my parents. I haven't done so for months, and I have even less reason to do so now that I'm here. I write them weekly letters and fill them with all sorts of details, but I am on some sort of automatic pilot. I have no idea what they do day to day, how they feel, or what, if anything, they're trying to do to reunite with us. And I really don't care to know. I feel this odd, fleeting emotion I recognize as some kind of love or attachment, some primal desire to stay connected with them, but it's much more like the attachment I have and the affection I feel for each and every one of my memories. All I can admit to myself is that Mom and Dad are nothing but memories. Yes, I know they're alive, but they might as well be on Uranus or Pluto, or one of the stars in Orion's Belt.

Why do I feel this way? No, I'm not asking any experts, much less doctors Freud and Jung. Sometimes I ask myself this question. I know it's strange to feel the way I do. I even make an effort to pretend that I still want to see them, or need them. But I know, deep down, that I'm feigning. None of my selves cares. Ask Carlos, Charles, Charlie, or Chuck and they'll give the same answer, if they're being honest. They're all quite happy with the way things are now. It's been only five days since I left the Palace Ricardo, but I already know that the time I spent there stripped me clean of any attachment I ever had to my parents. Bleached bones in the desert, buried by the drifting sands, that's all that's left of whatever I once felt for them.

Or at least, that is what I think and feel at the level of everyday awareness, and dreams. Some other part of me, some much deeper part, is bound and gagged at the moment, but it's just the opposite of bleached bones. It's very much alive, wounded, and screaming into its soundproof gag. And waiting for a chance to break free. This imprisoned part of me will escape, soon enough. It'll come roaring out, crazed and aching for revenge against Carlos, Charles, Charlie, and Chuck.

The Void will spring it loose and possess it, like a legion of demons.

But for now, I've got nothing to worry about. Nothing at all. I'm finally out of Plato's cave and living in the realm of light. Fall is just a few weeks away, and winter can't be too far behind. Just a couple of months, maybe three at most. Soon I'll be jumping into piles of red and golden leaves, maybe making a colossal bonfire with them. You can burn the leaves, Uncle Amado has told me. I'll be counting the leaves as they fall, the same way I count all of the perfect features on the girls at school. And I'll be just as transfixed by each multicolored leaf as by every perfect face and every perfect pair of legs. The pain will be exquisite. I'll be seeing snow soon too, counting the snowflakes as they fall, one by one. I'll be rolling in it as it piles up on the ground; I'll be sledding, making snowballs and snowmen; I'll be catching snowflakes with my tongue as they fall from heaven, letting each and every unique one of them dissolve like a consecrated host, with exactly the same reverence. Maybe even more.

I'm fine. Just fine. Perfect. I'm higher than a junkie on heroin.

I'm waiting for snow in Bloomington.

Twenty-one

I t happened so quickly. One day the leaves were green, the next day they staged a revolt against chlorophyll. The trees are all ablaze, and I'm on fire too. I pick up some of the leaves that fall to the ground. Many of them aren't just a single color, but practically the entire spectrum. The patterns on them remind me of kaleidoscopes. The maple leaves are the best, by far. They transfix me, each and every one of them.

I save the most spectacular ones, stick them into books, between the pages, hoping they'll never fade or crumble away. Some of them will actually stay in good shape for a while, and I'll be able to kick-start my euphoria many times over, simply by retrieving them from their hiding place.

The cold air also knocks me out. Especially at night. Seeing your own breath is something otherworldly to me. I don't care how ordinary it seems to those who live up here. To me, it's a miracle. I've seen frost again, several times. Another miracle. It's most easily detected on the garage roof first thing in the morning, from the breakfast nook where I toast up about half a loaf of American bread every morning. The toaster is right under the windowsill, on the table, and I just keep popping them in as fast as I eat them. Margarine, still. No butter. Refugees can't afford butter.

School is a constant high. Jerks and thugs are at a minimum, and the girls seem to get more beautiful with every passing day. No one has yet asked where I'm from. No one has made a single remark about my accent. Maybe I don't have one anymore? Hard to tell, and Chuck's not about to ask, "Hey, could you tell me, please, do I speak English with an accent?"

I continue to model my speech after that of Andy Griffith and the Beverly Hillbillies. Fortunately, those two shows are on the CBS network, the only one we can pick up with our ancient television set. I practice by myself, when no one is looking.

My new friend Gary is one of the nicest and funniest guys I've ever run into. Everything is a joke to him. But he lives far away on the edge of town, on the border with Normal, out near Route 66, near the Ewing Mansion, one of the town's tourist attractions. It's hard to get together with him. My other new friend, Eddie, is also a great guy. And he lives just a few blocks away on Olive Street, in my neighborhood, so we get together very often.

As the fall colors reach their peak, our family is invited to a picnic out in the countryside, at a place named Funk's Grove, where Abraham Lincoln once stopped to give his horse a drink from a sulphur spring. Poor horse. That spring stinks. And the stench is nothing compared to the taste. It's bad enough to make you spew whatever you've eaten, right there, on the spot. This picnic was organized by the folks who run the Americanization program in Bloomington, and one of them has driven us all out here in his car. These are the good people who introduce the few foreigners in town to the English language and the American system of government. Most of them are immigrants themselves who've been here for a long time. Uncle Amado and Aunt Alejandra go to these classes. How willingly they go, I don't know. These Americanization folk also help new immigrants in other ways, and it could be that Amado doesn't want to upset them.

Nearly all of these good people are German.

"Vould you like anozzer viener," the kindly old man asks me, as I sit near the small bonfire on which hot dogs are being roasted.

"A what?"

"A viener," he says. "A viener," he says again.

I catch on. "Yeah, thanks, I'd love another hot dog."

It's as fabulous a fall day as you might wish for, anywhere. Out here in Funk's Grove, which is a patch of trees surrounded by an ocean of seemingly infinite cornfields, the afternoon autumn sunlight makes everything seem on fire.

By now I know for sure that we're the only Spanish-speaking family in town. One day at Woolworth's, downtown, a little girl came up to us as we were talking to one another in Spanish, and she just stood there with her mouth totally agape, her eyes so wide open that I thought they were about to pop out of her head. Her mom tiptoed over to us, took her by the hand, and led her away without saying a word. Up in Normal there's another Spanish-speaking family, and they happen to be Cuban, but they've been here so long that they're barely Cuban. The head of that family is a Spanish professor at Illinois State University, and he and his wife have been in the United States since the 1940s. Their children don't even speak Spanish. We can't visit them because they live so far away, but the one time they came over to our house made me thankful for that. I was so bored, I had trouble staying awake.

Most of the other foreigners in town seem to be German. At Bloomington Junior High School, the only other foreign kid in seventh grade is a German too. And he's subjected to frequent abuse. Way too often, our classmates give him the Nazi salute and a *"Sieg heil!"*

No one notices me, for no one seems to know where Cuba is, or that it exists. So Chuck Neat-o sails right over potentially troubled waters, unnoticed. I'm just another guy, with one of those weird surnames that end in *O*. Good thing that no one seems to know anything about Cuba, or I'd be getting the clenched left fist salute and a constant round of *"Venceremos."* But I've checked out the history and geography textbooks in my social studies class to see what they have to say about my birthplace, and they're no different from the ones I'd used in Florida. According to these books, I hail from one of the most primitive, corrupt, and politically unstable countries on earth. All of Latin America, including Cuba, is like some starving child running amok, half-naked and three-quarters savage.

I dread the day when we'll get to this section in class. That's when I'll have to deal with the dumb questions for sure. And it'll be so hard to stay cool.

But I have other things to deal with here, in Funk's Grove, in the fall of 1963.

It's a perfectly named place, Funk's Grove. It may look to everyone—and to the camera—as if I'm having a grand old time, but the God's honest truth is that I'm in the bluest of blue funks. This morning, before we came out here to the countryside, the Void pounced on me without warning.

I woke up, made my toast and coffee, sat in the breakfast nook, looked at the backyard, and *wham!*

"Long time no see. Dukes up!"

Wham!

Jesus H. Crucified Christ, help me.

In the wink of an eye, the world around me loses its boundaries, and all of its details turn sour. All I can see and feel is this vortex of nothingness, emptiness, and utter loneliness. Pure Absence. I recognize it immediately for what it is, but I'm unable to deal with the enormity of it all. For starters, this house is totally full of people. I'm not alone at all. To top it all off, I've been so deliriously happy these past few weeks, and these autumn leaves have taken me even higher than I thought it possible to go with euphoria.

Where the hell did this come from?

I tell Tony how I feel. For the first time, I actually reveal this awful secret to someone. I go into great detail, the best I can. He doesn't know what to make of it. He tells me to ignore the feeling, that it's just some weird fluke, and that it'll go away soon enough.

All I can say is that I hope he's right, but that I don't think he really understands what I mean. He shrugs his shoulders and says, again, "Forget about it; it'll go away."

But the Void refuses to go away. It goes with me to Funk's Grove and ruins the picnic and all that's marvelous and divine in this otherworldly autumn day. Never before had the Void followed me anywhere, or tried to claim my soul while I was outdoors, or sitting in a car, so close to other bodies that I could barely move.

On the way home from Funk's Grove, as we're passing cornfield after harvested cornfield, and the golden light is glowing ever more fiercely, smothering everything with its hypercelestial glow, I knock out the Void with a single thought: *Tonight I'll be watching television with my family. I'm not alone. Ha. Take that.*

One television show in particular helps me win the match, for I picture it in great detail and use those images to disorient the Void. It's probably one of the stupidest shows ever to air on American television: *My Favorite Martian*. But it's not the show itself that makes the difference, it's the mere fact that I'll be watching it with family.

This time, I throw the sucker punch. And the Void's out like a light, and down for the count. Ha, there you go. Annihilate yourself, *cabrón*.

But this leaves me shaken. If the Void can spring on me so unexpectedly and intensely, when I'm surrounded by people, what can I do in the future if it happens again?

I respond by doing what I've learned to do best: I resolve to forget this incident and bury it as deeply in my Vault of Oblivion as possible. Unfortunately, the best I can do is to put it in a waiting room, way up the hallway from the antechamber to the Vault of Oblivion. It just won't go anywhere near the Vault, no matter how much I push and shove.

Life resumes its usual wonderful pace. And everything seems to speed up, as the days get shorter and the nights grow longer.

We try to burn some leaves on the street the next day, after the picnic at Funk's Grove, but all they do is smolder. Apparently, we don't know how to turn our leaves into incense. We give up after an hour or so, and just pile them up at the curb, where some truck from the town will pick them up and cart them off. I hope it's to someplace where they'll be burned in a huge bonfire.

Once the trees are bare and the air is crisp all the time, Tony and I step up our watch for snow. We follow the weather forecasts every night, hoping for good news. But the news isn't encouraging. Last year, the first snow came in late October. But this year, some stupid weather pattern known as Indian Summer is stretching way too far into snow season. Plenty of frost in the morning, but no snow.

I love my sweaters and the winter coat the Presbyterians gave me. It's from the 1940s, pure wool, and it keeps out the cold just fine. It looks like something that could have been worn to a polar expedition, and I don't give a damn about its style. It's the real thing: It's seen many a winter, and that alone makes it better than any new coat. I love my wool cap, and my scarf, and the gloves, and the earmuffs from Kmart, that huge store out there by Route 66, where Mrs. Junk takes us every now and then. It's the only store where we can afford to buy new stuff.

I constantly check the thermometer Uncle Amado has screwed onto the outside of the dining room windowsill. It keeps getting lower and lower, with every passing day.

Thank you, God.

November 17. Unforgettable. Snow flurries. The flakes come down sparsely and blow about. They look like small hosts, hundreds of them, wafting, twisting, turning in the wind, smacking into everything and melting right away. Not one of them survives its fall from heaven. I can't really gawk as much as I want to at school, when they first begin to fill the air, but once I get home, I park myself at the dining room windows and keep an eye on what's coming down. The Victorian house next door is a perfect backdrop, especially the blue spruce. It's snow, all right, but it's not piling up. I'm enthralled and horribly frustrated at the same time. There it goes again, this refugee thing: the constant irritating coincidence of opposites, the wonderful and the awful inseparably linked.

November 22, the day before my thirteenth birthday. If I were still living with the Chaits, maybe I'd be having a Bar Mitzvah. But I'm as far from such a ritual as I am from my parents, and all of my past. I'm about to turn into a man according to Jewish law, which, as I understand it, is the original deal between God and his Chosen People. I'm pissed that this part of *The* deal has been undone, and I'm disappointed, deep down, that my passage to manhood is not going to be appropriately recognized.

But, what the hell, I'm here, in the Promised Land, in this Corn Belt Jerusalem, and that makes me some sort of Jew and just as Chosen and no less of a man. Come to think of it, I've been a man since I first set foot in the fishbowl at the Havana airport.

At lunchtime, in the cafeteria, some of the women who dish out our food suddenly start to cry. One of them shrieks, another one howls. I'm at the same table as always, mooching leftovers from my new friends. They call me the "moocher" because anytime anyone at the table leaves something uneaten that I'd love to consume I say "Are you going to eat that?"

The word spreads like wildfire: President John F. Bay of Pigs Kennedy has been shot in Dallas. And he could be dead. Several of my table mates cheer. The rest don't look as terribly upset as the cafeteria ladies.

The loudspeakers in the cafeteria instruct us to go directly to our homerooms, immediately. So we all dispose of our trays and the trash on them, and we go where we've been told to go.

My flat-topped homeroom teacher tells us that he doesn't know any more than we do, but it is a fact that President Kennedy has been shot. Mr. Happy Birthday Mister President skintight–Marilyn Monroe–dress John Fitzgerald Kennedy. No doubt about it.

The principal breaks the news on the loudspeaker. President Screw You Cubans Kennedy is dead. Go home, all of you. Run home. Run for cover. Our history has just taken a sharp unexpected turn.

No one has to say it: This is bigger than us all. Here, in the land of Lincoln, presidential assassinations are taken much more seriously than elsewhere.

I pick up Alejandrita from her school, and we walk home together. On Evans Street, I look down at the red bricks with which the street is paved. I tell myself that I'll remember this moment till the day I die, and I'll see the bricks every time I recall this day. I turn out to be right. Mention President Let's Make a Deal with Russia Kennedy to me, and I immediately see those bricks. Each and every one of them, down to the nicks and dents and the grit in the spaces between them.

Walter Cronkite confirms that President Missile Crisis Kennedy is dead, again and again. I'm glued to the television, and so is everyone else at home, just like everyone throughout the land.

November 23. My thirteenth birthday is overshadowed by history. I don't really give a damn about the birthday. I'm past all such trivial things, especially since no one is ushering me into manhood with a proper ritual. I get a Tinkertoy set for a present, which comes in a tubular container, not unlike those used to enshrine single-malt Scotch whiskies. Not quite appropriate for my age, this child's toy, but I know how much it must have cost Uncle Amado, and I appreciate the gesture.

As soon as I see Lee Harvey Fair Play for Cuba Oswald shot dead right in front of me, on live television, I know for sure that Cubans had something to do with all of this. No doubt about it. And this conviction will stay with me for the rest of my life.

Accompanied by the icon of Corn Belt Jesus, we watch the funeral to end all funerals on channel three, the only signal that can reach our television. Aunt Alejandra is spellbound by the riderless horse, above all. I'm wondering if they've injected him with some kind of drug to make him so jittery. An impressive number of world leaders march in the funeral cortège. There's the emperor of Ethiopia. There's Charles de Gaulle. A bunch of Brits, too, including the queen's useless husband. The German chancellor. And even a Russian who had paid many a visit to Cuba, Anastas Mikoyan. Fidel is nowhere in sight.

Thanksgiving. November 28. Where's the snow, damn it? What kind of cruel hoax is this? The corny song about grandmother's house says you're supposed to have snow on Thanksgiving:

> *The horse knows the way to carry the sleigh,*
> *Thru the white and drifted snow, oh!*

And the Currier & Ives calendar on our kitchen wall gives me the same irritating message. *Home for Thanksgiving,* it says, or something like that, and the print shows a house and landscape knee-deep in snow.

Crap. It's just because I'm up here. The tropical sunlight trapped inside of my veins is warming up Bloomington a bit too much.

November 30. Saturday. My mother's birthday. She's forty-three today. Snow.

Holy God. It fell overnight, while I slept. It snuck up on me, just like the Cuban Revolution. Except this is the best of all surprises, not the worst. *Sanctus, sanctus, sanctus.* How is this kind of white possible? How is this whole thing possible at all? *Baruch atah Adonai.* It's a million, zillion times more beautiful than I ever imagined. Surely, this is what going to heaven will be like, this kind of extrasensory bombshell.

I grab my coat, gloves, and cap—finally, after so much waiting—slip the secondhand rubber galoshes over my shoes, and run out the back door. I'm not waiting for anyone.

Being in it is almost more than I can take. Every sensation is new. I'm overwhelmed. The sound it makes when you step on it. The way it muffles every sound around you, large and small. The way it feels underfoot. The very feel of it, on your bare hands. Its coldness, its wetness. The taste of it. The way everything is transformed by it, purified, redeemed. It clings to everything. It's the ultimate mercy. I make my first snowball and throw it against the side of the garage. *Splat*. Oh, man. *Splat*. How, how sweet. I run out to the street, making sure that I don't mess up the snow too much. It's so unforgiving. All you have to do is touch it, and you scar it. I listen to the sound the cars make as they roll over it. Our street hasn't been plowed, so the cars just squish it, with the most muffled sort of low roar. A car with chains on its tires. Holy God. Chains. And what a heavenly sound they make: *whirr, clank, whirr, clank* . . .

Tony and my two cousins come out. We throw snowballs at one another.

For this, and this alone, I was born.

A few days before Christmas Eve, Reverend Nordquist drives us up to Chicago with his son and a friend of his. We go to the Adler Planetarium and the Museum of Science and Industry, and as we arrive in the city, it starts to snow. It's a wet snow, and it clings to everything and melts immediately on the roadways and sidewalks. Everything is white, gray, or black, save for the Christmas decorations, which are red, gold, and green, and all lit up. Lake Michigan is gray and white too, and partly frozen. This city is even more impressive up close, at street level, and so incredibly huge. It makes Havana and Miami feel like small towns, or like Bloomington, come to think of it. Riding back through the Corn Belt at night, with the moon shining on the snow covered fields, so flat, seems like a dream within a dream. I pinch myself, and laugh, quietly.

Christmas Eve. We've had three snowfalls, so we have snow on the ground tonight, and plenty of it. It snowed a lot about five days ago, and everything is Christmas card perfect. But it's starting to warm up. What's this cruel last-minute twist? Isn't nighttime supposed to be colder? We go to a Christmas party sponsored by the Americanization program. It's in some basement in downtown Bloomington, near Montgomery Ward. I flash back to last year, same day, same hour, exactly. In my mind's eye I see the trees on Coral Way. No angelic trees here. But I can see snow, just outside these basement windows. No presents here, just a party, with some clown dressed as Santa Claus, telling the little kids about his sleigh outside and Rudolph's red nose, in a very thick German accent.

Holy crap.

We don't have a Christmas tree at home. Can't afford one, much less the decorations. So we do without. This party room has a Christmas tree, though, and it's a nice one. I don't hate it at all. As a matter of fact, I find it damn nice. I secretly revere it, as the idolater in me awakens once again.

Aunt Alejandra has a very bad migraine, so she's not with us. She's stayed at home, flattened by the pain. The Americanization Germans feel bad about this and decide to bring her some Christmas cheer. So, when they drive us back home, in a small caravan, they all get out of their cars and start caroling in the driveway. Three or four songs, at full blast, right under her second-story window. The snow around us is melting fast. *Drip, drip, drip* goes the snow on the roof. *Slish slosh* goes the snow underfoot. *"Alle zusammen,"* says one of the Germans.

"Angels, ve haf heardt on high . . .

"Silent night, holy night . . .

"Hark! Ze heraldt angels sing . . ."

Germans singing Christmas carols in English to a Cuban who speaks nothing but Spanish and has a blinding migraine, as the snow melts in the Corn Belt, under a starry sky.

Then, a sudden switch to a tongue that I fall in love with, instantly.

> *O Tannenbaum, O Tannenbaum*
> *wie treu sind deine Blätter!*
> *Du grünst nicht nur*
> *zur Sommerzeit,*
> *Nein auch im Winter, wenn es schneit.*
> *O Tannenbaum, o Tannenbaum,*
> *wie treu sind deine Blätter!*

Jesus H. God Incarnate Christ, can it get any better than this? Maybe. How about more snow now, instead of this thaw?

Lots of it—here, now—before the singing stops.

Beyond Number

Does every chapter need a number?
   No.
Those that deal with happiness don't. They're above that.
Happiness includes all numbers. It's infinite and eternal.
This raises another question.
Can happiness ever be adequately described?
No.
So say the greatest mystics.
But you don't need anyone to tell you this, especially men and women who eat too little, never get drunk, and shun sex. You know this already.
When the ultimate goal is reached, words fail. They crash against the zenith of your expectations and fall to the ground mortally wounded by their own feelings of inadequacy.
Happiness is our ultimate goal, even though it often eludes us.
Oh, but it *can* be found, now and then.
Or, better to say that it can find you. Pursuing it is often futile. More often than not, you have to wait for it to show up.
But when it does show up, the poetry dries up.
Ask any poet. No angst, no poetry.
No unrequited love, no great poetry.
No absence, no need to say anything.
Presence makes you shut up.

Ay. But the pain caused by absence can feel so good because it's a symptom of love.

Is there any pain more exquisite than that which is caused by the realization that what you desire most deeply will always be absent and totally beyond your grasp?

Is there any ecstasy higher than that which is caused by the sudden and unexpected presence of what you desire most deeply?

Is there any blessing more mixed than accepting any such ecstasy as fleeting? Or anything more painful and joyful than accepting its evanescence?

Where's the boundary between pain and ecstasy when you realize that what is fleeting is also somehow eternal? That no matter how fleeting it seems, this presence has always been and always will be? That it will never be yours to keep, but that you will feel its absence and ache for it forever?

Is there any pain or any ecstasy more divine than acknowledging that you can never, ever hope to hold on to what every fiber of your being tells you is the very purpose of your existence, the sole reason for your coming into being in the first place?

No.

Letting go is the ultimate happiness, and the ultimate pain.

I can't let go. No way. Not here in Bloomington. My attachment to this place runs deep. But, damn it, I have this book I carry around that tells me that I should let go of everything and everyone, including myself. It's the book my parents gave me when I left home, *The Imitation of Christ.* An awful book, really. They don't come much worse than this one. It scares me to death, every time I try to read it.

Let go of everything, says the book.

But everything in my life right now is everything I've always wanted. I know it can't stay this way forever, but all I have is now, and now is as good as it has ever been or may ever be. I was born to be here and to live this life.

To someone else it could seem like a hard life, but to me it's just perfect. I love everything about it, even the most painful things. By now I've figured out that pain can be a good thing—a blessing—if you accept it when it's inevitable. No pain, no joy.

I know nothing about yin and yang, or the coincidence of opposites, or Nietzsche's Law about what doesn't kill me makes me stronger, but I do know this: I've developed a fondness for pain, especially the kind that helps you realize that you're capable of doing all sorts of things that should be impossible for you.

I'm attached to my perfect pain and perfect joy, which are inseparable.

At age thirteen, I have an infinite list of perfect things I love being attached to, and want to stay attached to forever. Perfection, infinity, and eternity are as inseparable from one another as truth, beauty, and goodness, and the three persons in the Holy Trinity, after all.

I didn't go to Catholic school for nothing, for so many years, back in that hellhole in which I was born. I know a few things about theology.

My infinite list has no beginning and no end, and no rankings. Here's but an infinitesimally tiny slice of this list, the items chosen at random.

Secondhand clothes from Goodwill and the Salvation Army.

The toaster at the breakfast nook window.

The ten-cent loaves of bread at the A&P, which you buy with your own hard-earned cash and no one else in the house can touch.

Toasting up an entire loaf and eating it in one sitting.

MAD magazine.

Snow falling at night.

Freezing rain at night.

Seeing what freezing rain can do when you wake up in the morning and the world is entirely glazed, even each pine needle and blade of grass.

Sledding down a steep, snow-packed brick street recently glazed by freezing rain.

Missing a fast-moving car by just a few inches at the bottom of the hill.

Mr. Henker torturing you in gym class, calling you and everybody else "girls" all the time, stepping on your stomach as you're doing sit-ups or on your back when you're doing push-ups.

Swimming right after lunch.

The long pole with a hook at the end that hangs on the wall at the pool.

Mr. Henker holding this hook in front of the diving board, making you jump over it, raising it higher and higher each time.

Getting naked in front of thirty other guys, day in and day out, and not minding it.

The way some guys' gym lockers smell.

Delivering newspapers after school and on Saturday and Sunday mornings, especially when the temperature falls below zero.

Wearing long underwear.

Feeling your breath turn into ice on your woolen ski mask at fifteen below zero.

Folding the newspapers into squares and launching them like flying saucers onto porches.

Breaking windows with misfired folded-up newspapers.

Having newspapers swerve upward unexpectedly and land on the roof.

Hearing an old man who is sitting on his porch say *"Huuumpf"* when you hit him squarely over his heart with a misfired, folded-up newspaper.

Practicing your hillbilly English pronunciation as you deliver newspapers, and having customers catch you in the act of talking to yourself.

Learning that some of your customers call you "that strange boy."

Receiving complaints from customers who don't get their newspaper, or often find it on the roof or other odd places.

Taunting the mean barking dog that's always chained up.

Being chased by the mean barking dog that's broken loose from its chain.

Trying to collect the weekly subscription fee for the newspapers from your customers, and having them pay you with pennies, or not at all.

Having to fork over part of your earnings to the newspaper when you fail to collect from all of your customers.

Talking to cousin Alejandrita.

Watching cousin Marisol cut out coupons from newspapers and magazines.

Washing and waxing Uncle Amado's green-and-white 1958 Ford Custom two-door sedan, which he bought with the three hundred dollars he saved up by using coupons at the supermarket.

Having no telephone at home.

Walking four blocks to the nearest pay phone.

Saying hello to the scruffy old men who live at the transient hotel where this pay phone can be found.

Going to the movies every single week, either at the Castle or the Irving theater, both of which are only a few blocks from your house.

Seeing *Lawrence of Arabia* at the Irving theater with your entire family.

Seeing *Dr. No* and *Goldfinger* at the Irving theater with your brother.

Receiving only one channel on your ancient black-and-white television set.

Riding a bicycle with big fat tires that's older than your television set, has no gears at all, and is very heavy and hard to pedal up any incline.

Shoveling snow after a blizzard.

Jumping into snowdrifts.

Snowball fights.

Getting hit with an icy slush ball on an already nearly frozen ear.

Hitting your older brother squarely in the face with a tightly packed snowball.

Doing your own laundry at home in an ancient washing machine that requires you to put every single item through a wringer.

Watching your underwear go through the wringer.

Hanging your clothes on the lines that are strung in the perfect but drafty and unheated study with the stained glass ceiling light.

Contemplating the dragonflies on the ceiling light through your own condensed breath.

Ironing your own clothes.

Discovering that your cousins will do your ironing if you pay them five cents per item.

Being told by the nun at Sunday school that doing your laundry on Sunday is a mortal sin, no matter what the circumstances.

Riding your bicycle on a recently frozen lake, at Miller Park.

Hearing the sound of the ice as it cracks right under you.

Catching one hundred and fifty sunfish in a single summer day at Miller Park with your friend Eddie, and throwing all of the fish back into the lake.

Catching crayfish with nets in the creek behind your friend Gary's house.

Calling the crayfish "crawdads."

Falling into the deepest part of the creek and having to ride your bike home for five miles, totally soaked, in nearly freezing temperatures.

Making your own skateboard with a piece of scrap wood and old metal skates from the Salvation Army store.

Finding out that your homemade skateboard can't go in a straight line, even on the steepest hills, despite the nice straight green lines that you painted on its surface.

Falling and scraping your kneecap right down to the bone.

Girls with perfect features.

Absolutely perfect Peggy, in Mr. Noden's class.

All the other perfect girls whose names you don't know.

Falling deeply in love with a girl who has the most perfect eyes in the whole school, maybe the whole world, and a perfect sense of humor.

Thinking that she likes you back, maybe.

Spending a perfect afternoon with her, during which she touches your shoulder.

Never again wearing the shirt you wore on that day when she touched you because it's now a holy relic.

Vowing to remember the month, day, and year when this girl touched you, along with the time of day, 3:17 in the afternoon, and the temperature, seventy-two degrees Fahrenheit.

Realizing that you have no chance with her because you and your family are so poor.

Letting go of those perfect eyes and the girl to whom they belong.

Knowing that your brother is a carhop at the Steak 'n Shake in Normal, the very first Steak 'n Shake ever, the mother of all Steak 'n Shakes.

Knowing that your brother rides his bike to Normal every afternoon after school, and then rides home at midnight or one in the morning, no matter what the weather is, spring, summer, fall, or winter, even when it's below zero.

Knowing that your brother makes good money, especially in tips.

Knowing that your brother has taken a second part-time job at Casella's Italian Restaurant, where the tips are even better.

Seeing your first Ford Mustang ever on the day when Gary's family takes you skeet shooting out in the countryside.

Shooting at clay pigeons as they arc over a cornfield.

Feeling the kick of the shotgun on your shoulder when you fire it.

Missing the target.

Hitting the target.

Writing a letter to your parents every Thursday, in which you give them a detailed account of everything you've done, seen, heard, and felt.

Knowing that you'll never see your parents again.

Being visited by second or third cousins of your own cousins, from out of town.

Watching one of those cousins of your cousins—no blood relation to you—suddenly go into a trance at dinner and be possessed by the spirit of a long-dead German woman, who speaks through her in Spanish, with a thick German accent.

Hearing all sorts of prophecies issue from the mouth of this possessed woman, none of which pertain to you or your brother.

Feeling relieved that the dead German left you alone.

Watching stupid girls on television scream their lungs out at these four English guys who wear identical suits and call themselves the Beatles.

Seeing these other English guys on television who call themselves the Rolling Stones and remind you very much of the Three Thugs with whom you used to live.

Walking to the public library with and without your brother, and checking out books.

Paying fines for overdue books at the library, again and again.

Looking at the icon of Corn Belt Jesus that hangs above your uncle's chair and being strangely comforted by its presence.

Never going to confession, never examining your conscience or taking stock of your sins, one by one, or of their frequency or the circumstances in which you commit them.

Walking about two miles to church every Sunday morning with your brother.

Suffering through yet another unbearably long Good Friday ritual, and puzzling over all of the little foxes that are draped over the shoulders of little old ladies.

Noticing that many of the dead little foxes are biting their own tails.

Walking out of church on Easter Sunday into a snowstorm, and hearing everyone complain about it.

Being attacked by the Void time and time again.

Landing a few punches that make the Void reel.

Picking up that awful book of yours more and more often—that dismal *Imitation of Christ*—and finding it less and less frightening.

Thinking that this strange book that you've hated for so long may not be so bad or so crazy after all.

Thinking that what's really scary is not the book, but the world around you, not because your life is bad, but precisely because your life is so good and everything you hold dear could be gone in an instant, including that toaster that you use so much, and the table on which it sits, and the house in which you find yourself, and the people in it.

Thinking that attachment to this world might be your biggest problem, aside from the Void.

Suspecting that you might be able to knock out the Void more often if you let go of all of your attachments.

Suspecting that you're a total idiot.

Hoping that maybe you're not.

Hoping that you've got some time to figure out whether you are or aren't.

Dreaming of the girl with the blue eyes, often.

Never, ever dreaming of those you once loved the most.

Twenty-two

The car did it.

That green-and-white 1958 Ford Custom two-door sedan that Uncle Amado bought for three hundred dollars with money saved through grocery store coupons has changed my life unexpectedly.

It has unleashed the Void.

Suddenly, Amado and his wife and daughters can go places. Which means that I often come home to an empty house, because they love to do everything together, even if it's only a trip to the A&P for a dozen eggs.

And when I come home to an empty house, the Void pounces on me immediately.

I try fighting it off, but it always gets the best of me. Telling it that the house will be swarming with people soon doesn't distract it. Nothing does. When I walk through the door and find myself alone in the house, all of my defenses against Absolute Absence evaporate instantly.

Pow. I'm knocked out in a flash.

Instant replay, each and every time. It's an endless emotional and spiritual loop, an eternal Now moment of the sort no one wants to have. Absolute Absence, absolute pain.

One evening is different, however; worse than any other. I come home from Eddie's house and no one is home. It's wintertime, so it's already dark at five in the afternoon. Tony is at work, as always. Every-one else has simply disappeared.

So I go back to Eddie's house and pretend that I don't have a key and can't get into my house. There's no way in hell I can tell Eddie and his parents the full awful truth: I need to have people around me in order to stay sane.

I spend the next three hours going back and forth between Eddie's house and mine, getting more and more desperate with each passing minute, and each futile trek. Finally, on one of my sorties, as I'm reach-ing what I think is the end of my rope, I see some lights on in the house as I approach it from the alley.

Saved. Thank God.

But the same thing keeps happening. I come home to an empty house and I'm toast. And every time it happens, the Void has an ever greater effect on me. Pretty soon I'll be burned to a crisp, or worse. I'll be noth-ing but carbon atoms dispersing in all directions in the vacuum of space at the speed of light.

There has to be some way to beat this. But how?

The idolater in me, the superstitious troglodyte, whispers: "Pssst. How about that book that's supposed to have an answer for every ques-tion. The one your derelict parents forced you to bring along?"

Yeah, sure. All previous attempts to obtain divine guidance from that chamber of horrors had been irredeemable failures. That book was nothing but a source of fright and despair.

But my pain is so great, I'll try just about anything. Even this supersti-tious game, which, as experience has taught me time and time again, is not only futile, but always to be regretted.

So I open *The Imitation of Christ* at random, and my eyes spot this pas-sage: "Be prepared for the fight, then, if you wish to gain the victory . . . If you desire to be crowned, fight bravely and bear up patiently. Without labor there is no rest, and without fighting, no victory."

I'm astonished. For the first time ever, this book is speaking to me, and what it says makes sense. This has to be a fluke.

So I put the wretched text to the test again. I flip the pages back and forth, back and forth, and settle on a spot toward the back of the book.

Another passage that makes sense. No way. This, too, is mere coincidence. One more time. I flip the pages back and forth and find yet another text that speaks to me. This is too weird. Maybe there's something to this book, after all. Maybe? Just maybe?

Slightly unnerved by this thought, I put the book away, determined not to pick it up again anytime soon.

And the next thing I know I'm not just opening it at random, but reading it from front to back, little by little. The more sense it makes, the more I read and the more confused I get. What's wrong with me? This is crazy. Maybe I'm crazy? How can everything I've feared for so long now seem incredibly sweet, and so much like the key that unlocks all of the secrets of the universe? Nothing like this has ever happened to me before. Not even close to it. Nothing has flipped on me so completely as this book.

Things are what they are. What you see is what you get. Pain is pain. Evil is evil. Ugliness is ugliness. An iguana is an ugly-ass lizard, perhaps even a proof that God can't exist, or that if he does, then he's far from all Good. An iguana can't suddenly turn into Marilyn Monroe or Perfect Peggy in Mr. Noden's class.

Then how is it that this awful book has pulled this trick on me? Since when do self-denial, abject humility, self-emptying, devotion to a crucified God, and detachment from the world equal happiness? Since when does abstinence gain you anything but frustration?

I read the book gingerly at first, much like someone on the bomb squad might handle an explosive device. But before long I am deeply immersed in it, nodding in agreement even with the most repulsive of passages, which ask me to embrace suffering and to hanker for a cross like those of Jesus and Spartacus.

No way.

Years from now I'll read about Buddhist monks who are brought to sudden enlightenment when they're struck on the back of the head with a plank by their more advanced elders, as they meditate on illogical propositions. And I'll know what that blow to the head must feel like, more or less. I had no elder to whack me, but I did have a book that did exactly the same thing.

Everything changes, from top to bottom. A veil rips, loudly, and light pours through, and nothing looks the same. For the first time in my life I feel as if I'm master of my own destiny, not because I think more highly of myself, but just the opposite: Accepting my own limitations is key. So is accepting it as an unquestionable fact that some higher power is eager to help me overcome whatever the world throws at me, both from without and within.

It's close to Easter. My mind is reeling and so are my heart and my will. I'm in Bizarro World now, where everything is the opposite of what it should be. I'm no longer who I was two months before, and neither is the world itself.

Jagged is smooth. Bitter is sweet. Sorrow is joy. Dark is light. Black is white.

The unseen illumines what's seen.

Absurdity rescues logic.

Love of self leads to anguish.

Self-loathing leads to elation.

Abstinence becomes the highest thrill of all.

Praying becomes the only conversation that makes sense.

Believing becomes as natural and unstoppable as breathing.

Doubting becomes as unsurprising as exhaling.

Forgiving becomes the only sensible option.

Temptation drops its mask.

Remorse claims its crown.

Loss loses its sting.

Pain gains its wings.

Now becomes forever. Forever begins now, forever.

Slowly, ever so haltingly, I catch fleeting glimpses of Something so awesome that Carlos, Charles, Charlie, and Chuck all feel compelled to bow before It, thank It, and trust It without reservation. This response is a physical reflex, not just a spiritual one. Bowing, kneeling, prostrating oneself is as involuntary before It as closing one's eyes to the full light of the sun.

Holy Thursday. I come home, and the house is empty. I stare at Corn Belt Jesus, hanging there, above my uncle's empty chair. It's late afternoon, and the fast-sinking sun is shining through the dining room windows. It's a weird sort of light, for there are dark clouds out there, closing in on the sun, ominously. The kind of clouds that usually prompt tornado warnings.

The fear I've had for so long about being alone rises in me, in a savage rush. I feel the Void about to pounce. I know its ways all too well and can sense it approaching, faster than the speed of light.

"Dukes up."

Before I can do anything, in a flash, a Presence fills the room, and expands it to the size of the entire universe. Light streams in. The Void crashes into this Presence, and evaporates, instantly, in the blinding glow. The force of the impact throws me off balance, physically, and hurls me to the ground, on my knees, right there, by my uncle's chair, under Protestant Jesus, sweet Midwestern Christ, ever so human and infinite and present. As I gaze at him, the goddamned Void hisses and spits and sputters and vanishes.

This is no mere knockout, I think. This is some sort of annihilation. Way to go.

It will take me several years to figure out what happened there, in that living room. But I know for sure, as I rise from the floor, that I've just died again and that nothing can ever be the same. I also know that this new life will be much better than any of those that preceded it. Not because it'll be less painful from now on, but because the pain will make perfect sense, and even seem like a beautiful gift from that Presence I felt today, for the first time.

Good Friday. It's good, really good. Really, really. For the first time ever.

Easter Sunday. Now, finally, I understand what Easter is. *Resurrection* was an empty word before. Now it makes all the awful things—even the very worst, such as each and every crucifix—look bright.

I no longer need to fear Absence again, or so I think. But I have a lot to learn, yet.

Flash forward, two years, exactly. Spring 1967. I'm now living in Chicago, with my mother and Tony.

I've spent the past two months rereading *The Imitation of Christ*, slowly, methodically absorbing everything it has to say. Whatever effect that book had on me the first time around seems like a surface scratch on my soul compared to the nearly total immolation that's taken place this time. I'm on fire. It's not just because I'm older and have more deaths and rebirths behind me, but also because this time around, I've followed the book's instructions carefully and read the four gospels in the New Testament too. I've gone straight to the source, and what I've found there has blown me away. I'd been hearing snippets every week at church since infancy, but I'd never paid too much attention to those texts and their power. Not even after I first saw the light two years before.

If you're going to imitate someone, especially a Savior, you should at least read the few sacred texts in which his words and deeds are recorded.

Now, everything changes, again. Whatever I knew has been eclipsed, overpowered by a much brighter light, much like a tiny candle in a room that is suddenly filled with brilliant sunshine. And that metaphor doesn't even begin to cover the change that's taken place in me. Words fail. Every metaphor fails. If nothing like this has ever happened to you, no amount of explaining will help. It's a lot like trying to describe colors to a blind person. Try explaining green, in all its shades. And all the other colors too. Good luck.

If you've ever fallen deeply in love with anyone, however, you may be able to understand. How does one put *that* into words? Poets have been failing at it since the dawn of time.

And my great good fortune this Lenten season is that I'm falling in love in two ways at once: with a higher Presence who demands total surrender, and with the girl who sits right next to me in history class, who demands nothing but my constant and total enthrallment. The gospel burns me, incinerates me. This blond girl does the same, but not so totally. She can't. My bad luck is that these two kinds of love don't mix too well, especially when the girl's a senior and you're nothing but a sophomore, and you see her for only forty minutes, five days a week, in the tightly controlled environment of history class.

As I see it, the gulf between me and God is much narrower than the one that exists between me and this perfect girl, even though she sits less than two feet away from me.

So I do all I can do, given the circumstances. I yield totally to both kinds of love, and hope for the best. And in both dimensions, I'm on fire like Moses's burning bush—always aflame, but never consumed.

My daily life changes most radically in the spiritual dimension, where my contact with higher things is not limited to forty minutes five days a week. I start to attend Mass every morning before school, and I pray constantly whenever I can, filling every minute, every second, with a certain kind of mental conversation that Doctor Freud and most of his disciples would diagnose as pathological, delusional obsessive-compulsiveness of the worst sort, but that Doctor Jung and other experts would not. I also embrace fasting during Lent with all of the discipline of an Olympic athlete, and once Lent is over, I find it impossible to let go of that kind of letting go. The more I relinquish my will, the easier it becomes to tame it, the greater the peace I feel. I vow total surrender.

Ay. This surrender is harder than I thought. Giving up food and drink is one thing. But giving up the way this girl Christine makes me feel is impossible, despite the searing holy pain that comes with it. She is so beautiful, and so smart, and so, so funny, so . . . so . . . so everything. Name it: If it's something good, she's got it in spades. If only she weren't two whole grades ahead of me, I might have a chance to spend time with her outside of class.

Yeah, sure. Dream on.

I have no chance with her, I know, but I surrender to her all the same inside, and I ride the huge tsunami that's sweeping me away in the spiritual dimension. What's the use of opening up to her, of trying to spend more time with her? I really should let go. I should be a monk. Yes, definitely. Or maybe a priest.

I've got to sort out this dilemma.

So I talk to my pastor, Monsignor Picard. I tell him I'm torn between God and this girl. He advises me to enroll in Quigley Seminary, a high school run by the Archdiocese of Chicago in which boys my age are fast-tracked into the priesthood. He writes down the address on a piece of paper and gives it to me, much as a doctor hands a prescription to a patient.

"Go there as soon as you can," he says.

I carry this prescription with me on the subway all the way to the gates of the seminary, which happens to be wedged against Chicago's nightclub district, Rush Street. I stand at the gates and peer into the courtyard. Pure, heavenly gothic. Every detail directs your attention upward and inward and beyond. I look at the piece of paper in my hand, at the perfectly symmetrical stone tracery of the rose window, the large doors, the soot and grime that have settled on the imposing facade, the spires, the skyscrapers that surround it and dwarf it, and my hands begin to tremble. Then my whole body feels as if it's being squashed from above, below, and all sides, like a grape in a winepress. An overwhelming feeling I can't recognize surges from somewhere inside of me, and takes over.

It's not fear. It's not indecision. It's a certainty I've never had before, ever. It's as if an invisible hand is pushing me away, a silent booming voice is telling me to scram. *This is not for you. This isn't your calling. Go home, go back to Senn High School. There are other paths. Wait.*

So I run away, literally, back to the subway, as if I'm fleeing a raging fire or an avalanche, and I head back north to my unholy neighborhood, Edgewater, where I belong.

It's in history class, sitting next to Christine, that I will find my path. Gradually, it becomes clear to me as the days lengthen, the air warms up, the trees begin to bud, and Christine becomes ever lovelier, that I need to be a historian and a teacher, and that my focus should be the history of my own religion. That's why I'm on earth. Nothing anyone will say to me during the next ten years will dissuade me from following that path I see stretching before me, so nice and narrow and straight.

As for my path toward Christine, well, it's also very clear, unfortunately. Dead end. She graduates, at the summit of her class. College bound. I have two more years of high school ahead of me. That's it. *Adios.*

All I can do is savor each and every day and repeat my mantra: Let go. Let go. Let go.

When that awful last day comes around, I wrangle a ticket to the graduation ceremony and say good-bye, good luck. And so does she. We go our separate ways. Oddly, though, her absence only intensifies the feelings I have for her, and I'm mystified by this. How can it be so impossible to let go of someone who isn't there at all?

Years later, St. John of the Cross will explain it all to me in his poems.

I'll run into Christine three times after graduation, purely by chance. And every time this happens I will have had an uncanny premonition before it happens. To be honest, calling the certainty I felt a *premonition* is not to do justice to this intuition—something akin to calling Buckingham Palace a *house,* or a miracle a *coincidence.* Each of those encounters and our conversations leave me totally elated and baffled and paralyzed. It's all much too otherworldly.

I let go without ever really letting go.

She goes away. Several months pass. I have no more premonitions. Then, one day in late May 1968, as the end of my junior year approaches, I read a *Chicago Tribune* headline on a newsstand, on my way to school, which has no impact on me whatsoever: "Chicago Co-ed Slain." "Another piece of bad news," I say to myself. What else is new?

The instant I walk through the front door of my school, I sense something is wrong. The usual din and overflowing energy of the entrance foyer is missing, replaced by hushed murmuring and some sobbing. Everyone's moving in slow motion. No need to ask why. A friend breaks the news to me immediately: The murdered co-ed in the headline is none other than Christine. Stabbed to death on a lovely spring morning at an idyllic Midwestern college campus, her bloody corpse tossed behind some bushes, like a crumpled, mangled mannequin. Jesus H. Nailed and Speared Christ. A vast crevice opens in the fabric of space and time and it swallows me whole, instantly. My body falls back and hits the wall behind it. It knows that a wall's holding it up, but the wall isn't really there and neither am I or anyone else around me.

Fade to black. Pitch black.

Blessed Vault of Oblivion, highest gift from the highest heaven, how lovely you are. Please don't ever let that day out, or any of the others that immediately followed. I remember nothing past that point, up until the funeral. *Whoa.* What kind of cruel joke is this? *No me jodas.* The casket is a gross insult, as is the stupid organ music, and the putrid flowers, and the muffled sobbing, and the insipid words and prayers uttered in that offensive funeral home on Ashland Avenue. And these acrid, insufferable insults wake me up, much like smelling salts.

No! my soul screams upon awakening.

Idiot that I am, I'll finally see the big picture I couldn't see while Christine was alive, when her sister tells me, in a hushed tone, there, at that funeral: "You know, she really loved you; she really did."

Letting go acquires a whole new meaning that day, as do God and the universe itself, and the Void. Major surprise, major adjustment in attitude, but not in daily routine. No way. Mass every morning; unceasing prayer all day and night. Sometimes I fall asleep on my knees and that's how my mother finds me in the morning, at the foot of my sofa bed. No change in course, either: My path is still as straight and narrow and clearly illuminated as before. It just happens to have this peculiar dip that can't be fathomed.

I see crucifixes in a whole different light after that day, and I appreciate them all the more, especially the five wounds. And I stick to my quest, the one I vowed to pursue while sitting right next to Christine in history class. Life goes on; the world spins without her in it. I meet a girl who seems to be a soul mate, and we pair up. Love of a different sort takes over me—the kind that requires constant compromises and awkward moments and an untold number of arguments. I go to college, major in history and religion, get married to that girl, and then set out to earn a doctorate in history and religion.

And sometime in 1978, about ten years after Christine's murder, my path seems to come to an abrupt dead end. *Whoa.* Nothing but tangled brush and a dark heavy jungle ahead. And this choking nightmare forest envelops me, quickly swallowing up the brightly lit path I followed, which dead-ended as painfully as my time with Christine. All around, everywhere I look, there's nothing but a stinking, vine-strangled jungle on all sides, and I have no compass to follow or sharp-edged tools with which to clear it. I can't find a teaching job. My marriage falls apart. I lose interest in everything I'd once loved, including history. I've stopped praying. No one to talk to anymore, as I see it. No Presence. Just more sucker punches from the Void, now and then. And when I finally do find a job, it's at the edge of the world, in Nowhere, Minnesota.

All I have left to like is long-distance running, and I take that up with the same passion I had once reserved for prayer. I run therefore I am.

Flash forward, June 1980. I'm now twice as old as I was when I came home on that Holy Thursday back in 1965. I've been teaching in Nowhere and frequenting the Buckhorn Bar far too often. I've given up on letting go. Forget it. Evanescent beauty is all I seek, for that's all that cheers me and all I'm certain of.

Soul mate, schmoul mate. Sure. Dream on. There's no such thing. A path? Maybe for some, but not for me. God? Yeah, sure. He definitely exists. But only on my terms.

I'm in Paris, traveling alone, living like a bum. I don't have a hotel at which to stay tonight, but I couldn't care less. It's a sunny day in June, and Paris is as heartbreakingly full of itself as when it's gray and cold and damp. The weather never makes a difference here. Nothing makes a difference. Paris is what it is. Too much.

Way too much.

I'm sitting on the ground, my back against a tree. I'm in the Square du Vert-Galant, a small park at the western tip of the Île de la Cité, which looks and feels just like the prow of a ship. The Seine River flows at my right and my left and meets up to form one stream directly ahead of me as it runs undivided under the Pont des Arts. I've been writing letters and postcards for hours, drawing pictures in them and taking in the scenery, reflecting on how strange it is that this place I've never visited before should feel so much like home, more so than any other spot on earth. I feel rooted, for the very first time in ages, and more firmly anchored to this tiny island, here, than I ever felt to that large lizard-shaped island where I was born.

I suspect my late father, Louis XVI, has something to do with this.

I feel tendrils extending from the core of my soul, growing, burrowing into the soil beneath me, swiftly and doggedly branching out in all directions, reaching down, down, to the core of the earth itself. I don't ever want to leave, and I vow to stay put. To hell with that teaching job in Minnesota. I'll work as a street sweeper here, if I have to.

Yet, I don't know a soul in this city, and the locals stubbornly refuse to understand the way I speak their language. If the Void really wanted to do me in, it could do it right here, in this strange place where I'm more alone than I've ever been. It could drive me mad with Absence, push me into the Seine and drown me, as it's done with many a forlorn lover.

"Come and get me," I whisper, in English. "I dare you."

Nothing.

The air is perfectly still. The harmonious din of Paris reverberates down here, so near the water. It's as if all of the sound waves tumble down to this spot because they feel as much at home here as I do. I try to detect the presence of my dead father, the onetime decapitated King of France, who may or may not have enjoyed being in Paris again. He's not here. Absent, as always, despite his profound influence.

"Dukes up, bitch," I whisper again. "I double dare you."

Nothing.

Instead, the Presence that first banished the Void from my life years ago quietly begins to snip away all the tendrils that had just sprung from the core of my soul. Silently, wordlessly, It severs each and every one of these fast-growing roots and forces me to stand up and walk away.

Snip, snip, snip. I hear no voices, I see no apparitions, but I know that It is everywhere and has always been and will always be, especially in that spot deep within me that had tried to root itself in this one place. How I know this, I don't know. But I'm as certain of this Presence and Its boundlessness and Its nearness as I am of the fact that I'm right smack in the middle of Paris, walking up the steps to the Pont Neuf, headed for the locker at the train station where I've crammed my duffel bag.

It doesn't need to speak at all. It doesn't have to say *let go*. I already know this, just as I know that the Void will stalk me for life, but never prevail. I reach for a passage I first read a long time ago in a certain book, which is etched somewhere in my memory.

With my third eye I search for that text in my Vault of Remembering. I see Louis XVI and Marie Antoinette. They hand me a small brown book engulfed in flames, then hurl me across a turquoise sea to a strange and wondrous land, as they cry a river of tears wider and deeper and murkier than the Seine. I open the burning book at random and read the text in question, which, curiously, is no longer in Spanish:

"He who knows best how to let go will enjoy the greater peace, because he is the conqueror of himself, the master of the world, and an heir of heaven."

The flames from this passage leap up and scorch all the stubble left behind by the severed tendrils. The light is blinding. The fumes are sublime. And the pain is absolutely exquisite.

Heavenly.

Twenty-three

M y mother, Marie Antoinette, is in Rome, at the Vatican. It's 1984, and she's traveling with a large group of her Cuban friends from Chicago. The end point of her tour will be Madrid, where I've been living for the past eight months with my lovely wife, Jane. She's going to spend several weeks with us, once she's done with this European tour, which she's managed to finagle from a travel agency free of charge to herself because of the high number of other travelers she roped into joining her.

His Holiness John Paul II is out and about, on foot, in some corner of the Vatican, despite the attempt on his life by some Turk that the Kremlin hired to kill him.

As divine providence would have it, my mother and her tour group cross paths with His Holiness.

"*Papito, Papito,*" she yells, at the top of her lungs, which is about three times louder than the average human being can manage to scream.

Hard to translate. "Little pope, little pope" comes close, but doesn't really do it justice. It's at once a term of endearment, in a spiritual sense, but also highly irreverent, as far as papal protocol is concerned. English has no such suffix for a term of endearment. Stiff upper lip and all that. You know.

"*Papito, Papito, por favor reza por Cuba,*" she shouts, again and again. Please, dear little Pope, pray for Cuba.

His Holiness stops dead in his tracks, turns around, and finds the crazed woman who keeps calling him *Papito*.

He speaks to her in perfect Spanish. "Are you Cuban? What are you doing here? How did you get out?"

She tells him that she left Cuba a long time ago and is now living in the United States, and that her homeland needs his prayers.

In perfect Spanish, as he holds her hands, he tells her he prays for Cuba every day.

She plants several kisses on his cheek, leaving it smeared in bright red lipstick. None of her friends snaps a photo of this earth-shaking event.

Too bad. This moment sums up her life.

Marie Antoinette, my mom. Maria Azucena Eiré Gonzalez. Conceived somewhere between La Coruña, Spain, and Havana, Cuba, on a transatlantic ship. Her parents eloped because they came from different social classes and no one in the Old World would allow them to get married. Her very existence was always an affront to propriety and the status quo, to everyone else's notion of what was supposed to happen.

Told she would never be able to walk after being stricken with polio, she proved everyone wrong. Told she would have to wear metal braces after she dared to prove everyone wrong, she shirked the braces and made do with a simple cane instead. It wouldn't be until she was in her sixties that she had to resort to two canes. Told she would never wed because of her crippled leg, she found herself an eccentric judge to marry. And she carried two pregnancies to full term despite her frequent falls, some of which were pretty serious.

God only knows how many times I banged my head against the ground, really hard, before I was born, or what I might have made of my life without those prenatal bruises.

Her resolve and self-confidence knew no bounds, and neither did her desire to prove everyone wrong, even when it came to learning English. She never, ever learned more than a few words and phrases, all horribly mangled in the thickest Spanish accent ever heard in any English-speaking land. Why should she learn it? She wasn't going to stay in the United States. No way. She was no immigrant, but a refugee, waiting for Castrolandia to become Cuba again. Besides, why shouldn't all Americans learn *her* language?

LEARNING TO DIE IN MIAMI   269

Marie Antoinette never took no for an answer. She never accepted anything she thought was wrong or stupid either, such as learning English. So, when the exit door to Cuba was slammed shut in the fall of 1962, just a few days before she was about to leave, she never stopped trying to find another way out.

And she managed to do it, not once, but twice, only to be thwarted at the last minute. Sometime in 1963 she somehow gained an exit through Spain and actually got to the airport, thinking she had succeeded, only to find that the all-wise and compassionate Revolution had already given her seat to someone "more important." Months and months of scraping and bowing and going here and there, all reduced to a brusque rebuff, and a simple confirmation of her insignificance. "Try again," said the jerk at the airport, smirking, knowing that this was tantamount to saying "grow a new leg." Then sometime in 1964 she wrangled another bona-fide exit through Venezuela, only to have exactly the very same thing happen again at the airport. "Try again," said the compassionate Revolutionaries, smirking, as always.

Somewhere in there, between the first and second—and third—attempts she was attacked by a mob while waiting in line outside the Swiss embassy. Such harassment was routine. Those who wanted to leave were reviled as *gusanos*, or worms, and were fair game for the so-called Cuban people, *el pueblo cubano*. Reporting these mob attacks to the authorities was futile, even when you were injured. In fact, if you reported any such attack, you were just digging a deeper hole for yourself, for the mobs were directed by the authorities.

As Marie Antoinette struggled to leave, Louis XVI did nothing. Leaving was never part of his plan. His only plan was to stay put and guard our valuable inheritance.

"This can't last much longer," he said, year after year.

Anyone who applied for a visa or permission to leave the country had to surrender his job and all of his property. Men, especially, had a high price to pay, for they were forced to pay their "debt" to the Revolution by performing slave labor in the countryside for anywhere from three to six years before being allowed to leave.

For many, many years, no family could ever leave Cuba intact.

This makes it hard for me to judge my father harshly for betting on the collapse of the Revolution, rather than on an exit visa.

Sometime in early 1965, Marie Antoinette runs into someone who knows someone at the Mexican embassy, and she pounces on her, asking for that ultimate favor: an introduction. Once again, for the third time, it pans out. She obtains a visa and an exit permit. Fearing a repeat of the previous attempts, trying to buffer herself from disappointment, she approaches the airport with a healthy measure of skepticism. This time, the authorities allow her to take her seat. No one "more important" had to travel that day, apparently. She bids farewell to her husband of twenty years, her parents, her brother and sister, her husband's sister, boards the plane and actually manages to take off, at just about the same time that her youngest son's life is being radically changed by a certain book.

As has been the case since the early days of the Revolution, those who leave Cuba aren't allowed to take anything out of the country, save for a few changes of clothing. Marie Antoinette has a tiny suitcase, no money, and no clue how she's going to get to the United States once she reaches Mexico. Fortunately, she has a good childhood friend in Mexico City, Carmencita, who has agreed to house and feed her while she searches for a visa to the United States.

Lucky Marie Antoinette. She owes this good twist of fate to none other than Che Guevara. Back in 1959, in the earliest days of the Revolution, Carmencita's husband, a businessman, went to visit Che, the new treasury minister, full of fervor for the new changes that were taking place, like so many other Cubans.

"I want to invest in Cuba," he told Che. "I want to build up our industrial base, and make us less dependent on foreign investments. What are your plans? What new industries would you like to see developed?"

"*Carajo*, you can invest in anything you want," said Che. "But whatever you create will be taken from you. We're not going to allow any private enterprise."

So, while he still had a chance, Carmencita's husband took all of his money—with only a few weeks to spare—and fled to Mexico, where he invested it wisely and grew fabulously rich.

At the very same time Che spoke to him this way, Fidel Castro was strenuously denying that he or his so-called Revolution were communist. And the world believed him because the world's press was so easily and willingly duped. Who can resist the charm of cigar-chomping bearded revolutionaries who never shed their green fatigues, even after their Revolution has toppled the universally hated dictator and wiped out anyone who challenges them, including other bearded colleagues in green fatigues?

Good thing that my mom's friend's husband didn't have to rely on press reports.

Carmencita welcomes my mom to Mexico City, generously lodges her with some of her relatives in a fancy high-rise building near the Bosque de Chapultepec, and offers to help her get a visa to the United States.

In Bloomington, Tony and I get the news in a tersely worded telegram. We don't dare talk about this to each other. It's been three years since we left Cuba and neither one of us is sure that this is good news, though deep down we know that it is, sort of. Do we really need her? What about our life here in Bloomington? Better not to talk about it.

Our ambivalence is colossal.

Within days of her arrival in Mexico, Marie Antoinette begins to hemorrhage. At first it's blamed on the altitude, since Mexico City is one of the highest cities on earth, but as the bleeding intensifies there's no choice but to take her to a hospital emergency room. A hysterectomy seems to be the only solution. So she goes under the knife. And Carmencita pays for the surgery.

The loss of blood has been substantial, so transfusions are called for. Several pints of anonymously donated blood are pumped into Marie Antoinette's veins. What no one can see or even suspect—given that this is 1965—is that some of the blood is infected with hepatitis C. There aren't any tests for this virus, which will slowly destroy her liver and kill her forty years later.

As soon as she recovers from surgery, Marie Antoinette returns to the apartment she shares with Carmencita's relatives. It takes her a while to get back on her feet, physically and emotionally. Having to undergo an emergency hysterectomy is tough enough under the best of circumstances. When you've just landed penniless and alone in a foreign country it's a bit tougher. And when you're immediately hit by an earthquake, it's even harder.

It was the toilet that offered Marie Antoinette some clue as to why she was feeling so dizzy. Water was sloshing out of the toilet. Until she saw that, she thought the swaying and the noise were all in her head, yet another post-surgical dizzy spell.

She was already shaken in more ways than she could count, but she wasn't about to let any of these setbacks stand in her way. As soon as she could, she made her way to the American embassy and applied for a visa. Having two sons in the United States and being a political refugee put her on some sort of fast track.

Not too fast, though. It wouldn't be until September that she'd get to leave Mexico City. And during all that time, her friend Carmencita had to cover all of her expenses.

In the meantime, Tony and I are living life to the fullest in Bloomington. We have great friends and enjoy our lives as much as possible. Tony has a wild set of friends—they cut school often, and know how to have a good time, even out in the cornfields. My friends are far from wild, but we know how to have a good time too. At some point during this time, as my mom is in Mexico, Gary and I hear of a barn near his house that's supposed to be full of circus gear. We decide to see for ourselves whether this is true or not. Never mind that the barn is on private property. We find a way in by climbing up through a high window. What we find is otherworldly. The whole damn barn is filled with circus stuff all right. Dusty as hell in there, but so eerily beautiful. Wagons. Cages. Signs. A whole circus asleep, or in a coma. All of this equipment, hidden from the world, illuminated by the sharply angled, dust mote–filled shaft of light that streams from the window that we just jimmied open. Things that delight and transport you beyond the mundane, all stacked up, hidden in the dark, like a pharaoh's mummy within a pyramid, looking ghostly under tarpaulins, like the furniture in my aunt Carmela's house back in Havana. How much fun is buried in here? Who owns this? How much trouble will we get into if someone finds us in here? We climb back out, and I carry the images with me in a place of honor in the Vault of

Remembering, along with the number one song on the charts that week, "Satisfaction," by the Rolling Stones, which I never tire of hearing, again and again and again, even as an old geezer.

Hey, hey, hey. That's what I say.

Ambivalence about our mom? You bet. Ever more staggering as she gets closer and closer to us.

Sometime in September, as I'm starting ninth grade and riding on cloud nine, Marie Antoinette flies from Mexico City to Miami. Her plan is to find a job and a place where the three of us can live in Miami. But, as had often been the case in my mom's life, surprises of all sorts derail her plans.

Marie Antoinette arrives in Miami penniless, totally dependent on the kindness of friends and the Cuban Refugee Center, a federal welfare agency that hasn't been too busy lately. It's been three years, more or less, since Miami has taken in many Cuban refugees. When the doors in Cuba slammed shut in the fall of 1962, the flood had dwindled to a trickle. The only Cubans who made it to Miami during those three years were those who fled in boats and on rafts, or those lucky few who managed to leave via some other country, and somehow made their way there, such as my mom. This means that Miami has adjusted to a fixed number of Cubans, and it's relatively easy for all new arrivals to find work. Compared to 1961 and 1962, Miami is now a refugee paradise. Gone is the need to send all arriving Cubans as far from Miami as possible, to places such as Bloomington, Illinois.

As soon as Marie Antoinette sets foot in Miami, however, everything changes. Irony of ironies: The doors are once again opened in Cuba. Much to everyone's surprise, the United States and Castrolandia reach an agreement that allows for emigration from Cuba. The so-called Freedom Flights begin, which will eventually ferry a quarter of a million Cubans to the United States. And as this begins to unfold, in the euphoria and confusion caused by this sudden unbolting of the prison gates, Cubans in Miami rush to Cuba in boats, pick up their families, and bring them to South Florida.

Mayhem. Suddenly, the Cuban Refugee Center can't handle the influx, and Marie Antoinette is lost in the shuffle.

And that's not all that stands in her way.

First, there's Hurricane Betsy. As soon as she sets foot in Miami, the place is hit hard by a category four hurricane, the worst that Marie Antoinette has seen in her forty-four years in the tropics. Miami shuts down for a while.

Then, there's the place where she's living. She's with her friends Marta and Juan Becquer, who were so good to Tony and me, especially when we were living at the Palace Ricardo. Marta and Juan are now working on graduate degrees while they carry full-time jobs, and they're very, very busy. My mom spends a lot of time waiting for them to take her to the places she needs to go to, like *El Refugio* on Biscayne Bay, the Refugee Center, which was once the customs house and will later be turned into a museum called Freedom Tower. Weeks pass. Nothing. A month. Nothing.

In the meantime, I'm flying high in Bloomington, not thinking of her at all. Same with Tony. I've got two successful paper routes, I'm in all honors classes, and I've got more good friends than I can count, and more infatuations than I can handle. And I'm even buying my clothes at Montgomery Ward. I've got new Levi's jeans, shirts with button-down collars, crew neck sweaters, and penny loafers; everything I know I should not be attached to or care about, all purchased with my own hard-earned cash. Let go. Yeah. Sure. I know I should let go, but I can't. Especially when I know that my mom is about to bring my current life to an abrupt and bittersweet end.

I'm torn and deeply confused, but prefer not to dwell on it. There's too much to enjoy in the here and now. Too much that will soon evaporate. As Doctor Freud would put it, "Transience value is scarcity value in time. Limitation in the possibility of an enjoyment raises the value of the enjoyment." Yeah, he had a formula for this irksome problem.

Back in Miami, finally tired of waiting for a ride to *El Refugio*, Marie Antoinette figures out how to get there on a bus and she borrows the bus fare from Marta's mom. Once she gets there, she finds out she's only one of a horde of recent arrivals, even though she landed in Miami before all of them did.

A kindly social worker with the surname of Sandoval sets up Marie Antoinette with what she needs: a Social Security card and a job search.

Staying in Miami is out of the question. Too many Cubans, all at once. Everyone has to be resettled.

"Do you know anyone outside of Miami?"

She mentions her cousins in Queens, New York. But that doesn't work out, for some reason. Dead end.

"Who else?"

She mentions her friends, the Puron sisters, who are in someplace called North Adams, Massachusetts. The Puron sisters had a chain of bedding stores in Havana and a beautiful house we used to go to all the time. They had movie parties on Saturdays and showed theater-quality films in their enormous living room. Now they're in a mill town in the Berkshires, where they think they can get Marie Antoinette a job as a seamstress at a dry cleaning shop.

So Tony and I prepare for a move to North Adams. We look it up in the encyclopedias at the public library, the same way we had looked up Bloomington at the Miami library. It seems exotic enough. Promising, maybe. Mountains. That would be a change. New England. Sounds less American than the Corn Belt. More European. That could be good, but it could also be bad.

No matter how certain North Adams looks, Tony and I press ahead with our lives, as if nothing is going to end abruptly. Day to day. Seize the day. Live it to the fullest.

As divine providence would have it, the seamstress job fails to materialize and North Adams fizzles. Tony and I are not the least bit surprised or fazed. Par for the course. Both of us know that when social workers are involved, things have a tendency to get screwed up. Our rescue from the Palace Ricardo was an exception to the rule, as we see it.

With North Adams out of the picture, Mr. Sandoval runs out of options. Marie Antoinette doesn't know anyone else in the United States, save for our uncle Amado. But there are no jobs in Bloomington for someone who doesn't speak a word of English. That option—the one that would make me happiest—is tossed aside.

"Are you sure you don't know anyone else, anywhere?"

Having a personal connection makes any abrupt transition out of Miami much easier. All of the social workers at *El Refugio* know this.

"Well, my friend Carmencita, in Mexico City, has these cousins who've gone to Chicago. I don't know them very well at all, and they just moved there, very recently, but we did spend time together in Mexico."

Chicago it is, then. Lots of jobs. Factories on every street, practically, all of them full of workers who speak all sorts of languages except English. And you sort of know someone. That seals it: Chicago, city of the Big Shoulders, Hog Butcher, Tool Maker, Stacker of Wheat, Player with Railroads. Under the smoke, dust all over his mouth, laughing with white teeth. Carl Sandburg got it right, all right. There are more jobs in Chicago than there are ever people to fill them. Even unskilled cripples who don't speak English can get a job there.

When Tony and I find out that we're going to Chicago, we feel exactly the same way we did when we first toured the Palace Ricardo. Christ, no. Please, no.

This can't be happening. Not again. Not another hellhole.

Everyone in Bloomington thinks of Chicago as an awful place, and that small-town attitude has rubbed off on us. And Tony and I once caught a glimpse of what Chicago looked like, away from the museums. Reverend Nordquist had taken us on a tour of some of the slums on the West Side, along the Eisenhower Expressway. It was a scary place, no doubt about it. We're not going to live in the museums, after all, or anywhere near them. We know that we're headed straight for the low-rent districts, with a mom like ours. Maybe even the West Side, or worse.

Holy crap. This is not how it should turn out, not after all the gains we've made. We're devastated. I can't let go. Not this much. No.

But Marie Antoinette can't wait to see us again. Our absence has been eating away at her, gnawing at the core of her soul. She's waited so long, endured so much. She didn't dig a tunnel under the Florida Straits with her bare hands, as she vowed to do, but she's come damn close to the equivalent. Two departures denied at the last minute. Waiting, and waiting, and waiting. Being attacked by a mob. Visiting embassies all the time. Pestering everyone. Leaving all by herself, abandoning all her other loved ones, including her husband. Emergency surgery. Earthquake. Hurricane. *El Refugio*. Resettlement. She really would prefer to stay in

Miami, so much, but it turns out that she can't because of all the new-comers who got out the easy way.

She'll make our lives so much better, finally.

Yeah. Sure.

Flash forward, forty years. Marie Antoinette is near the end of her life, and she knows it. Pope John Paul II has just died. He and she were born in the same year, and both have declined in tandem. In three weeks she'll be dead.

"I think my time is up," she says, as I'm driving her around Chicago in a rental car, on the way to see Tony in his nursing home way up near Wisconsin, in Waukegan. "Papito is showing me the way."

All I can say is, "No, not yet."

"Are you glad I sent you away?" she asks for the one millionth time. She's been asking me this question constantly ever since she showed up in 1965, and more and more frequently in the past few years as her health steeply declined, along with Tony's.

"Yes," I say for the millionth time. "I thank you and God for this gift every single day, often more than once a day. No gift can compare with it, ever."

"Tony doesn't think so," she says. This, too, is something I've heard way too often.

I say nothing.

She asks: "Are you glad I joined you here in *Los Estados Unidos?*" That's a new question. Totally new.

I feel a buzz saw slicing through my brain and a blowtorch scorching the core of my soul.

"Yes, sure, of course. Are you crazy?" I say. "Yes, yes. Thank you for that too." In Spanish, of course.

And, damn it, she knows she just made me lie.

Twenty-four

Union Station, Chicago. It's the third of November, 1965, around seven in the evening. Tony and I meet up with our mom after one thousand three hundred and seven days apart from her. She looks so much older, and smaller; her presence, here, in this enormous train station lends the world itself an unfamiliar feel, a lack of definition.

She exudes pure love, but enwraps space and time in a thick, menacing haze.

All I know is that whatever lies ahead is going to be unlike anything I've known up until now. So I thirst for some certainty other than that. This is a whole new Void, unexpectedly generated by the one soul on earth who loves me the most. I can't yet recognize it, but I know I don't like it. I want to imagine a better future so I can enjoy this long-delayed reunion, but my apprehension snuffs out whatever flame could be kindled by the sight of my beaming gray-haired mom and her cane. *If only we could see into the future*, I say to myself.

Better not to know what awaits us, of course.

Better for us, in late 1965, yes. But certainly not for you, now. You need to see what lay ahead then, and what came to pass.

So, fasten your seat belt.

Whoosh. Flash forward again, forty years. It's the merry month of May, in the year 2005. I've just given a talk on the Pedro Pan Airlift at a public library, and the place is full.

"I'm sick of *you people*," shouts the old man in the third row.

He speaks with an Eastern European accent, and he reminds me of Triumph the Insult Comic Dog.

"*You people* are ruining this country," he yells, his voice trembling. "It's because of *you people* that we have Bush as president. It's because of *you people* that we're stuck in this war in Iraq. It's because of *you people* that this country is being ruined in every way and the world hates us. Why don't *you people* shut up, go back to where you came from, and leave us alone?"

Whoa, dude.

I'm in Westport, Connecticut, on the east bank of the Saugatuck River, within sight of Long Island Sound. It doesn't get more genteel around here than this town, save for Greenwich, perhaps. Furs in every closet, jumbo gems in every safe. More money in trust funds than one can find in most tropical nations. Outbursts like this are as rare around here as plastic pink flamingoes on a front lawn.

I take a closer look at the old coot who seems to hate me, simply for being Cuban. I notice something odd on his bare forearm. Is that a tattoo? *What gives?* This is Westport. Only teens and twenty-somethings have tattoos in this town, and then only in hidden places. Wait. Are those numbers? Yes, damn it.

Someone, please, kill me now, before my head explodes.

I've seen those numbers before on the parents of some of my Chicago schoolmates, and they can mean only one thing: This guy is a Holocaust survivor. He's wrestled with the devil and pinned him to the mat. If anyone on earth should understand bigotry and its place in the master plans of the Prince of Darkness, it should be this guy.

So I ask him point-blank about the tattoo, after the question-and-answer period is over, as he gets up from his chair. And he confirms my hunch.

"So what?" huffs the geezer. "What do you care if I'm a Holocaust survivor? That has nothing to do with *you people* and what you've done to this country. *You people* voted for this Bush, and the other one, and Reagan, and Nixon, and you're all stupid, and always vote for the wrong side. I'm sick of all of *you.*"

The old man turns his back to me, shrugs his shoulders, and walks away, and maybe that's a good thing. Nothing I can say will change his mind. Bigots have no way of processing any information that contradicts their thinking, even bigots who've been abused by other bigots.

Bastard. *Cabrón. Imbécil.* I have to forgive him.

As this is taking place, my mother is dying in Chicago. *Tick tock,* every second is part of a countdown, much as in a rocket launch. She's been in a coma for several days, and the doctors have told me that she won't be coming out of it this time, as she's done before. "She's got about another week to go, that's it; maybe two," a young Pakistani doctor said to me, without flinching.

After spending nearly a week in Chicago, I've rushed back home to Connecticut so I could fulfill this speaking engagement and spend a couple of days with Jane and the kids. My Calvinist impulses are too strong. And this has been a tough call to make: Do I stay in Chicago and watch my unconscious mother breathe in and out, day after day, *tick tock,* or do I come home to my conscious loved ones and my professional obligations, and make myself useful for a couple of days?

Being useful is such a great virtue. The greatest perhaps, especially for a spic. We have such a bad reputation to overcome. God forbid we miss an appointment. *Tick tock.* Someone might say, "I should have known better than to invite one of *you people* to speak to us."

The venom spewed by the Holocaust survivor is worming its way through me. Pretty soon, it will make me feel physically ill. I know it, expect it. When things like this happen, it always gets to me, eventually.

But images of my dying mother block out the poison this time. She's the only thing on my mind—other than the traffic—as I drive home on Interstate 95. The venom will hit much later, after she's dead and buried.

The boundary between past and present burns away, like morning fog.

Whoosh. It's summer 1969, and the Chicago Cubs seem headed for the World Series, for sure. Marie Antoinette is working at her factory, screwing machine parts together. *Whirr, whirr, whirr . . .* She's an artist with that pneumatic screwdriver, just as with her sewing machine at home. Her dexterity is a lot like an athlete's, or a musician's, or a ballerina's. She moves so fast, so fluidly, so perfectly in harmony with the pieces of metal that she's handling. She's one with those parts, and with her tool.

There's no screwdriver and there are no screws or parts to bind; there's also no Maria Azucena Eiré de Nieto. *Whirr, whirr, whirr* . . . There's no stool under her, no workbench, no assembly line; no cavernous, stifling hot factory humming and ringing and clanging and thumping with the rhythmic noise of hundreds of workers piecing together photocopy machines; no foremen giving orders, no inspectors with clipboards, no clock on the wall, *tick tock*; no shafts of sunlight streaming in from the windows high above; no coworkers, no husband back in Cuba, no mother, father, sister, brother; no beautiful house left behind; no recently married Tony working at a print shop twenty miles to the south, on Lake Street; no Carlos looking at her from just a short distance away, here in Evanston. The salt pill she took a few minutes ago to prevent dehydration in this colossal oven never existed to begin with. Nothing exists but her motion, and the feeling of it, and the sheer elation it brings, which is eternal and beyond description.

She knows nothing about Zen. *Whirr, whirr, whirr* . . . Nothing, not even the word. *Whirr, whirr, whirr* . . . But she's mastered the Zen of assembling. And no one else in that factory can keep up with her. No Greek, no Pole, no Serb, no Czech, no African-American, no redneck. *Whirr, whirr, whirr* . . . No Cuban, either, and the factory is full of them.

Nearly two-thirds of our fellow workers here in this factory came from Cuba too, and most of them, like her, never did this kind of work before. Most of them were lawyers, or shopkeepers, or pharmacists, or teachers, or office clerks, or housewives. All of them had been better off in Cuba, before it became Castrolandia. I'm there for the summer, filling in for those who go on vacation. All the others are here for good. They can't hope for anything better than this. Unlike my mom, I hate the place and the work. Sheer drudgery for me. But I need the money, and my mom reminds me of that way too often.

I so envy her constant ecstasy. *Whirr, whirr, whirr* . . .

My only raptures in that stifling factory come when I'm opening boxes that contain parts wrapped in newspapers and I spot some interesting article to read, on the sly, when the foreman's eyes are focused elsewhere.

After I leave the factory, I go to the Jewel supermarket on Morse Avenue and work some more, as a stockboy. Sum total, I put in somewhere between sixty and seventy hours of work per week. My mom has trouble understanding why I'm not happy with this arrangement, at the age of eighteen, right between high school and college. She also can't fathom why my girlfriend and bride-to-be is giving me such a hard time about working so much.

She knows nothing about Calvinism. *Whirr, whirr, whirr*... Not even the name of John Calvin. *Whirr, whirr, whirr*... But, Jesus H. Ever-useful Christ, my mom makes all Calvinists look like slackers and reprobates.

Whoosh. I hear my mom's voice. It's 1974, and she's speaking to me on the phone. I'm in New Haven, and she's in Chicago. She's in a total panic—hysterical—a lack of control I've never witnessed before.

"Your brother has vanished!"

"What do you mean?"

"He's gone. He didn't come home two days ago and no one has heard from him. He's disappeared!"

"He'll show up. Don't worry. He's probably having a good time, somewhere. You know how he used to disappear like this when he was a boy."

"No, no! This is different. He's never vanished for this long. I have a very bad feeling about this. I think he's dead, somewhere!"

"Has anyone called the police?"

"Yes, his wife called, and I had someone call for me, but they won't do anything. They say he's a grown man and that he has a right to disappear without telling anyone."

"See, I told you, there's nothing to worry about. He'll show up."

"No, no, no. You don't understand. Something awful must have happened to him. And I'm not the only one thinking this way: My friend Carmen said that his head is probably floating in the Chicago River!"

Ay. Leave it to Carmen. Goddamnit. So graphic, so poetic, so overblown, so Cuban.

Marie Antoinette begins to sob, and then to weep and howl, uncontrollably. All I can do is assure her that everything will be all right, and predict that when Tony finally does show up, he won't even think that he has anything to apologize for.

Sure enough, Tony eventually shows up, weeks later, and acts like everyone was a fool for worrying about him. Tony says he went to Florida with a woman he met at the airport, whose charms he couldn't resist. Mom believes him, of course, and forgives him. God knows why his wife takes him back, but she does.

Repeat at least a dozen times, only with different details. Tony keeps vanishing, time and time again, and making up ever less credible tales. And our mom worries just as much each and every time, and weeps, and howls, and forgives; and she gives Tony whatever he asks for, along with things he doesn't even know he should ask for.

Whoosh. Twin images flash before my mind's eye: my mom in a coma, dying, *tick, tock;* my mom hugging Tony when he's just an empty husk, a faint brainless shadow of himself, trapped in a useless and ridiculously fat body, a changeling if ever there was one on earth.

Another image suddenly bursts into view: a braided rope with three strands, one is Tony, another is my mom, and the third is my dad. It's the weirdest braid in the world, for one of the strands—my dad—is totally invisible, but just as evident as the other two, maybe even more so. His absence is his presence, and it defines the twists and turns of the other two. It's taken my third eye a whole lifetime to see this so clearly. Yes, damn it, my brother's long sad downward slide and my mom's response to it are tightly and inextricably intertwined with my father's gross non-occurrence. He's a lot like God, my Louis XVI, insofar as he can't be seen but can certainly be felt or simply intuited by reason. But he's totally unlike God, insofar as he never, ever, sends anything good your way. All he can do as a father is haunt our memories and serve as a convenient scapegoat: the efficient cause of everything that's ever gone wrong in our lives.

Marie Antoinette is married to a specter, but won't acknowledge it. Even worse, she's trapped in a disembodied union and convinced that she must play a dual role to Tony and me, as mother and father, to make up for his ghostliness. Convinced that she's taking care of us and making our lives better, she's blind to the fact that Tony and I are so fully Americanized that we treasure our independence from her, and that Tony, especially, resents the way in which she ripped our lives apart by turning us into her caretakers. Tony also hates our dad so much that I fear he might kill him if he ever shows up, and he hates Uncle Amado too, and the Rubins, and the Ricardos, and anyone else—good, bad, or indifferent—who ever assumed the role of parent or guardian in his life. The anger bottled up inside of him is immeasurable.

I hate no one. I *love* everybody. *Sure.* Yeah. And I can stand back and look at this weird braided rope as if I'm not one of its strands. *Sure.*

This rope is tied, tightly, around my chest, right over my heart. Sometimes it slips up to my neck.

Whoosh. Tony plummets downward, at breakneck speed, faster than any Olympic bobsled, taking the tightest, steepest curves at what seems to be the speed of light, defying all the laws of motion, denying, demolishing, pulverizing every fate his mother and father ever hoped would be his. Marie Antoinette watches in horror and does whatever she can to reverse his course, never accepting it as irreversible, not realizing that her love freights him down, often making him plunge all the faster and steeper. Louis XVI, far, far away, clueless, heartbroken, helpless, does nothing but get sicker and sicker as he guards our ephemeral inheritance—that goddamned art collection that's no longer his, but still fills our former home, which isn't his either. King Louis, stuck for this lifetime in the tropical communist heat of Castrolandia, a mere custodian of valuable loot that belongs to all of the people of Cuba—not to him or to us—can't tell shit from Shinola, as his son Tony puts it. Louis XVI can't understand why Tony stopped writing to him back in Bloomington, can't cope with the distance and the silence, can't express a single feeling to any of the three of us, and, least of all, to his wife, Marie Antoinette. The last time he tried, during a three-minute phone call, the Cuban security agent listening on his end laughed when he said to her, "I miss you so much." Prolonged, outright laughter on the Cuban end.

Ha, ha, ha. Guffaw. Yes. *Viva la Revolución!* To me, this cold-blooded belly laugh is the footnote to every Che T-shirt.

I'm the only one King Louis writes to regularly. He tells me how sick he is, how his heart is failing, and how much stuff he's crammed into the house, illegally. "It's worth millions," he dares to say in one letter. All of his letters are hard to open. Cuban security agents have rifled through them and then resealed them sloppily—intentionally—with thick glue that binds the paper sheets to one another and to the envelope. Whether someone has actually read them is anyone's guess. Your fellow countrymen in charge of mail surveillance just want you to know that every word is potentially subject to inspection, so you'll keep your most important thoughts safely bottled up in your head. Separating the letters from the envelopes requires patience and the skill of a neurosurgeon.

And I answer each and every one of his letters. I tell Louis XVI how much I long to be with him again, and how much I love history, and how obsessed I am with the past.

Whoosh. It's nineteen seventy-something and Tony is drinking heavily. O'Hare airport is one hell of a nonstop party. According to him, booze and drugs flow more abundantly than tap water. During these golden years of his, he gets to fly everywhere for free, as long as there's an empty seat not taken by a paying customer. And often, it's a first-class seat, with unlimited drinks and easy access to attractive flight attendants who are very eager to party, not just during the flight but also at whatever the destination happens to be. I'd only find this out later. While this is happening, he's not talking to me. Tony, my brother, flight attendant magnet, has vanished from my life, completely, and I from his. The force field he began to wrap himself in back in Miami has grown ever more impenetrable, and the difference between his life and mine has created a vast gulf between us, as colossal as that between one end of the universe and the other. While he's flying around the world carousing with flight attendants, I'm slaving away at my doctorate, reading everything ever written by and about John Calvin and the Protestant Reformation of the sixteenth century. The most fun I have is returning books to the library after I've drained all of their blood out of them. The contrast between the two of us stuns me, each and every day, and the more stunned I become, the further Tony and I grow apart.

The braided rope in my mind's eye begins to fray.

Marie Antoinette fills her basement apartment with broken, wounded souls who need company. First it's my brother's friend John, fresh from war and mayhem in Vietnam. He joined the Marines and volunteered for duty in Southeast Asia so he could shoot at communists. He got to fire at them, all right, and to kill a few, but they also got to shoot back, lob mortars, blow up his jeep, and fill his body up with shrapnel, and all of this has left him off-kilter. He'll recover just fine, living in that basement. I was still there, then, but his path and mine seldom crossed. He was finishing his degree at the Art Institute of Chicago and I was majoring in theology and history at Loyola, just seven blocks up Winthrop Avenue. I worked at the Jewel supermarket every night and came home late. He drove a taxicab at night and came home even later. After John went off on his own, all healed, and after I got married and left the basement apartment, Marie Antoinette took in a long string of wounded souls: a girl from Colombia; a Peruvian priest who was questioning his vocation; her brother's sister Lucía—my aunt—who left Cuba at the age of seventy-five and couldn't stand living in Bloomington with her brother Amado; this friend, that friend, and perfect strangers foisted on her by friends. I'd lose track of who was living with her, there were so many of them. And she'd also make hundreds of friends, mostly Cuban, who became like family to her. Maybe it's more accurate to say that they became a better family than any she could hope to have with Tony and me.

At her funeral, at St. Ita's Church—where I once prayed for hours on end every day and where Tony and I had our first weddings—nearly every pew will be full. It'll be a sight to behold, as impressive a testimony to the love she doled out, naturally, unconditionally, as might make most of us feel grossly inadequate.

Whoosh. Tony turns dissoluteness into an art. He lies and cheats, and drinks and parties, gambles himself broke time and time again, and collects guns as if they were baseball cards. He also collects parking tickets with a nearly apocalyptic sense of urgency, and his name ends up in the news as one of Chicago's most wanted parking criminals. Seventy thousand dollars in unpaid fines land him in jail. Marie Antoinette can't stop crying about that and helps him pay the much smaller sum that he negotiated with some lenient judge. It's the first of many stints in the hoosegow for Tony. Most of the others will be for drunk driving and domestic violence. He and his second wife have a very rough-and-tumble life together, but, somehow, for some reason unfathomable to me and Marie Antoinette, and anyone who knows the full story, the two of them remain as inseparable as Romeo and Juliet.

Whoosh. It's 1975, and Louis XVI retires from his judgeship, due to his ever-worsening heart condition. God only knows what compromises he's had to make in order to work as a judge in Castrolandia, or what his life must have been like, stripped of his wife and children. Years and years later, I'll get a furtive glimpse of him from a woman who writes to me out of the blue and tells me that my father once rescued her from a ten-year prison sentence. Her crime? Selling her weekly meat ration to a neighbor. This woman will also tell me that she went to *my* house, to thank my father in person, face-to-face, and that he never once mentioned that his wife and children were in the United States.

In the final year of his life, Louis XVI will write to me about his plans to leave Cuba and his efforts to find a perfect home for his art collection. "Would you object if I just accept the inevitable and let go of your inheritance?" he'll ask me. "Go ahead and let the bastards set up a nice museum," I'll respond. He'll tell me about his dealings with the Ministry of Culture, and his search for an abandoned mansion large enough to house *my* noninheritance. I'll tell him how much I long to see him again, and how glad I am that he's decided to leave Castrolandia. What I don't tell him is how I fear he'll get screwed by the Ministry of Culture. What he doesn't tell me is how sick he is.

Whoosh. It's 1976, mid-September. As Tony continues his steep descent and Marie Antoinette ministers to wounded souls in her basement apartment and I bury myself in sixteenth-century Latin, French, and German texts, a large truck pulls up to *my* house in Havana one day. It parks directly in front, where the ficus tree used to be that Tony and I climbed just about every day. Without a tree to block it, the scorching sun blasts the front porch and the door to the house, howling in self-satisfaction, aggressively. Men emerge from the truck and knock on the door, with the door-knocker I used to play with as a child. *Tick tock.* My father, who's in the living room talking to a diplomat from the Peruvian embassy, gets up, opens the door, and sees the large truck parked at the curb. The men tell him that they've come for his art collection. Louis XVI tells them that there must be some mistake, for no place has yet been found in which to house all of this art he's been collecting since he was a teenager. The men say that there's no mistake at all, that they've been charged with emptying the house of its treasures and taking them to a warehouse. As the Peruvian diplomat listens to this exchange— which he can't make much sense out of—Louis XVI crumples and dies on the spot, right there, by the front door, on our black-and-white marble floor, just beyond reach of the scorching sunlight. All attempts to revive him fail.

Louis XVI laughs and laughs as he leaves this body, in which he hasn't ever been very happy, and spits, spiritually, on the truck parked at the curb.

The truck drivers flee the scene immediately and abandon their mission. Somehow, in that mysterious way in which corrupt workers' paradises work, the bureaucrat who ordered the looting of *my* house gives up, and no one ever returns to take my dead father's art collection anywhere. The museum never comes to be; Ernesto, my adopted brother, gets to stay in the house with all the stuff; and he earns the unfair, un-communist right to sell it all on the black market, piece for piece.

Three cheers for the so-called Revolution and its Ministry of Culture!

Whoosh. It's 1980. Marie Antoinette's factory goes bankrupt and closes down, and she loses her pension. All of her contributions to the factory's retirement plan had been invested in company stock, and she and everyone else are left with nothing. *Nada, nada, nada.* She can't find another job, but lucks out, big-time. She ends up in a brand-new apartment, in the near North Side of Chicago, in a plush building run by the Little Sisters of the Poor. The monthly rent is a negligible slice of her ridiculously low Social Security income. And all of the views from that building are priceless. The red, orange, and purple sunsets from my mom's fifth-floor picture window are beyond sublime, as are all of the smokestacks and church steeples that punctuate the cityscape to the west, in what was once the heart of industrial Chicago but is now the exclusive domain of yuppies and their offspring.

I get a job in Minnesota, a short ten-hour drive from Chicago, and begin to reconnect with Tony and Marie Antoinette.

Tony's force field begins to burn away, much like a meteor hitting the atmosphere, as he plunges deeper into his abyss. One image bolts out of my memory: Tony and I take the elevated train to the Art Institute of Chicago, along with Kenny, one of his friends from the airport. Tony jokes around, and sometimes he's funnier than the comedians at Second City, but he's wearing slippers on his feet. Goddamned slippers. And he's got pajama pants under his slacks. He pauses for a long time when we come to Grant Wood's *American Gothic* painting, and says, after minutes of silence: "Hey, look, it's Uncle Amado."

Whoosh. Tony begins to tell me about his work for the Central Intelligence Agency, and about his covert work as a spook in Central America. "That's where I went when I disappeared," he confesses. "I was an operative, working off the record. I'm one of those expendables that the Agency will deny is working for them if caught or killed in action." I refuse to believe him. He also tells me about all of the music he's composed for Pink Floyd, and how they've never paid him for it. I have trouble believing that too, even though he seems to know an awful lot about Roger Waters, Syd Barrett, and David Gilmour, whom he claims to have befriended at O'Hare airport, along with Ronald Reagan, Frank Sinatra, and Don Rickles.

Whoosh. It's 1981. Tony crashes and burns. Rock bottom. He checks into Resurrection Hospital, on Easter, his drinking totally out of control. As I chat with him, I glance out the window and see a rabbit jump out from the bushes. Peter Cottontail, at Resurrection Hospital, on Easter. Is this a good omen, a mere coincidence, or a cruel joke? It's only the first of many such stints in clinics for Tony, and none of the others will be graced by Easter bunnies or omens of any kind, or any real healing. As I say good-bye to Tony that night, at Easter Bunny Hospital, I see the same look in his eyes as he had when we were separated at the Miami airport, back in April 1962.

Whoosh. It's the late 1980s and early '90s. Marie Antoinette's health takes a sharp turn for the worse. Bum liver, infected with the hepatitis C she picked up from a blood transfusion in Mexico, back in 1965, just after she left Cuba. Crippling pain in her back and legs makes her life miserable, and on top of that fatigue too, caused by post-polio, a resurgence of the disease that ravaged her in infancy. Toxins invade her brain, sometimes, and scramble her thinking. She falls and breaks a hip—her good hip, the one to which her only useful leg is connected. She learns how to live in a wheelchair.

Whoosh. She's visiting me in Connecticut in 1996. I've just moved here from Virginia, and I want to show her the ducks in the swamp that borders my new house. I park the car at the top of the hill, at the end of my road, take out her wheelchair, help her get in, and set both of her brakes as tightly as possible. I turn around to shut the car door, and when I turn back to grasp the wheelchair handles, she's not there at all. *Tick tock.* I lift my head slightly from that shockingly empty spot to see my mom careening down the steep hill in her wheelchair, at about twenty miles per hour, straight toward a clump of tall oaks at the edge of the swamp. She's headed straight for the biggest, fattest tree of all. I see *her* life flashing before my eyes, and *my* eternity in hell as well. "I've just killed my mom," I say out loud as I dash down the hill. But before I can take more than three steps, her wheelchair veers sharply to the left and rolls into a large pile of freshly ground-up mulch. She's thrown from the chair, flips in the air, and lands on top of the mulch pile. The empty chair tumbles to the very edge of the murky water, like a rogue die tossed by an angry gambling deity. When I reach her, a few seconds later, we both start laughing as I brush off the mulch from her sweater. "You know," she says, "you shouldn't really push the chair that fast." All I can say is: "You need a new chair with brakes that work."

Whoosh. It's the late nineties: the end of the millennium, and the end of the road for Tony. He crashes through rock bottom and vanishes from his body, his soul snatched by the drugs that the doctors prescribe. "Post-traumatic-stress-syndrome," say some doctors. "Anxiety disorder," say others. "Schizoaffective disorder," say yet others. It makes no difference what the doctors say, the end result of their ministrations is the creation of a zombie who doesn't even look at all like Tony. All of his teeth fall out. His hair turns white. His now-diabetic body turns into a gross caricature of a blimp, or of our father, the very fat Louis XVI. He shakes all the time and rubs his leg constantly. His tongue darts in and out of his mouth like a lizard's. His speech is slurred. His attention span is reduced to a minute, at most, and his responses to questions become grunts. He stops bathing or shaving, or cutting his hair, changing his clothes, or controlling his blood sugar. A stinking Bizarro Santa Claus, he scares people on the street and the nuns in our mom's building. Even worse, his wife insists that he's getting the best of care and that there's nothing else to be done for him. And she views all advice as hostile meddling.

Whoosh. New century, new millennium. The braided rope in my mind's eye is so frayed now, so tightly wound around me. Marie Antoinette declines rapidly, alongside Tony. As her visits to the hospital become more frequent and the care she requires intensifies, I fly to Chicago, back and forth, almost as a commuter, and search for a solution. She insists on remaining in Chicago so she can be near Tony, even though she can't really do anything for him, not even visit unless I fly all the way out there and rent a car. All along, as her health has worsened, she's been thinking she'll eventually move into the nursing home that's attached to her apartment building. But it doesn't turn out that way. She falls into a coma, her brain awash in toxins. The doctors offer no hope. This is it. Curtains. *If she comes out of it, she'll be a vegetable,* they say. The Little Sisters of the Poor decide that she can no longer keep her apartment and refuse to take her into their ultra-plush nursing home, where Cardinal Bernardin's mother is living out her final days on earth. Tony scares them too much, they say, and so does my mother's bright red lipstick, and her Cuban loudness, and her inability to speak English. No amount of pleading by me or her friends can change their nun minds. They give me three days to clean out my mom's apartment, and they offer no help in finding her another place to live.

Her friends and I dispose of her few belongings, as if she were already dead.

Marie Antoinette regains her senses and is fully back to her old self, but she has no place to live. Given that there's no such thing as a truly nice nursing home—save for the one the nuns have barred my mother from—I find one that's as close an approximation of "nice" as one could hope for. For the brief remainder of her life on earth, Marie Antoinette will constantly say, "You know, I lost everything twice; first when I left Cuba, then when the nuns kicked me out."

Her roommate at the nursing home is paralyzed and unable to speak. The best she can do is mumble and moan. Marie Antoinette becomes her best friend. The fact that my mom can't speak English is of no consequence: Eventually, Mom will be the only one in the nursing home who understands each and every one of her roommate's primal grunts.

Whoosh. It's 2003. Despite his dire state, Tony manages to drive himself to liquor stores and get into all sorts of jams at home and on the road. His wife is there, on the front lines, much like an infantryman in a trench, constantly shelled, unable to stop the shelling, convinced that there's nothing anyone can do to improve the situation, suspicious of any attempts to intervene. All of the policemen and emergency room doctors and nurses in his town, forty miles north of Chicago, come to know him and his wife very well. One night, a diabetic blackout knocks him unconscious while he's driving on the Northwest Tollway, and he rams his car head-on into a concrete barrier. Like Marie Antoinette on the mulch pile, he escapes unscathed. But his driver's license is revoked by the state of Illinois. Never a stickler for the rules, Tony keeps driving anyway. Then, sure enough, he blacks out again one night while driving home from the liquor store and crashes into a parked car. As soon as he comes to and sees what's happened, he limps away as fast as he can and leaves the two smashed-up cars behind. Nabbed at home by the cops and found guilty of driving without a license and fleeing the scene of a crime, Tony is declared a danger to himself and others. The options offered by the court at this crossroads are as limited as they are hard to accept: jail, a state-run mental hospital, or a nursing home. So, Tony ends up in a nursing home—and not a very good one at that because he limits his choices to those that allow smoking.

Whoosh. It's 2004. Tony and Marie Antoinette fade away at a fast clip, in their nursing homes. Marie Antoinette fades only physically, but Tony fades in every way. I fly to Chicago so often that I begin to think of cars and jet airplanes as no different from each other. Both have seats with seat belts and get you where you're going. Unfortunately, air travel costs a lot and it eats up my income. Fortunately, at the Chicago end of my commute, John, the wounded Marine my mom took in years before, helps me out and lets me stay in his lakefront high-rise apartment. He's done very well for himself. And he's a constant companion to Marie Antoinette and Tony. Truth be told, he's the only real brother I have. Tony's gone. He's died a thousand deaths with every pill he's taken and is now one of the living dead.

I bring our mom to see him and the three of us go to the International House of Pancakes, each and every time. What a strange sight the three of us exiles are, here, at this table. What an abhorrent, unforeseen tableau, here, at the International House of Pancakes in gritty Waukegan, Illinois—2662 Belvidere Road—in the smoking area. Had anyone told us back in 1962 at the airport in Havana that this is how our family would end up, we couldn't have believed it. Had anyone shown me this scene back in 1962—at the International House of Pancakes in the Westchester

Shopping Center in Miami, on the corner of Eighty-seventh Avenue and Twenty-fourth Street Southwest, where all the different syrups brought me to the edge of rapture, or at Union Station in Chicago on the third of November, 1965—I could never have recognized it as my future, *our* future.

Not even Louis XVI and his Ouija board could have fathomed this grotesque ending, this frayed and tattered braid. All the same, however, we're always seated at a table for four and I can't help but feel the ever-absent presence of my father in the empty seat.

"Tremenda sorpresa, no?" he whispers inside my head. What a surprise, huh?

Doctors Sigmund and Carl, you gnostic guides, bogus high priests, you and your disciples have nothing to offer us here, at this well-lit table with its fake wood-grain finish, paper place mats, and scuffed-up stainless-steel forks and spoons. Your insights are as valuable as the smoke curling up toward heaven from my brother's Camel cigarette, which I bought for him on the Internet from a Native American reservation in upstate New York. *Tick tock.* Shut up and go away, headshrinkers. I'm sick of *you people.*

This is not the way it should end. But this is the way it's ending, all right. And there's a blessing in this wretched dénouement, a glowing otherworldly gift. Each of us at this table has been reduced to the barest essentials, under these bright, bright lights, which remind me so much of those above the table at the Pedro Pan camp in Florida City, that first night of mine in the United States, when I ate my first and last chicken sandwich.

Marie Antoinette and Tony have been stripped clean, down to the core of their souls. It's all they have left, really, the spark of the divine in them, and their lingering faults and quirks, so human, irksome, and inevitable. Their bodies are a great burden to them: noisome, painful, unsightly husks. They've had no choice but to let go of their belongings and their flesh: It's a self-denial that's been imposed on them, and their plight, which is also mine in a very real sense, has forced me to empty my pockets, draw inward and upward and outward and backward and forward and to be stripped clean in a different way. Watching them disappear this way—so far away from where their exit point on the map should have been, so far from all other kin, so far down at the very bottom of the heap, so destitute, so crucified—rubs my third eye raw, and it allows me to see what's most essential, here and beyond, through a blissfully painful haze.

We're seeds sown in fertile, stinking soil. *No doubt about it.* Dying is our lot, but not our end.

It's only the beginning. *It has to be.*

Or else that number tattooed by Nazis on the Holocaust survivor who accused the three of us of ruining *his* country might as well be the cruelest, darkest joke in the universe. And his words nothing but an echo of God's summary judgment:

"I'm sick of *you people.*"

Twenty-five

H ow about this one?"
    It's a real Christmas tree, like all the other ones in this parking lot. The lightbulbs strung above our heads cast the blurriest and flimsiest of shadows, as insubstantial as the warmth that emanates from the steel barrel in which a lazy fire burns. All but a few of the trees look acceptable. None is perfect.

There's no snow on the ground. It hasn't snowed yet, at all, and it's already late December. What kind of cruel hoax is this?

Par for the course, here in Chicago, where nothing has gone right for the past two months. Until now, that is. Shopping for this Christmas tree is the best thing that's happened since we met up with our mom back in early November.

We had to leave Bloomington in a hurry, almost as if we'd committed a crime. Our mom arrived in Chicago on Halloween, and we were tossed aboard a Chicago-bound train three days later. No chance to say farewell to anyone, really. No time to get ready for this death.

The sweet flame wasn't very sweet this time. It's still burning me up, in fact, and it hurts like hell. I didn't want to die; couldn't let go. Still can't. I don't want to be transfigured this time. No. Jesus H. Resurrected Christ, why have you abandoned me? Corn Belt Jesus, above my uncle's chair, what have you done?

All of my friends were shocked by the abruptness of my departure. "What? Tomorrow?" I'm sure it was no different for Tony's many friends. Our uncle and aunt and our cousins seemed stunned too. Who wouldn't be?

Oh, but this Christmas tree might be the turning point. We pick out a very nice one and carry it for a block and a half to the basement apartment we've just rented at the southeast corner of Hollywood and Winthrop. It's a beautiful building, English Tudor style, red brick, with turrets and bay windows and limestone trim everywhere. Once upon a time, it was an elegant residence, you can tell. Top-notch. But the basement was always the basement, and now it's our home. Our radiators are on the ceiling, which is crisscrossed by pipes. We have very little furniture, all secondhand: a sofa bed, where Tony and I sleep, a cot for our mother, and a folding table and chairs. We've also just picked up an old television set from a Puerto Rican lady we met at a secondhand shop, down in Uptown, the nearest slum, which is brimming over with junk shops.

At least here in Chicago we get about seven channels. Now, finally, I'll get to see shows on networks other than CBS.

You've got to look at the bright side. Tony has found a job at a print shop. He's quit high school and works there full-time during the day. I'm looking for a job too. I'm too young to drop out of high school, like Tony, so I'm supposed to find a full-time job at night. It's what the social worker downtown told us to do. Our mom is also looking for work, sort of. The truth is she has no clue how to do that. She means to, but doesn't know what to do.

My mom's friends, Luis and Ada Serrano—the ones she didn't know too well—put us up at their tiny apartment for a month and a half while we looked for a place of our own. They're wonderful people, and their son Luisito—who's about ten years older than me—is one of the nicest guys I've ever met. He'll be my older brother, and a damn good one, as Tony vanishes down his abyss.

It takes a month and a half to get our own place because no one wants to rent to an unemployed handicapped single mom with two teenage sons, especially as soon as Tony and I switch from English to Spanish as we translate what is being said to Marie Antoinette. Many a door has been slammed in our faces, impolitely, Chicago style.

We bring the Christmas tree into our empty living room. Save for the sofa bed, the tree is it. No competition. It dominates the room. With money from Tony's first paycheck, we buy lights, simple solid-color glass ornaments, and tinsel at Woolworth's, on Bryn Mawr Avenue. We also buy a cheap, but very well made, Italian porcelain Nativity set. No real Christmas would be complete without one.

While we're making these purchases, a fellow Cuban approaches us and makes small talk. Before you know it, he's solved my job-search problem. He tells me that right after New Year's he can get me a full-time job as a dishwasher at the Conrad Hilton Hotel, where he works as a freight elevator operator.

Back in Cuba, his father owned a sugar mill, which he thought he'd inherit.

I'll work at the Hilton for nearly a year, full-time, at night, as I attend high school during the day.

The tree is more than wonderful. More than heavenly. It's the only nice thing in the world. I know I've reverted to my idolatrous ways, but hell, once we hung the ornaments and plugged in those lights, and the living room lit up just the way our living room in Havana used to at Christmastime, I had no choice. This is no hollow idol, like the one in that upper room in Coral Gables, or the one in that basement in Bloomington, or all the others I've seen since then. This is my idol, and it's full of my memories, which, at this time, is about all I have that can make me happy. This Christmas is all about returning to the way things used to be. Our mom came here and uprooted us just so we could go back to that: the golden past we lost.

So what if no one else from the family is here? At least the three of us are together, and we have a Christmas tree. In English class, where our very young teacher screams constantly at us, I concentrate on images of our Christmas tree in order to block out her rants. The way the Christmas lights paint a bare wall with splashes of color is really like nothing else on earth, especially when every one of those splotches is linked to some distant memory.

All I need is an army of angels, like the ones on Coral Way. Here, in this gritty place, I sure could use them. Little do I know that a whole legion of them will soon walk with me through skid row and ride the subway with me every night, unseen, their bright shining weapons joyfully unsheathed.

Christmas Eve. Christ, yes. We dine with the Serranos. It's something of a homecoming, returning to the apartment where we lived up until a fortnight ago, during our first trying weeks in Chicago. It's so good to see Luis, Ada, and Luisito. So what if they don't have a Christmas tree? We do, in our basement apartment, two blocks down Winthrop Avenue. It's a real *Nochebuena,* with all of the traditional Spanish and Cuban goodies. Each and every one of them, down to the walnuts and filberts and four or five different kinds of *turrón.*

We're all upset that it hasn't snowed yet. Damn it, where's the snow? It's Christmas Eve and we're up north. If we're going to be exiled this far from home, we should at least get a white Christmas.

Crap. It actually starts to rain. What kind of insult is this? God, where are you? The wind begins to pick up, seriously. Ada Serrano jokes about being in the Windy City. We can hear it howling, and we also hear the raindrops being driven into the windowpanes. I get up at dessert time and look out the window. I can't believe my eyes—the rain is turning to snow. Big fat flakes, falling horizontally.

"*Nieve!*" I yell out.

Everyone comes to the window. We see a man across the street, at the entrance to Swift Elementary School, struggling against the wind. He's not making much progress. The wind is so fierce that it pushes him back while he holds on to his hat with all of his strength.

We all have a good laugh at his expense when the wind knocks him down and his hat escapes, flying away from him like a hawk after prey.

The snowflakes soon outnumber the raindrops, and then quickly replace them. It's a blizzard out there, an honest-to-goodness blizzard. And we stand at the window, all of us, and take in the miracle. Then we return to the table and enjoy our dessert—*flan* and the nuts and the *turrón*—as the snow piles up outside and sticks to everything, like superabundant grace.

A couple of hours later, the storm is over. Everything is covered in snow. It's not only on the ground and on all of the parked cars, about four inches deep, but it is also plastered on all vertical surfaces: trees, light posts, street signs, buildings. And it looks like fluffy stucco. Not even Currier & Ives could have come up with a more perfect Christmas landscape, even though Winthrop Avenue is an orderly jumble of densely packed buildings rather than some bucolic village or farm.

Tony and I walk home with our mother under a starry sky. She can slip in the snow very easily, and none of the sidewalks has been shoveled yet, so we hold on to her tightly. We leave very odd tracks in the freshly fallen snow, like some seven-legged beast with one clubfoot. As soon as I walk down the steps into our living room, I turn on the Christmas tree. It lights up the whole space, including the crèche underneath, on the floor. Little Baby Jesus, his chubby arms upraised, blesses us all, bathed in all colors, all at once. Mary and Joseph, as always, simply look stunned.

Presents? Who needs them.

Flash forward, three years. Christmas 1968. Three earthmen are circling the moon, for the first time in the history of the universe. I've just had an essay published in the *Chicago Tribune* about the real meaning of Christmas. It's been one hell of a year, one damn thing after another, yet the *Tribune* stoops to publish such a thing in its *Voice of Youth* column. Never mind Vietnam, which is bad enough. The world is falling apart. Riots after the assassination of Martin Luther King Jr. Chicago on fire. Curfews. Riots in Paris. Robert Bay of Pigs Kennedy gets shot to death too. Riots at the Democratic Party convention. Blood on the streets of Chicago. Russian tanks on the streets of Prague. My very first transcendent love, Christine, my first true soul mate, murdered, stabbed seventeen times in Madison, Wisconsin. In her absence, I've picked up a girlfriend I think might also be a soul mate, broken up once, and gotten back together. Tony has gotten engaged to a girl my age who's totally wrong for him.

My *Tribune* essay ignores all this. It's all about the way in which the stable in Bethlehem must have stunk to high heaven, and how essential it is to keep that in mind when celebrating Christmas. Forget the decorations on State Street and Michigan Avenue, forget the store windows at Marshall Field's and Carson Pirie Scott and Company, forget the tinsel, and the gift wrap, and all that stuff. Smell the manger. That's Christmas.

Hypocrite. Blind fool. Deep down inside I'm still an idolater and worship all that stuff I deride. Which is why I'm not in a seminary or a monastery. The sad truth is that I can no more let go of what I like in 1968 than I could in 1965, or 1962, or 1956. And I have no burning desire to smell a stinking stable either. No way. I just can't admit it to myself.

I'm a success story, damn it, and I'm as deeply entangled in the world and as addicted to praise and recognition as the shallowest, most materialistic, money-grubbing cretin in the world.

"I" this and "I" that. Moron. *Comemierda*. I have a long list of accomplishments that begin with "I." I'm vice president of student council. I've designed the yearbook cover. I'm in about ten clubs and on the honors and advanced placement track in all of my classes. I've received a special prize for being engaged in so many social service programs, like playing basketball with handicapped kids every week. I also go to church every single day, pray compulsively, and work at a grocery store about thirty hours a week. Not only that, I've managed to find jobs for about twelve other Cubans at my grocery store, where I'm only one of four guys named Carlos.

Yes, Chuck Neat-o is dead. He died the day I left Bloomington. And he stayed dead too, along with Charles and Charlie.

Now, at the Jewel food store on Morse Avenue, it's just Carlos Nieto (*Knee-a-toe*, not *Neat-o*), along with Carlos Mendez, Carlos Trelles, and Carlos Montoya.

Somewhere down the line, in 1978, Carlos Nieto will become Carlos M. N. Eire, and then, later, just plain old Carlos Eire, when I stop writing books with footnotes.

Flash forward to the present. Right now, as I'm writing.

This book has come to an end at chapter twenty-five. It's an arbitrary number. I haven't aimed for it, or bothered to look up its meaning in the Chinese-inspired Cuban lottery known as *la charada*, or *la bolita*, in which every number from one to one hundred is assigned a symbol. Number one, for instance, is *caballo*, or horse; thirteen is *pavo real*, or peacock;

seventy-eight is *sarcófago*, or coffin; ninety-six is *puta vieja*, or old whore; and so on. Ideally, the way this is supposed to work is that if a certain image shows up in your dreams, you can safely bet on its number equivalent and win the lottery. Normally, I pay no attention to this nonsense. But when I wrote my first book without footnotes, a friend passed on the *bolita* number list, by chance, and I glanced at it. Much to my amazement, I'd stopped at chapter forty-one, the number for *lagartija*, or lizard, the central metaphor in that book. It was too perfect, too much of a coincidence. So out of sheer curiosity I've checked to see what surprise the number twenty-five holds in store for this book.

And once again, I'm blown away: It's *casa nueva*, or new home.

No me jodas. This is too much. Too much of a coincidence for a book about life in a new country and the journey to one *casa nueva* after another.

How awesome, this coincidence, and how annoying. It makes you question everything and ache for certainty, maybe even yearn for the once sacred art of augury to return. But why plumb a number for meaning? Or a name?

On some days, I wish I could change my name to McKinley Morganfield, the baptismal and legal name of the chief god of the blues, Muddy Waters. And I often regret not giving that name to my firstborn son, even though that son often thanks me for not having done so.

Most recently, I've pined for the name José Candelario Tres Patines, that of the main character in *La Tremenda Corte*, the Cuban radio show I used to listen to with Tony every night before going to sleep, back in Plato's cave. In case you don't know, by the way, *Tres Patines* means "Three Skates." A perfectly nonsensical name, for a perfectly nonsensical world, in which we all commit nonsensical crimes and receive nonsensical punishments.

"For the crime of nameicide, I fine you fifteen grande-no-fat-triple-shot-no-foam lattes from Starbucks, six unrequited loves, and one daylong oral exam on Immanuel Kant, in German. And may this teach you never, ever to kill your name again."

What's in a name? Who are you, after you die over and over and are gloriously reborn, time and time again, in the same body? What's a life, anyway? All of the cells you and I were born with are long gone. Our bodies are never the same: We're in constant flux, physically. So who are we? If all of the cells and atoms in my body and yours are not the same ones we were born with, and if these minute building blocks we have at the moment are constantly replaced, including those that make up our brains, then how can we be the same person, the same self?

"Software," the die-hard materialists will say. The hardware changes, but the software and the information it contains remains the same. In other words, all we are is memory.

Ay. This always gives me trouble. If all we are is memory, and memory contains one death after another, rebirth upon rebirth, how can we ever hope to speak of "I," "me," or "myself"? Shouldn't we speak of "we," "us," or "ourselves"?

This would be so confusing, but so much more accurate.

Proving the existence of God is fairly easy. Any idiot can take a stab at that. As one might say in Chicagoese: *What, you think all of this made itself up? Yeah. Sure.* Proving the existence of the soul and its immortality is much harder. After all, we perish and vanish from view just like all of the plants and animals on earth. *Poof.* Dust we are and unto dust we return, just like the pets we love, and the chickens we eat, and the cockroaches we squash, and last summer's heirloom tomato plants. The universe insults us by carrying on and on, as if we had never existed. How galling: Many astrophysicists now say that its eternity is undeniable, as undeniable as God's used to be.

Ay. Tremendo insulto. What an affront.

In another book, which I wrote two deaths ago, I came up with several contemptible proofs for the existence of God. But in this book, I've wrestled with the harder challenge posed by the human soul, that most painfully evanescent entity. And here, at the end, I have only one proof to offer concerning the soul and its immortality: this whole book, from cover to cover, and its readers, including you.

Go ahead, call this proof ridiculous. I double dare you.

Dukes up.

Having just died an utterly exquisite and surprising death a few days before I began to write these pages, while biking through the Tiergarten in Berlin—a park with a name that comes too damn close to sounding like *Tear Garden* in English—I can't help but see it this way: If one can recall how one learned to die, and remember dying again and again, then death has no right to be absolute. None at all. It would be the ultimate poetic injustice.

And the stupidest, cruelest, grossest joke ever, totally out of sync with the order we can perceive in the universe.

Learning to die is as necessary as learning to breathe, but a lot harder. It's not just because of the pain involved, but also because death calls for opposite reactions all at once, something none of us is well equipped to handle. Death gives you no choice but to embrace it and hate it and thank it all at once. Letting go is the key to dying well, and so is never letting go. Never is the only door to forever. Never surrendering and always surrendering. Dying is the only option and not an option at all. Something to be fervently desired and something totally unacceptable. Dying is constant. But it is summed up only once, at physical death, when the body begins to dissolve. Then, and only then, will we know if we've learned our lessons well, when our vulnerable bodies are also transformed by another sort of sweet flame. Then, and only then, can all our dying lead to deathlessness and an enduring life in which there is no Absence whatsoever. None. Forever.

Presence. Sheer presence. Light. Love eternal.

Flash back, forward, sideways, up, down, inward, outward, any way you want. Forget directions, time, and space.

I'm at a Christmas tree farm with the four sweetest souls in the world: my lovely wife Jane, my son John-Carlos, my daughter Grace, and my son Bruno. The trees are all planted in perfectly straight lines that extend in all directions—horizontally, vertically, diagonally, infinitely—over gently undulating ground, on an earth without circumference, the center of which is everywhere. There's snow underfoot, lots of it, and the bright, sublime light that envelops us doesn't melt it. Not even in the least. Every snowflake remains intact. Every tree is perfect. Each and every tree, each and every branch and needle, perfectly shaped, and gleaming, as if from within. We have trouble deciding which tree to cut. We argue, as we always do. "No, not this one, that one. No, not that one, this one." We trudge through the snow up and down the endless rows of pines. And everyone we know and love shows up and tries to help, as each and every tree shouts, "Pick me!" And, simultaneously, we five try to help everyone we know and love to pick out their prize tree, as the angels laugh and all the perfect evergreens cry out, "Pick me!" and our saws sing, in perfect harmony, "Use us, now!"

This goes on forever.

Por siempre jamás.

Without end.

Without end, when all is said and done.

You know.

Acknowledgments

Ever since the publication of *Waiting for Snow in Havana*, I've been asked countless times, "When will you continue the story?" or "When will you write another book without footnotes?" My response has always been the same: "Maybe tomorrow; maybe never. I have to wait for the inspiration."

Out of the blue, the inspiration finally came at an unlikely time, in a most unlikely place: Berlin, in early June 2009, after a two-week journey on the Elbe River, up from Prague. I must thank my travel companions on this tour—in which I was a lecturer—for helping me realize that all genuine pilgrimages ultimately lead to the core of the soul through a linking of heaven and earth; past, present, and future; self and other; dreaming and waking; and the here-and-now with the then-and-there.

As a refugee from the former Soviet Empire I was overwhelmed by what I found in its former colonies. Knowing that my Cuban brethren are still trapped inside a grotesque relic of that totalitarian nightmare, and knowing that my parents had sent me to the United States so I wouldn't end up in these places through which I was traveling, I couldn't help but feel a constant twinge of something I couldn't identify: a strangely mixed emotion—part sorrow, part envy, part gratitude, and part rage—that drew me inward and made me feel more like an exile than ever.

I must therefore thank you Czechs and Germans who were bold enough to rid yourselves of your oppressors twenty years ago: The legacy of your accomplishment brought me in touch with my own past in a very immediate way, and it gave me hope for the future of the ruined land I was forced to leave behind and from which I've been barred, along with my books.

I'm especially grateful to the Museum of Communism in Prague, in which I never set foot. I only saw posters advertising its existence, but that was enough for me. It knocked me off balance just to know that such a museum exists, in which I and every Czech over the age of twenty-one could be at once a visitor and an exhibit. You realigned my thinking and my center of gravity, Museum of Communism, as all great paradoxes tend to do. So thanks to whoever created you, a place at once so ludicrous and meaningful, and so perfectly designed to awaken my full identity. I must thank the Berlin Wall too, or what's left of it. Its sorry remains—including the small chunks I purchased at souvenir shops and brought home with me—were a constant source of inspiration.

Infant of Prague—miracle-working icon of the Christ child brought to Bohemia from Spain by Carmelite nuns in the seventeenth century, exile reified, tucked away in such a peculiar spot, which I had such a hard time finding—I thank you too, much more than the Museum of Communism or the Berlin Wall. If I hadn't stumbled into your shrine on that Pentecost Eve, this book wouldn't have been written. *Mil gracias.* You know why. *Tú sabes.*

Others have done more than inspire me: They've actually helped shape this book and enabled its creation.

First, I'd like to thank Alice Martell, my agent. Thanks, Alice, for your advice and all of your efforts on my behalf. And once again; I can't thank you enough.

I'd also like to thank my editor, Martin Beiser, for his support, and guidance, and unerring advice. I can't thank you enough either.

Deeply heartfelt thanks also go to my colleagues in the Virginia Seminar in Lived Theology, funded by the Lilly Foundation: Charles Marsh, Mark Gornik, Patricia Hampl, Susan Holman, Alan Jacobs, Chuck Mathewes. Our spirited conversations during the past four years have guided the writing of this book, and your response to just one small part of it has improved the whole considerably. Thanks, friends.

Thanks also to Father Robert Pelton, of Madonna House. You've helped in so many ways, so constantly, from far away.

Here, in my own house, I found the greatest help and inspiration of all.

As happened before, with *Waiting for Snow*, my children, John-Carlos, Grace, and Bruno, played a key role. I couldn't read this book to you as I did with the other one nine years ago, when you were so much younger, but your eagerness to read the emerging text, day by day, and your honest responses meant more to me than you can imagine. You guided me and kept me fired up, you three. This is your story too: Thanks for helping me tell it.

Finally, I owe the greatest debt of all to my wife Jane, whose love and encouragement and advice helped me find the right words in their hiding places and allowed me to corral them and string them together in the best possible order, under the best possible circumstances, during a wonderful summer that slipped away much too quickly but will forever be with us, no matter what.

As always, *thanks* doesn't even begin to cover it, lovely Jane, my Jane. The right words with which to end this sentence aren't hiding; they simply can't be found on earth.

About the Author

BORN IN HAVANA in 1950, Carlos Eire left his homeland in 1962, one of fourteen thousand unaccompanied children airlifted out of Cuba by Operation Pedro Pan. After living in a series of foster homes in Florida and Illinois, he was reunited with his mother in Chicago in 1965. His father, who died in 1976, never left Cuba. After earning his PhD at Yale University in 1979, Carlos Eire taught at St. John's University in Minnesota for two years and at the University of Virginia for fifteen. He is now the T. Lawrason Riggs Professor of History and Religious Studies at Yale University. He lives in Guilford, Connecticut, with his wife, Jane, and their three children.

Learning to Die in Miami

Confessions of a Refugee Boy

Carlos Eire

Reading Group Guide

Author Q&A

ABOUT THIS GUIDE

The following reading group guide and author interview are intended
to help you find interesting and rewarding approaches to your reading
of *Learning to Die in Miami*. We hope this enhances your enjoyment and
appreciation of the book. For a complete listing of reading group guides
from Simon & Schuster, visit http://community.simonandschuster.com.

INTRODUCTION

In *Learning to Die in Miami*, Carlos Eire explores the consequences associated with the emergence of a new American identity at the expense of the "death" of his old Cuban self after he emigrates to the United States during the Cuban Revolution. Along the way, Carlos must learn to navigate the differences between his past and present lives—redefining his relationship with his distant parents, mastering a new language, and adopting foreign customs and traditions. As Carlos is plagued by intense bouts of loneliness and abandonment while struggling to find his footing in his new homeland, readers cannot help but be moved by Eire's compelling first-person account of immigration in America. *Learning to Die in Miami* is a universal story of not only the pain of letting go, but also the rewards it ultimately brings.

TOPICS AND QUESTIONS FOR DISCUSSION

1. Reread the poem by Emily Dickinson at the beginning of the book: "Death is a dialogue between/The spirit and the dust.... An overcoat of clay." Why do you think Carlos Eire chose this poem to open his memoir?

2. Describing his experience of arriving in Miami as finally crossing over into "the real world" (p. 9), Eire then perceives Cuba as part of "some other dimension" (p. 9). What first impressions of the United States may have inspired this perspective?

3. Throughout the memoir, Carlos Eire refers constantly to the father and mother he left behind as Louis XVI and Marie Antoinette. Why did he choose these nicknames? Do you find them apt?

4. Eire describes a popular Cuban comic radio show called *La Tremenda Corte* (p. 36), which became unavailable under the Castro

regime. How did the plot of this show compare and contrast with the events that were occurring in Havana during the time that Eire was growing up? Why do you think it was removed from the air despite its tremendous popularity?

5. One of the themes *Learning to Die in Miami* explores is the relationship between parents and children. After separating from his parents, Carlos writes poignantly, "We had letters, yes, but letters are a very poor substitute for parents when you're eleven . . . children need to press the flesh and to have Mom and Dad there. . . . Without that sort of contact, Mom and Dad become ciphers, mere concepts" (p. 44). How did his time with his various foster families shape his experience? Were any of them real substitutes for his parents?

6. One the main goals Eire had when he arrived in America was to master the English language. Why was this so important to him? How do you interpret Eire's emotion as he demands, "Don't ask me what I think about my fellow Hispanics who insist on bilingual everything, or about how I feel every time I see a public sign in Spanish or am asked to choose between English or Spanish on the telephone" (pp. 54–55).

7. Eire experiences an intense conflict of personal identity during his first three years in America. How does Eire progress from identifying himself as Carlos, Charles, Charlie, Chuck, and then, finally, Carlos once again? What events in his life were pivotal in shaping his method of self-expression?

8. Among the many emotions that Eire struggles with as he adapts to his new homeland is "the feeling of being utterly alone and abandoned forever, of being stuck with no one but [himself] for eternity. The Void" (p. 91). When does the Void first enter Carlos's life? What does the Void represent to him, and how does he handle it? Does he ever ultimately overcome the Void?

9. Why do you think Eire describes Christmas as "the darkest day of the year?" (p. 118). What was Eire's relationship with this holiday that usually embodies tradition and joy?

10. One of the terms Eire comes up with to describe his "death" in Miami is "self-squashing" (p. 163). How does this term describes his situation?

11. Adding to the richness of this memoir is how Eire plays with time throughout the book, layering his adolescent experience through both young and more mature eyes. How different would Learning to Die in Miami have been if he had not used this storytelling technique?

12. How does Eire's experience of leaving Cuba behind mold his opinion of President John F. Kennedy as a "knucklehead"? (p. 191). Do you feel that his attitude of bitterness toward the president is justified?

13. What do you think Eire is referring to specifically when he proclaims, "Letting go is the ultimate happiness, and the ultimate pain"? (p. 248).

14. In what way does religion play a role in the narrative?

ENHANCE YOUR BOOK CLUB

1. Learning to Die to Miami is a brilliant follow-up to Carlos Eire's first memoir, the National Book Award–winner Waiting for Snow in Havana. Read Eire's first book and discuss how the two narratives ultimately come together to form his story.

2. Eire makes references to Plato's cave during his first few years in America. As a group, read Plato's Allegory of the Cave in The Republic and discuss how the various stages of the allegory correlate with the stages of Eire's journey.

3. One of the most important influences of Eire's coming-of-age is Thomas à Kempis's *The Imitation of Christ*. Select passages from this classic and discuss how they relate to or have influenced your own lives.

4. Television shows such as *The Twilight Zone*, *The Andy Griffith Show*, and *The Beverly Hillbillies* were an important part of Eire's childhood identity and his experience of America. What television shows had a direct effect on who you are today?

A CONVERSATION WITH CARLOS EIRE

Where did you encounter Emily Dickinson's poem included at the beginning of your memoir? Why did you choose to open your memoir with it?

I discovered Emily Dickinson in high school, about forty-four years ago. Although I had a tin ear for poetry back then, I knew instinctively that her poems had something that was lacking in most of the other poetry that was assigned to us: an intuitive grasp of paradox and of our deep-seated longing for transcendence. Over time, as I matured, her poetry stayed with me, and especially this poem, since I have always been drawn to the conundrum of our mortality. As I was writing my *Very Brief History of Eternity* two years ago, the poem surfaced many times, both in my mind and in my reading. So, when I began writing *Learning to Die*, I didn't have to search for the perfect opening epigraph. It had been there all along, guiding my thinking. It seems perfect, not just because it influenced me, but because it sums up the central theme of this book: that of the immortality of the soul.

In this memoir we see your struggles defining yourself as a Cuban living in America. Today, do you consider yourself Cuban American, Cuban, or American? Why so? Do you still consider yourself a refugee?

I'm always amazed when anyone asks me this question, for the chief assumption behind it is that one's identity can be neatly packaged and one can simply be either *this* or *that*. I realize that for someone who has spent his or her entire life living in a single culture, it must be hard to imagine what it feels like to be an immigrant, and to absorb cultures other than the one you were born into, but in many ways, asking this question is a lot like asking whether the tongue is for speaking or for tasting. Many things in life and in nature—like the tongue—cannot be explained in terms of either/or. Being an immigrant in the United States is not an either/or proposition, but rather a both/and. No one ever ceases to be part of the culture from which they came, save for infants who are adopted and taken to another country shortly after birth. Immigrants add other layers to their identity, other "selves," and depending on age, personality, and circumstances, these layers or "selves" assume all sorts of different configurations in each individual. In this memoir, I try to deal with this complexity, and with the fact that one's identity is always fluid in exile, and that there are times when the different selves converge or collide. Immigrants know firsthand that the "I" or "me" is not simple or uniform: it's a riotous mess.

So, to finally answer the question point-blank: I have a complex identity. Of course I'm American. Of course I'm Cuban. Of course I'm Cuban-American. I'm also Spanish and European, for my grandparents were immigrants from Spain, and they and my parents and relatives always reminded me of the fact that I was not *really* Cuban, but a displaced European with various identities: Gallego, Catalan, Basque, French, and Irish, with the constant hint of some distant Jewish *converso* ancestry. And to top it off, as a historian, my professional self is wholly enmeshed in European history and culture: my research takes me to Europe constantly, which oddly feels like home and, at the very same time, like a double exile.

I am still a refugee, too, and will continue to be one until Castrolandia ceases to exist. I came to the United States to escape from a nightmarish existence. As long as my place of birth remains enslaved by an oppressive totalitarian regime and the nightmare continues, I cannot return, and therefore remain a refugee. Throw into this bargain the fact that the Cuban authorities have pronounced me an "enemy" of their so-called Revolution, and that my books are banned in my homeland, and my refugee status is doubly confirmed.

What was the process behind writing this memoir? Did you rely solely on your recollections, or did you have some kind of journal you kept during the time? Were there any people you interviewed to enhance your storytelling?

I followed the same process as in *Waiting for Snow*: I wrote straight from memory, late at night, over the space of three months, during my summer break from teaching. No journals. No notes. No research. No interviews. I did share a few stories with my brother Tony as I was writing, and sometimes he had some details to contribute. But even this doesn't count as research, for we talk on the phone every night and often reminisce about the past. It's an ongoing thing, our connection with a common past.

Norma and Lou were the first foster parents who truly made you feel welcome in America. How did their Jewish influence and traditions help you to integrate with the American culture? How did their love and nurturing, despite coming from a different religious background, influence your beliefs?

Even though I lived with them for only nine months, Norma and Louis Chait had a profound influence on me, so profound, in fact, that it is difficult to measure it. This question is related to the second question above, the question of identities. I knew they were Jewish and American. Their parents were immigrants from Eastern Europe. And they were New Yorkers, too. This mixture of identities became the norm for me: this is what it means to be an American, to be many things at once. The fact that they not only respected my faith, but forced me to observe it may be the most significant thing of all. It put religion in another dimension for me, at that early age. Their love and nurturing proved to me, in the most practical way possible, that real goodness transcends religious beliefs, and that differences in religion do not necessarily cancel out faith, but can actually enhance it. Above all, they taught me to respect other faiths, and they did so by example rather than by lecturing me about it. They also showed me that love and self-sacrifice and concern for others matter more than doctrines or rituals; yet, at the same time, they exposed me to the significance of doctrines and rituals by sending me to church and taking me to Bar Mitzvahs. In the Gospel of John, Jesus says that God is love. The other gospels also affirm that the highest commandment is love of neighbor. These Christian values are derived directly from Judaism, one of the most philanthropically inclined religions on earth. In *Waiting for Snow in Havana* I refer to Norma and Lou as a proof for the existence of God. I still think of them this way. My professional interest in religion, especially my interest in the religious differences that emerged in the sixteenth century, derives from my experiences in the Chait household.

Besides your struggle to get rid of your accent, were there any other remarkable difficulties that you recall which perhaps you didn't express in your memoir?

Yes. In this book I provide only brief glimpses of another great difficulty that I and every Cuban exile face: our constant encounter with ignorance about Cuba and all of the monumentally stupid stereotypes that dominate American thinking about Cuba, pre- and post-Castro. Having to contend with people who see you as some sort of backward *primitive* from an *inferior* culture is just the tip of the iceberg. As I point out in this book, I encountered the very source of this ignorance in my school textbooks, all of which were filled with incorrect and very negatively biased information about Cuba and Latin America in general. So, it is not really a question of ignorance that stems from lack of information, but rather of ignorance derived from false information that keeps being drummed into young minds.

Many Americans still harbor all sorts of prejudices toward "Hispanics" because their exposure to the full complexity of the Hispanic world is limited and misinformed, and most Americans aren't really aware of the fact that their culture has constructed an artificial category—"Hispanic"—which is extremely broad and a gross distortion of reality. Chief among the errors committed by Americans is that of conceiving of "Hispanic" as a race, or of all "Hispanics" as the same, more or less, despite the fact that there are eighteen different Spanish-speaking countries in Latin America, each with their own particular ethnic mixture and culture, not to mention one European country in which Spanish is the official language but other languages are also spoken. Whenever I am confronted with any document or news piece in which "Hispanic" is conceived of as a "race," my head feels as if it's going to explode, for that is so totally wrong. Whenever this happens, I am also reminded of the one time that the mother of one of my high school friends expressed her prejudices openly, saying, with a sigh of relief, "Oh, but you look just like all the other boys," when she first met me. And that is just one such incident, though specially poignant; I've lost count of how many times I've been told that I don't look like a Cuban. And it's not just Americans who harbor these prejudices. Several of the European publishers of *Waiting for Snow* refused to include any of my childhood photographs in their translated editions because, as one of them put it, I don't look Cuban enough.

But all of this is a minor irritation when compared with the real torture that comes when Cuban exiles meet Americans, Canadians, Australians, Europeans, and others who admire the Castro brothers and their so-called Revolution, and lecture us about the wonderful achievements of that murderous, soul-crushing regime from which we've fled. Again, I've lost count of how many times I've had to confront this ignorance, which always includes hostility toward me personally, for those who praise the Revolution tend to see me and all other exiles as "oppressors" who were justly driven out, selfish bastards who simply didn't want to share their possessions with the poor. The guiding principle undergirding such prejudice is usually called "social justice," a very loose concept that refers to the redistribution of wealth in Third World countries, which are all imagined as equally corrupt and poor and as peopled by nonwhites. This hideously misguided conception of "justice" is itself derived from a host of other prejudices, including that which I like to call the Mussolini principle, which is the assumption that *underdeveloped* or *inferior* nations need strong leaders and draconian measures in order to function properly. So, just as the Italian fascist dictator Mussolini was constantly praised in Europe and North America for finally making the trains run on time in unruly, darker-skinned Italy, Fidel Castro and his henchmen are praised for finally bringing health care and education to the even unrulier and darker-skinned Cuban people. The chief assumption behind such praise, of course, is that such people are essentially different, and congenitally incapable of enjoying the same kinds of rights and freedoms as *more advanced* light-skinned Europeans and Americans. Another wrong assumption that guides such thinking is that Cuba was a Third World country before Fidel came along and "improved" it. The real truth is just the reverse: on many accounts, Cuba was on a par with or ahead of many European countries, and ahead of most other Latin American nations, in 1958. Nothing proves this more convincingly than the fact that, between 1900 and 1958, more than one million Europeans migrated to Cuba, seeking a better life, and between 1959 and today, more than two million Cubans have fled the island while no one, from anywhere, has migrated to it.

This glorification of Castrolandia is pervasive and, oddly enough, the higher one goes in the social scale here in America, the more one is likely to encounter it. In my profession, it is absolutely impossible to escape it, for most academics—though bright and well educated—are predisposed to champion the Mussolini principle unflinchingly and unquestioningly when it comes to Cuba and Latin America in general. Seven years ago, for instance, the University of Wisconsin revoked an invitation to speak they had offered me earlier because, as the dis-invitation e-mail put it—I would represent "the unjust oppression of the Cuban people by the exile community." Four years ago, when Fidel Castro fell gravely ill, I was approached by the Op-Ed editors of the *New York Times* and asked point-blank if I would be willing to condemn my fellow exiles who were celebrating Fidel Castro's imminent demise on the streets of Miami. As the editor put it to me: "We don't think these revelers are right; after all, Fidel Castro *allowed* them all to leave with his blessing back in the early 1960s." When I proposed a different essay, in which I would evaluate Fidel Castro as the ultimate Machiavellian prince, the editors said that "would not be right," and sent me packing. In essence, they were not interested in my opinion, but merely looking for a Cuban who would express *their* wrongheaded, unjust opinion. And when I wrote an essay exposing the duplicity and bias at the *Times*, no other newspaper in the United States would publish that essay.

Among the many ways in which we Cuban exiles encounter such prejudices and blatant ignorance, none is more constantly irritating than that of seeing the face of Che Guevara emblazoned on T-shirts and all sorts of other merchandise. Che was Castrolandia's chief executioner, the very embodiment of ruthless slaughter, the exact opposite of the idealistic hero so many people take him to be. Yet, I and other Cuban exiles constantly run into these bitter reminders of the world's foolishness and of the racially based prejudices that allow falsehoods to endure and turn into myths. The depth and breadth of such ignorance is staggering, and very troubling, especially for a historian. When falsehoods become history, and psychopaths like Che are turned into saints and pop icons, the whole world is in trouble, not just Cuban exiles, for then we are all one step closer to George Orwell's *1984* or already in it.

You always had the desire to come to America even at a young age; was there anything in particular about America that you were eager to experience?

I was eager to experience everything, not just something in particular. As I point out in this book, the United States had projected itself into my consciousness through its films, television shows, comics, and toys. It was the *real* world, where nearly everything important took place. In my early childhood years, up to 1959, I was aware of the fact that the United States was more stable than Cuba and that there was no cretin running the country, like Batista, and no need for a violent revolution across the Florida Straits. And then, after Batista left and Fidel made everything worse, the United States began to look even better to me. As the repression increased under Fidel in 1960, and as his policies drove Cuba back into the Stone Age economically, intellectually, and technologically, the United States became even more of a Utopia in my eyes. So of course I longed to go there, and not just to experience it but to live in it.

Do you feel that Spanish-speaking people living in America today are getting too comfortable with having translation readily accessible to them, reducing the urgency to learn English and perhaps progress further and faster through American society?

Yes, I think Spanish-speaking immigrants are digging a deep hole for themselves, collectively, by clinging so steadfastly to Spanish in every way. America as a whole is helping with the digging, too, especially those who define and guard political correctness. This sad mess resembles the dysfunctional relation between addicts and the people who enable them. What the enablers and the addicts won't admit in this case is that the only way to gain equality in the United States is to be fluent in English. This is how every other immigrant group has climbed its way up. And that doesn't just apply to the past: it is still happening with immigrants from places other than Latin America. Right now, here at Yale University, 18 percent of our undergraduate students are Asian, most of them first or second generation. Asian immigrants don't insist on being addressed in their languages the way Spanish-speakers do, and they always ensure that their children have full command of English. Imagine if Asians insisted on bilingual everything: "for Cantonese, press one; for Vietnamese, press two; for Korean, press three," and so on. Imagine if Jews, Poles, and Italians had done the same a century ago. "For Yiddish, please press four." How many of our undergraduate students at Yale are "Hispanics"? Only between 1 and 3 percent. And many of these are third or fourth generation. The language issue alone is not responsible for this disparity, but it contributes to it significantly. I am angered by bilingual signs in Spanish (many of which are grammatically incorrect, anyway), by phone lines in Spanish, and especially by schools that stress bilingual education. All of these accommodations are wrong, and extremely prejudicial to Spanish-speaking immigrants in the long run. As I say in this book, while this attitude persists, Spanish-speaking immigrants will continue to be second- or third-class citizens and to be perceived by the rest of the population (including immigrants from other places) as deserving of nothing other than the lowest place at the bottom of the heap.

What is your view on Arizona's stringent law on immigration?

Fortunately, this is a question that will become increasingly irrelevant with the passage of time, as the United States comes to terms with the lunacy of current immigration policies. Today this Arizona law is a volatile issue that has caused tens of millions of knee-jerk reactions, guided by emotion and ideology rather than reason or a knowledge of the facts. In reality, two factors drive illegal immigration into the United States from Mexico and Central America, and both are economic: the need for cheap labor on this side of the border, and the relatively poorer economies south of the border. It's a basic supply-and-demand question. Not many in the government or the news media want to admit this, but the United States has lost control of its southern border and of the lowest rung of its labor force. So it's the marketplace, rather than government policy, that is driving this immigration. The market and the law need to be brought into greater harmony. Perhaps a guest worker program, like those in place in Europe, would be in everyone's best interest.

Unfortunately, things are very messy right now. The current flap over the Arizona law—which allows police to ask for immigration papers from anyone suspected of a crime—is an irrational response to an eminently reasonable measure. The law in question does not call for random checks or racial profiling. It simply puts into effect at the local level what is already the law of the land: the identification and deportation of illegal aliens. And it actually does so within limits, for its intention is not to round up all illegal aliens, but only those who might be breaking the law.

I am not opposed to this law or offended by it. What really offends me is the way in which this very reasonable policy is being opposed, and how this controversy only helps to perpetuate the notion that "Hispanics" are hapless victims or helpless, inferior people who are so incapable of taking care of themselves that they can't even be expected to play by the same rules as everyone else. The real solution to the problem is not the abolition of this law, but rather its enforcement, coupled with the overhaul of the current system, which allows for uncontrolled immigration.

What other memoirs have inspired you?

Surprisingly, very few memoirs have inspired me. In fact, I hardly ever read memoirs, save for those from the distant past, in my work as a historian. At the top of the list is the ultimate memoir, which is also one of the oldest of all: the *Confessions* of Saint Augustine, written in the late fourth century. But Augustine skips over his childhood and adolescence, devoting only a few pages to that period of his life. What inspired me, then, is not how he thinks about his earliest years, but how he places all of his existence into a larger metaphysical and religious framework. His honesty is also exceptionally inspiring, for he is all too painfully aware of his worst faults and makes an effort to come to terms with them through his writing. It's a book I can read over and over again and always learn something new. I assign it to many of my classes. The other items on my list are not memoirs, but rather novels that might as well be memoirs: Mark Twain's *Tom Sawyer*, Charles Dickens's *David Copperfield*, Guillermo Cabrera Infante's *Tres Tristes Tigres* (Three Trapped Tigers). One semi-autobiographical novel in particular taught me how to see past, present, and future as interconnected plot lines: Kurt Vonnegut's *Slaughterhouse-Five*. One quasi-autobiographical film in particular had a profound effect on me: Fellini's *Amarcord*.

The last part of Plato's Allegory of the Cave is the proposition of Returning to the Cave. Have you been back to Cuba since you left? Would you ever consider living there again?

I have never returned to Cuba. I can't. First and foremost, right now, I am a *persona non grata*, an avowed enemy of the state. The Cuban authorities would never allow me to set foot on the island, and if they did, I would end up in prison in just a matter of days, maybe even within the first hour. The place is such a monstrous living hell, so repressive, so much a negation of all of the principles proclaimed in the Universal Declaration of Human Rights, that I would be unable to keep my mouth shut. Speaking your mind in Cuba is illegal, a crime punishable by decades of imprisonment or death. This is why even before I wrote *Waiting for Snow in Havana* and was proclaimed a criminal by the authorities in Castrolandia, I could never set foot in the place: I knew I'd be headed straight into prison. That is where I would have ended up if I had I stayed. I know that for certain, and so did my parents, which is why they felt compelled to send me away as quickly as possible.

As if this were not enough, I can't return for another reason: I think it is immoral to travel to places such as Cuba that have no regard for human rights. To travel to despotic locations, no matter how exotic or how deeply familiar, is one of the worst sins imaginable. First, one's presence legitimizes the oppressive regime, making it seem somehow "normal" or on the same level as other countries. This goes for everyone, whether they were born there or not. Tourists, especially those who go to enjoy themselves or sample the local color, are guilty of the worst sin of all, for they not only lend a sheen of respectability to the oppressors, but they also fill their coffers and keep them in power. In essence, anyone who travels to a place like Cuba is an accessory to oppression and exploitation. Since the government controls absolutely everything in Cuba, every penny spent there goes directly into the pockets of the oppressors, and only a tiny fraction goes to the Cuban workers. It's exactly the same setup as slavery, where the masters reaped the profits of captive labor. Moreover, a very strict apartheid is observed in Cuba, in which foreigners have access of all sorts of rights, facilities, and commodities that are denied to Cubans.

In the 1980s the oppressive apartheid of South Africa was brought to an end largely because of the boycott enforced on that nation by the rest of the world. Cuba's oppression and apartheid should—and could—be brought down in a similar way. Yet, in 2009, more than two million tourists visited Cuba, to sun themselves on beaches that are off-limits to Cubans, to rent cars and jet skis, and to eat and drink to their hearts' content in secluded air-conditioned hotels, while eleven million Cubans sustain themselves slightly above starvation on a government-controlled diet, deprived of all of those things that the tourists take for granted as rightfully *theirs* to enjoy. I don't know whether to laugh or cry when I see that many of the very same people who call for a boycott of Arizona because of one law that does not violate any human rights also call for a lifting of all travel restrictions to Cuba, a country that has been violating every human right for over fifty years, with abandon.

I don't see myself living in Cuba ever again. Cuba has changed way too much, irreversibly, and so have I. Home is here, in the United States. As for visiting, I will not set foot on the island again until the country is free of its current dictators and their henchmen, elections are held, and free enterprise and the free exchange of ideas are allowed. But I would love to visit a free, prosperous, tolerant, and intellectually vibrant Cuba some day, maybe contribute to its rebirth. The sooner the better.